# The Secret of the Jews
## Letters to Nietzsche

by David Ben Moshe

# THE SECRET OF THE JEWS
## LETTERS TO NIETZSCHE

by David Ben Moshe

gefen
publishing house בית הוצאה לאור
JERUSALEM ♦ NEW YORK

Layout: Marzel A.S. — Jerusalem
Cover Design: Robert Aulicino
Jacket illustration: Ken Meyer, Jr.
Author photo: Valerie Thompson

ISBN: 978-965-229-432-6
Edition   1 3 5 7 9 8 6 4 2
www.secretofthejews.com

Gefen Publishing House Ltd.          Gefen Books
6 Hatzvi St.                         600 Broadway
Jerusalem 94386, Israel       Lynbrook, NY 11563, USA
972-2-538-0247                    1-516-593-1234
orders@gefenpublishing.com      orders@gefenpublishing.com
**www.israelbooks.com**
Printed in Israel                *Send for our free catalogue*

*Dedicated to my children,*

*Marc and Valerie*

*With great love and respect*

# Contents

# Acknowledgments

I am very grateful to Rabbi Mendel Deren, who accompanied me from the brainstorming phase of this manuscript to its completion. Rabbi Dov Berkovits carefully reviewed every line of every chapter and contributed his considerable knowledge to both content and process. I deeply appreciate his time and advice. Gilya Gerda Schmidt, Ph.D., head of the Department of Religious Studies at the University of Tennessee, Knoxville, and an expert in German philosophy, provided excellent suggestions on all aspects of the manuscript. I am thankful for her generous help. This is my second manuscript to benefit from the professional editing of Esther Herscovics, and again I am grateful for her dedicated work. Michael Carr edited and Kezia Raffel Pride proofread the final edition. Their erudition, sharp eyes and professionalism enhanced the manuscript considerably. Mistakes that remain are solely my own. My heartfelt thanks go to Ilan Greenfield, my publisher, whose support and advice have been invaluable.

— David Ben Moshe

# A Note on Transliteration

Transliteration has to do with representing a word from one language in the alphabet of another. There are in use today multiple sophisticated, scholarly methods of transliteration. In this book, the method of transliterating Hebrew words into English is entirely practical. The author's aim is to use the English spelling that will give the reader the best opportunity to hear the word as it is pronounced in the Hebrew spoken in Israel today — to hear the music of the language.

For those familiar with the "usual" transliterations, it may at first jar the eyes to see the word "*Shema*" written as "*Sh'mah*." However, someone unfamiliar with transliteration from Hebrew might easily read the first syllable of "*Shema*" as "she," as in the feminine pronoun. In this book, the apostrophe indicates a silent vowel, so the first syllable of "*Sh'mah*" becomes the sound "sh," without any vowel sound, as if one were trying to tell someone to be quiet. Another example is the first word of the Torah: "*B'raysheet*." This word often appears transliterated as "*Bereishit*." But "*Bereishit*" is open to many possible mispronunciations, whereas "*B'raysheet*" almost forces us to read the word as it is pronounced in Israel today.

Vowel sounds cause much of the confusion in transliteration from Hebrew to English. In Hebrew there is no short "a," as in "as" or "action," but rather a broader "ah" sound. The word for Sabbath, "*Shahbaht*," is often transliterated as "*Shabbat*." This would understandably be misread by many Anglophones as the "a" sound in "bat." Using "ah" in both syllables offers the reader a better likelihood of reading/hearing the word correctly. The other common "a" sound in Hebrew is the sound of the letter itself, as spoken in English. In *B'raysheet*, the English word "ray" is reproduced, making it easier for the reader to hear the sound as pronounced in modern Hebrew.

As with "a," there is no short "i" in modern Hebrew; thus, as written, the word "*tallis*" (the prayer shawl worn in synagogues) could be read and pronounced with the second syllable sounding like the "i" in "list." And indeed, the word is pronounced this way in the Ashkenazic Hebrew more familiar to American readers. But modern Hebrew in Israel uses the Sephardic pronunciation; thus, in this book, the word will appear as *tahleet*.

The letter "u" is especially ambiguous, since Hebrew contains neither the short "u" sound in the English words "but" and "custom," nor the "u" sound in "purr" and "burden." Thus, the common transliteration of the holiday "*Purim*" is rendered "*Pooreem*." Because the letter "*u*" is so problematic, it is not used at all for transliteration in this book. And the double "*oo*" used in its stead is pronounced as in "soon" and "choose," *not* as in "book" or "foot."

Readers familiar with the word "*Elohim*" will recognized this as a Hebrew word commonly translated as "Lord." However, for most readers, the question arises: what is the pronunciation of the first syllable, "E"? And the third syllable could be read as the English word "him." Thus, to remove ambiguity, the transliteration in this book is "<u>*Ehloheem*</u>."

One Hebrew sound is not reproducible in English: the guttural sound in the Jewish toast "To life!" We are accustomed to seeing the Hebrew word transliterated as "*l'haim*," or "*l'chaim*," but Hebrew has no "ch" sound, as in "choose" or "change," so these letters are not used in transliteration in this book. It is common to transliterate the Hebrew letters "ח" and "כ" differently; this is because the beautiful and "pure" Sephardic pronunciation makes a distinction between the sounds of these Hebrew letters. However, because this distinction is gradually being lost, and because the untrained ear does not hear the difference anyway, in this book we will use "*kh*" as the transliteration for both letters. Simply by trying to make these two letters into a single unit, we come very close to the sound. However, the trick, when encountering this combination, is to "hear" the gentle throat-clearing sound in the lovely toast "*l'khahyeem*," "To life!"

Leaving explanations aside, by simply reading each unfamiliar syllable as the spelling would suggest in common English words, the reader will most closely approximate the sound heard in modern Hebrew.

Since the transliterations used here are unlikely to have been seen in other works, a glossary follows that shows some of the transliterations used in this book, and their likeliest counterparts found in other works.

# Transliteration Glossary

In the following glossary, several representative transliterations used in this book are found, followed by the transliterations likely to be encountered in other writings.

| In this book | In other works | English definition |
| --- | --- | --- |
| Ahdahr | Adar | Hebrew month |
| Ahmeedah | Amidah | Central prayer of Jewish worship service |
| Bahmeedbahr | Bamidbar | The fourth book of the Torah (Numbers) |
| Bayt Meedrahsh | Beit Midrash | Study hall of the Jewish learning institution where holy texts are studied |
| B'rahkhah | Beracha | Hebrew word for "blessing" |
| Beerkaht Hahmahzohn | Birkat Hamazon | Prayer of thanksgiving after a meal that includes bread |
| Breet Meelah | Brit Milah | Circumcision performed eight days after the birth of a male |
| B'raysheet | Bereishit | The first book of the Torah (Genesis) |
| Cahlev | Caleb | One of the spies sent by Moses to survey the land of Israel |
| D'vahreem | Devarim | Fifth book of the Torah (Deuteronomy) |
| Ehlee'ayzehr | Eliezer | Common Hebrew first name |
| Ehrehv | Erev | Hebrew word for evening, eve |
| Ephrahyeem | Ephraim | Common Hebrew first name |
| G'mahrah | Gemara | Exposition on the Meeshnah: Meeshnah + G'mahrah = Tahlmood |
| Hahshehm | Hashem | Hebrew term for the ineffable name of God; literally, "the Name" |

| In this book | In other works | English definition |
|---|---|---|
| Hahlahkhah | Halachah | Jewish law |
| K'dooshah | Kedusha | Hebrew word meaning "holiness" |
| Kahdeesh | Kaddish | Jewish prayer honoring a loved one who has died |
| Kahbahlah | Kabbalah, Kabala | Jewish esoteric wisdom |
| Kahlah | Kallah | Hebrew word for "bride" |
| Keedoosh | Kiddish | Hebrew prayer of sanctification, usually using wine |
| Keedoosheen | Kidushin | Hebrew word for "betrothal" |
| Keepah | Kippa | Skullcap worn by Jewish males |
| K'toobah | Ketubah | Hebrew word for "marriage contract" |
| Khahgeegah | Chagigah | One of the tractates of the Talmud |
| Khahtahn | Chatan | Hebrew word for "groom" |
| Khahfetz Khahyeem | Chofetz Chaim | Revered eighteenth-century Polish rabbi |
| Khahlah | Challah | Special braided bread for Sabbath |
| Khahyeem | Chaim, Haim | Common Hebrew first name |
| Khoopah | Chuppah | Wedding canopy |
| Khahseedism | Chassidism | A branch of pious Jewry that arose in the eighteenth century |
| Kohen | Cohen | Jewish priest; common Jewish family name |
| Lekhah Dohdee | Lecha Dodi | Song welcoming the Sabbath |
| M'zoozah | Mezuzah | Hebrew scripture, in an oblong casing and affixed to door of Jewish homes |
| Meekvah | Mikve, mikvah | Jewish ritual bath |
| Mehrkahvah | Merkavah | Hebrew word for "chariot" |
| Meenkhah | Mincha | Afternoon Jewish prayer service |
| Meenyahn | Minyan | A group of ten men required for a full prayer service |
| Meeshnah | Mishnah | Part of the Jewish Oral Law; Meeshnah + G'mahrah = Tahlmood |
| Meetzvah | Mitzvah | Hebrew word meaning "commandment" |
| Menahsheh | Menashe | One of the thirteen Hebrew tribes |
| M'shee'ahkh | Mashiach | Hebrew word for the "anointed one"; Messiah |

| In this book | In other works | English definition |
|---|---|---|
| Mount Khorev | Mount Horev | Mountain where Moses received the Torah; also called Mount Sinai |
| Nahzeer | Nazir | A man who, like Samson, takes a vow of abstinence |
| Neesahn | Nissan | A Hebrew month |
| N'teelaht Yahdahyeem | Netilat Yadayim | Ritual hand washing |
| Ovahdee'ah | Ovadiah | Common Hebrew first name |
| Pahrahshah | Parasha | A portion of the Torah; each week a different pahrahshah is read |
| Pehsakh | Pesach | Hebrew word meaning "Passover" |
| Pehsahkheem | Pesachim | A tractate of the Tahlmood |
| Pooreem | Purim | Jewish festival when the Book of Esther is read |
| Rabbi Ahkeevah | Rabbi Akiva | Revered rabbi of the first and second centuries of the Common Era |
| Rahmbahm | Rambam | Acronym for Rabbi Moses ben Maimon, a revered rabbi of the thirteenth century |
| Rahmbahn | Ramban | Acronym for Rabbi Moses ben Nakhmahn, revered rabbi of the thirteenth century |
| Rahshee | Rashi | Acronym for Rabbi Shlomo Yeetzkhakee, the most authoritative of all commentators on sacred Jewish texts |
| Rohsh Hahshahnah | Rosh Hashanah | Jewish New Year, the first day of the month of Teeshray |
| Rahv | Rav | Hebrew term for "rabbi" |
| Sanhehdreen | Sanhedrin | The highest Jewish judicial body; one of the tractates of the Tahlmood |
| Sah'ahdee'ah Gah'ohn | Saadiah Gaon | Revered rabbi of the tenth century |
| Sahndak | Sandak | Person honored to hold an infant male at the time of his circumcision |
| Seevahn | Sivan | A Hebrew month |
| Sayfehr Y'tzeerah | Sefer Yetzirah | An ancient Hebrew text of esoteric wisdom |
| Shahkhahreet | Shacharit | Jewish morning prayer service |
| Shahbaht | Shabbat | Hebrew word for "Sabbath" |

| In this book | In other works | English definition |
| --- | --- | --- |
| Shahvoo'oht | Shavuot | Hebrew spring festival commemorating the giving of the Ten Commandments |
| Sh'mah | Shema | Central Jewish prayer proclaiming God's unity |
| Sh'moht | Shemot | Second book of the Torah (Exodus) |
| Sh'vaht | Shevat | A Hebrew month |
| Sookah | Succah | Temporary structure used during Sookoht |
| Sookoht | Succot | Fall Jewish festival commemorating the children of Israel living in booths during their wandering in the desert |
| Shnay'oor Zahlmahn | Shneur Zalman | Revered eighteenth-century rabbi who founded Khabahd Khahseedism |
| Tahnahkh | Tanach | Jewish Bible, which includes the five books of Moses as well as Psalms, Proverbs, and other sacred texts |
| T'feeleen | Tefillin | Phylacteries worn on the head and arm by Jewish males during morning prayer service |
| Tahleet | Tallit, tallis | Jewish prayer shawl |
| Teekoon Ohlahm | Tikun Olam | Jewish concept of "fixing the world" in partnership with God |
| Teeshray | Tishre, Tishrei | A Hebrew month |
| Tehveht | Tevet | A Hebrew month |
| Tzahdeek | Tzadik | Hebrew term for a righteous person |
| Tzeetzeet | Tzitzit, tzitzis | Undergarment with fringes worn by Jewish males above the age of thirteen |
| Vahyeekrah | Vayikra | The third book of the Torah (Leviticus) |
| Yeetzkhahk Looreeah | Yitzhak Luria | Revered rabbi of the sixteenth century |
| Y'sheevah | Yeshiva | Educational institution for teaching sacred Jewish texts |
| Yohkhahnahn ben Zahkai | Yochanan ben Zakkai | Revered rabbi of the first century of the Common Era |
| Yohm Keepoor | Yom Kippur | Jewish fast day; Day of Atonement |

"The observation of the laws in the Old Testament was very simple at the time of its inception.... Today, it is utterly impossible to live in accordance to the viewpoints of that time. The last 'Jew' has been dead for a long time now; yet the descendants, with a mixture of obstinacy, arrogance, malice, self-conceit appropriate to their race, hold fast to their inherited laws."

— Otto Rank, psychoanalyst born Otto Rosenfeld in 1884

# Introduction

"It's kind of a miracle! I've experienced it a thousand times, and yet it still seems new to me. Some find fault with me for being a Jew; others forgive me; still others go so far as to compliment me for it; but every last one of them thinks of it. They seem caught in this magic circle of Jewishness; none of them can get out of it."[1] So wrote Ludwig Borne, a German journalist in the nineteenth century.

Indeed, there is this remarkable obsession with Jews throughout history. Despite the fact that Jews constitute less than 1 percent of the world's population, Borne's words could have been written in any era. Tacitus, a Roman historian of the first century of the Common Era, complained, "The Jews are extremely loyal toward one another, and always ready to show compassion, but toward every other people they feel only hate and enmity. They sit apart at meals and sleep apart, and although as a race they are prone to lust, they abstain from intercourse with foreign women."[2]

The fourth-century Roman emperor Julian saw in the Jewish people "those whose minds are turned to the doctrines of their Jewish religion and are so ardent in their belief that they would choose to die for it, and to endure utter want and starvation rather than taste pork or any animal that has not the life [i.e., blood] squeezed out of it immediately; whereas we are in such a state of apathy about religious matters that we have forgotten the customs of our forefathers."[3] Julian was, of course, referring to the pagan traditions of his people.

Martin Luther, the sixteenth-century German leader of the Protestant Reformation, thought he knew what should be done with the Jews: "What then shall we Christians do with this damned, rejected race of Jews...? First, their synagogues or churches should be set on fire, and whatever does not burn should be covered or spread over with dirt.... And this ought to be done for the honor of God and of Christianity in order that God may see that we are Christians, and that we have not wittingly tolerated or approved of such public lying, cursing, and blaspheming of His Son and His Christians.... Secondly, their homes should likewise be broken down and destroyed...they ought to be put under one roof or in a stable, like gypsies, in order that they may realize that they are not masters in our land...."[4] Four centuries later, other Germans, the Nazis, also lumped together gypsies and Jews in their attempt at a "final solution."

However, one of the most influential and admired German cultural figures of any era, Johann Wolfgang von Goethe, 1749-1832, understanding the influence of negative attitudes toward Jews early in his life, distanced himself from those external factors, noting, "Every Jew, no matter how insignificant, is engaged in some decisive and immediate pursuit of a goal.... It is the most perpetual people of the earth...."[5]

And what should we make of Karl Marx, whose paternal uncle was the last in a long line of chief rabbis of the Rhineland city of Trier? This famous father of socialism also sought the secret of the Jews: "Let us look for the secret of the Jew not in his religion, but let us look for the secret of religion in the actual Jew. What is the secular basis of Judaism? Practical need, self-interest.... What is his worldly god? Money."[6]

Mark Twain also wondered about the secret of the Jews, but from a completely different perspective: "The Egyptian, the Babylonian, and the Persian rose, filled the planet with sound and splendor, then faded to dreamstuff and passed away; the Greek and the Roman followed, and made a vast noise, and they are gone; other peoples have sprung up and held their torch high for a time, but it burned out, and they sit in twilight now, or have vanished. The Jew saw them all, beat them all, and is now what he always was, exhibiting no decadence, no infirmities of age, no weakening of his parts, no slowing of his energies, no dulling of his alert and aggressive mind. All things are mortal but the Jew; all other forces pass, but he remains. What is the secret of his immortality?"[7]

Henry Ward Beecher, a United States clergyman, abolitionist, and brother of Harriet Beecher Stowe, author of *Uncle Tom's Cabin*, agreed: "You cannot find another people in America among whom the social virtues are more rigorously taught and observed than among the Israelites.... They are a temperate people, and we largely tend to be a lascivious people. They are a people excessively careful of their children, and there is a great laxity among us in education of the household. We may well take lessons from them...."[8]

The second president of the United States, John Adams, wrote: "I will insist that the Hebrews have done more to civilize men than any other nation. If I were an atheist, and believed in blind eternal fate, I should still believe that fate had ordained the Jews to be the most essential instrument for civilizing the nations. If I were an atheist or of any other sect, who believe or pretend to believe that all is ordered by chance, I should believe that chance had ordered the Jews to preserve and propagate to all mankind the doctrine of a supreme, intelligent, wise, almighty sovereign of the universe...."[9]

Leo Tolstoy was in accord with President Adams. The great nineteenth- and twentieth-century Russian author of *War and Peace*, *Anna Karenina*, and other widely read literary masterpieces, wrote, "The Jew is the emblem of eternity. He whom neither slaughter nor torture of thousands of years could destroy, he whom neither fire nor sword nor inquisition was able to wipe off the face of the earth, he was the first to produce the oracles of God, he who has been for so long the guardian of prophecy, and who transmitted it to the rest of the world — such a nation cannot be destroyed."[10]

Indeed, reports of slaughter and torture fill Jewish history. This report could have come from the twentieth century or any century before it: "So excessive were the sufferings of our people that anyone who spoke of them [i.e., of the Jews] as undergoing wanton violence and outrage would be using words not properly applicable. [Such a man would lack] adequate terms to express the magnitude of cruelty so unprecedented that actions of conquerors in war, who are also merciless to the conquered, would seem kindness itself in comparison...."[11]

The above account is from a pogrom in Alexandria over two thousand years ago. That this report could be from Germany or Russia in the twentieth century speaks to how little progress mankind has made in rejecting cruelty.

These quotes — only a few of the thousands that can be cited from notable personages over the centuries — testify to Borne's comment that began this introduction: "...but every last one of them thinks of it. They seem caught in this magic circle of Jewishness; none of them can get out of it." In this book, we must get at the why — the "secret" — of the Jews. But has this not been amply done already? Have not others writing of the Jews explored this question? And if not, what is missing?

Max Dimont, an eminent twentieth-century Jewish historian who wrote the well-researched *Jews, God and History* and *The Indestructible Jews*, correctly pointed out the uniqueness of Jewish history: "There have been twenty to thirty civilized societies in the history of mankind, the number depending on how one defines a civilization. The usual life span of a civilization as a culture-producing entity has been between 500 to 1,000 years. Then the civilization has either stagnated or disintegrated. The Jews are seemingly the only exception to this 'rule.'"[12]

Dimont provides a creative set of ideas for conceptualizing Jewish history differently from previous historians, but he deals mostly in the intellectual realm. This is an important aspect certainly, though not sufficient to explain the continued existence of the Jews.

Eric Voegelin, a twentieth-century political scientist and philosopher, also went beyond conventional history. He considered the Greek discovery of the centrality of reason one of the great "leaps in being" in Western history. The second great leap Voegelin identified was the covenant between God and Israel. The Sinai experiences were "real events in history and so are open to empirical analysis. Revelation was experienced as a divine intrusion from beyond the cosmos."[13]

Dimont and Voegelin are historians who succeeded to a great degree in rising above inevitable biases, and thus, they leave us serious works to ponder. But pity poor Arnold Toynbee, a twentieth-century British man of letters whose lifework was a twelve-volume series of studies of civilizations. The continued presence of the Jews stuck in his craw like a peach stone: "Upon the advent of Christianity or, alternatively, of Islam, the 'mandate' of Judaism and the Jews 'was exhausted' (to use an apt Chinese formula). Now, in God's own good time, the true 'Chosen people' had arrived on the scene, and the Jews' duty was clear. They ought to have accepted Jesus or, alternatively, Muhammad."[14]

James Cahill, in *The Gift of the Jews*, provides an admirable attempt to study early civilizations. One problem is that he writes "popular history" — history without footnotes. The reader should have the *option* of joining with the writer in the process of discovery, of following footnotes and reading pertinent references, but Cahill rules out this option. He assigns to the Jews the role of "the inventors of Western culture…there is simply no one else remotely like them; theirs is a unique vocation."[15] However, he tells us, "To most readers today, the Bible is a confusing hodgepodge…. More than anything, because the Bible is the product of so many hands over so many ages, it is full of confusion for the modern reader."[16]

Much is wrong with this statement, but let us concentrate on two aspects pertinent to the current work. For whom is the Bible a "confusing hodge-podge": for non-Jews or for Jews? And if for Jews, is it for them all or just some of them? And who is "the modern reader"? In exploring the secret of the Jews, we will delve deeply into the concept of time. All time period designations, such as "medieval," "ancient," and "modern," are inventions. At the time of the "ancients," were they not modern? Did Yehhoodah HahLayvee, a brilliant twelfth-century rabbinic scholar, physician, and businessman, consider himself "medieval"? While these historical shorthands can be useful heuristic tools, they obfuscate and mislead more often than they elucidate. It is easy, for instance, to be seduced into sharply differentiating between the histories of the nineteenth and twentieth centuries. And yet, those reading these words close to the time of their publication, early in the twenty-first century, have experienced that the passing of December 31, 1999, into January 1, 2000, brought no great epiphany — the sun set on one day and rose on the next, just as it had every day of the preceding century.

More important is the question of whether all peoples live equally "in time." Is part of the secret of the Jews their unique experience of time? If this question seems strange, then we are on the right track, for conventional questions and their vague answers will not bring us closer to our quest.

A young child can relate only minimally to the concept of time. Tell him his fourth birthday is in "a week," and he may well ask, "How long is a week?" As adults, we develop more sophisticated concepts of time, though we remain tightly bound to the present as defined by our own life and surroundings. In this book, the concept of time is closely examined and, in fact, plays a central part in understanding the secret of the Jews.

Concepts of time, from a scientific point of view, were greatly elucidated in the twentieth century, beginning with Albert Einstein, a brilliant Jewish physicist. Is it a coincidence that a significant proportion of Nobel Prize winners are Jewish? It is fascinating that the "rational person" tends to accept science as the "ultimate wisdom." When an issue is not so complicated, we often hear, "It doesn't take a rocket scientist to know that," implying that the rocket scientist knows everything. For millennia, scientists have ridiculed the Jewish notion that God created the world *ex nihilo* — from nothing. Here men of science were questioning not simply the existence of God but also the concept that the universe could have come from nothing, rather than working from the more "reasoned" assumption that the universe has always been in existence and has slowly evolved.

But what happens when scientific man discovers that the universe did indeed come into existence *ex nihilo*, from a "big bang"? Would the Jews not be justified in asking, "What took you so long?" In this book, we will explore the wonderful writings on this subject by physicists such as Aryeh Kaplan, Nathan Aviezer, and Gerald Schroeder, men steeped in the knowledge of Jewish sources as well as science.

Who is a Jew? *What* is a Jew? This book provides an overlooked aspect of these questions, returning us to the concept of time. Given that the Jews have survived for thousands of years, we must get beyond the time-bound, contentious discussions that often mar such discourse. Jonathan Sarna, in his 2004 book about American Jewry, dutifully informs us of the parameters for his study. For one thing, "...the term 'religion' needs to be construed broadly, so as to include not only 'secular' movements but also those opposed to religion altogether. Jewish secularism, communism, and what came to be known as 'Jewishness,' or 'Yiddishkeit,' are, from the historian's perspective, religions...."[17]

It is not surprising that by the end of his book, Sarna seems confused about the future of America's Jews and closes with what amounts to a pep talk: "With the help of visionary leaders, committed followers, and generous philanthropists, it may still be possible for the current 'vanishing' generation of American Jews to be succeeded by another 'vanishing' generation, and then still another."[18]

In 1990, fifteen years before the above-mentioned book, the same Professor Sarna, then teaching history at the Cincinnati campus of the Reform movement's Hebrew Union College, conducted a study of lay leaders of the Reform movement, with a focus on those who had converted to Judaism. At that time he was much less sanguine about the trend he was studying: "Frighteningly, about 80 percent of converts or those married to converts...would not, by their own admission, feel too badly if their children married non-Jews.... In the Reform leadership study, more than 50 percent of the converts responding — leaders, I remind you — would not even be bothered a great deal if their children converted to Christianity.... Let us make no mistake; the data we have at hand should serve as a dire warning.... We will be held accountable to posterity, if knowing what we now know, we close our eyes and do nothing."[19]

Was the very broad definition of religion that framed Sarna's more recent history of American Jewry the antidote against coming up with the same painful realities he uncovered in his 1990 study?

The vast array of "Judaisms" existing today can indeed be bewildering. There are Orthodox Jews, Reform Jews, Conservative Jews, Reconstructionist Jews, and cultural humanist Jews. And the categories have their own offshoots as well. The Reform and Conservative movements have their left and right wings, Orthodoxy has its Khahseedic Jews and Lithuanian Jews, and Khahseedism branches further into its many sects.

We can get a clearer perspective by looking at Jews and Jewish survival from beyond the constraints of a limited time span. If we roll backward through the centuries with a time-lapse camera, stopping periodically, what do we see? What do we *not* see? Is there today a consistently generative Jewish community — that is, one that is able to grow and continue its existence into the future? Have there been, throughout the ages, Jews who have come and gone *without* being a part of this generative Jewish history?

Only by looking as objectively as possible beyond our own biases and preconceptions can we get a meaningful look at the secret of the Jews. Why have past expressions of a pluralistic Judaism not been generative? And is the pluralism of today condemned to the same fate?

Relying *only* on long-range examinations of history in general, and Jewish history in particular, provides an important yet incomplete picture. That is, along with the view from thirty thousand feet, we must at times also draw close to the edge of the forest, to peer in and try to understand the specific community under study. Indeed, we have to wander into the forest, get right in among the trees, and encounter the Jews as individuals.

What do the Jews of the culture of the Bayt Meedrahsh — "Orthodox" Jews, "traditional" Jews, "Torah-true" Jews — believe? What do they do from day to day? How do they interact with other Jews and with the non-Jewish world? There is no single source the reader can consult to learn in any depth about the Jews of the Bayt Meedrahsh. Most people, even scholars, know very little about the communities of the Bayt Meedrahsh as a culture, or about the individuals who make up that culture. The physical Bayt Meedrahsh is the study hall where Orthodox, or observant, Jews study sacred texts. But these terms, "Orthodox" and "observant," are inadequate to convey the secret of the Jews; thus, "Jews of the culture of the Bayt Meedrahsh" will be a more useful descriptor in studying this centuries-long facet of Jewish history.

## Why "Letters to Nietzsche"?

Writing this book as letters to Nietzsche is attractive from a number of perspectives. The brilliant German thinker's productive life ended in 1889, when he lapsed into dementia until his death in 1900. The son and grandson of Lutheran ministers was born in the Prussian province of Saxony on October 15, 1844, and was named Friedrich Wilhelm, after King Friedrich Wilhelm IV of Prussia, whose birthday he shared.

Nietzsche and his era are far enough removed that readers of this book can see him as someone who is not "modern" or contemporary. He lived at a time when Reform and Conservative Jewish innovators were leaving the culture of the Bayt Meedrahsh to establish alternative Jewish methods of worship — alternatives that arose in response to the Enlightenment. Nietzsche's German contemporary, Rabbi Samson Raphael Hirsch, vigorously contested the validity of these movements, exhorting Jews to continue educating their children just as they had for centuries, that is, in the Bayt Meedrahsh. Was Nietzsche aware of these controversies? By following these issues, which were still nascent in his day, into the present, we can gain a useful perspective on the secret of the Jews.

Nietzsche was on a lifelong quest for something that he never found: the *Übermensch*. His prolific translator and commentator Walter Kaufman explains that for Nietzsche, man, unbridled, is not the goal; "man is something that should be overcome."[20] In this study, we will take a much closer look at Nietzsche's concept of the *Übermensch* and at what he meant by "overcoming." He was not aware of how much this concept had in common with central tenets of Jewish learning, and it is worth noting that despite his close acquaintance with many assimilating Jewish intellectuals, he never found a single *Übermensch*. It is one of the great tragedies of cross-cultural history that Nietzsche did not know the Jews of the Bayt Meedrahsh, for there he would have found the *Übermensch* he was looking for.

Nietzsche's works speak for themselves. Of his positive attitude toward Jews and his loathing of anti-Semitism, there is no question. However, scholars are flummoxed by his negative portrayal of "priestly Judaism" — a conundrum that will finally become clear in the course of this work. This work will also examine for the first time the startling similarities between Nietzsche's writings and those from Jewish sources, as well as the similar values that Judaism and Nietzsche share.

"But wait just a moment!" we might well object. "Aren't you talking about Nietzsche the nihilist, who called for a reevaluation of *all* values? Didn't his *Übermensch* become a model for the Nazis?"

There are almost as many misperceptions about Nietzsche as there are about Jews. Max Dimont, whose works are mentioned favorably above, writes, "A whole new school of apologists has recently arisen, making Nietzsche the ethical successor to the humanists. Nietzsche, however, with all due regard for his nervous, brilliant prose, is the 'father' of Nazism, and his ethic is not the ethic of Torah and Testament, but the limited code of the Nazi."[21] This misrepresentation shows a serious lapse in scholarship that is difficult to explain. We will read later how Nietzsche's avowedly Nazi sister, Elisabeth, who became the administrator of his literary estate, dedicated herself to distorting her brother's writings and became an active accomplice in the co-opting of his literary legacy by the Nazis, who came to power in 1933, thirty-three years after his death. In Nietzsche's lifetime, his sister was a "pre-Nazi" — something that caused him great distress.

Nietzsche takes his understanding of religion and his concept of God from Christianity — and rejects them both. His search for the *Übermensch*, and our search for the secret of the Jews, lead us together toward the Bayt Meedrahsh. This is a direction, but only that; we have much work yet to do to find the secret of the Jews.

Before moving on to the letters to Nietzsche, here are two quotes — one from Nietzsche and one from the *Tahnahkh*, the Jewish Bible. But which is which? The answer will come in the body of one of the letters, thus no footnotes are included here.

1. Wisdom cries aloud in the street; she utters her voice in the squares; she cries in the chief place of concourse, at the entrances of the gates; in the city she utters her words, saying, How long, you simple ones, will you love being simple? And how long, O scorners, will you delight in scoffing, and fools hate knowledge? Turn at my reproof: behold, I will pour out my spirit to you, I will make known to you my words. Because I have called, and you refused; I have stretched out my hand, and no man regarded; but you have set at naught all my counsel, and would none of my reproof: I will also laugh at your calamity; I will mock when your fear comes upon you; when your fear comes like a storm and your calamity comes like a tempest; when distress and anguish come upon you. Then shall they call upon me, but I will not answer; they shall seek me early, but they will not find me; for they hated knowledge.

2. But why do I speak where nobody has my ears? And so let me shout it into all the winds: You are becoming smaller and smaller, you small people! You are crumbling, you comfortable ones. You will yet perish of your many small virtues, of your many small abstentions, of your many small resignations. Too considerate, too yielding is your soul.... And when you receive it is like stealing, you small men of virtue.... But why do I speak where nobody has my ears? It is still an hour too early for me here. I am my own precursor among this people, my own cock's crow through dark lanes. But their hour will come! And mine will come too!

# Letter One

May 27, 2005

י״ח באיר תשס״ה

Dear Nietzsche,

It has been over a century since you left us. I am drawn to you as the interlocutor I cannot have, so I must write to you. When I think about Jews and when I think about you, Nietzsche, my thoughts run together. There is this great secret about the Jews, known to few, which is that no one knows them; therefore, no one knows the even deeper secret: why the Jews are eternal. You, a great thinker who understood the crucial importance of developing the human mind to its fullest possible extent, you did not know Jews.[1]

In *The Genealogy of Morals*, you wrote, "I have been on the lookout for learned, bold and industrious comrades in arms — I am still looking. The object is to explore the huge, distant and thoroughly hidden country of morality, morality as it has actually existed and actually been lived, with new questions in mind and with fresh eyes. Is not this tantamount to saying that that country must be discovered anew?"[2]

You justifiably object that there must be some mistake. Of course you knew Jews, a fair number of your acquaintances were Jews, and you wrote about Jews. So I must explain myself.

It is important that I explore with you the secret of the survival of the Jews. To begin with, we must begin to discern between different Jewish identities. There are those Jews who assimilate, with greater or lesser speed and intensity, into the larger surrounding culture. These were the Jews that you knew, Nietzsche. They have been present in every generation since the beginning of Jewish culture. They are still Jews, and they often play a key role in the interaction between Jews and non-Jews — that is, they are still Jews until their descendants actively sever, or passively lose contact with, their roots. A century later, the branches of these family trees not only do not identify themselves as Jews, but in many cases they do not even know that they are descended from Jews.

You knew of the Samaritans, Essenes, Sadducees, and Pharisees — Jews of the beginning of the Common Era. The Samaritans, Essenes, and Sadducees disappeared entirely from Jewish history. Now, at the beginning of the twenty-first century, there are Reconstructionist Jews, Reform Jews, Secular-Humanist Jews, and Orthodox Jews. We will explore and identify how to make the necessary distinctions so that we may know where among these groups to look for the secret of the Jews.

Your vigorous condemnation of the anti-Jewish sentiment of your day is well documented. We will avoid the term "anti-Semitism," because so many people want to quibble about who is a Semite. In *The Genealogy of Morals*, you wrote, "I do not like the 'New Testament.' ... The Old Testament — that is something else again: all honor to the Old Testament. I find in it great human beings, a heroic landscape, and something of the very rarest quality in the world, the incomparable naïveté of the strong heart; what is more, I find a people."[3] In *Beyond Good and Evil*, you are equally clear: "In the Jewish 'Old Testament'...there are men, things, and speeches in so grand a style that Greek and Indian literature have nothing to compare with it.... To have glued this New Testament, a kind of rococo of taste in every respect, to the Old Testament to form one book — the 'Bible,' *the* book — that is perhaps the greatest audacity and 'sin against the spirit' which literary Europe has on its conscience."[4]

And if casual readers are still uncertain, they have only to read *The Dawn*: "They themselves have never ceased to believe in their calling to the highest things, and the virtues of all who suffer have never ceased to adorn them. The way in which they honor their fathers and their children and the rationality of their marriages and marital customs distinguish them above all Europeans."[5]

In *Beyond Good and Evil*, you separate yourself from most of your fellow Germans in very clear terms: "I have not met a German yet who was well disposed toward the Jews.... The Jews, however, are beyond any doubt the strongest, toughest, and purest race now living in Europe."[6]

You recall, Nietzsche, the letter you wrote to your sister, Elisabeth, about her own involvement with Jew haters. It was on Christmas Day, 1887: "One of the greatest stupidities you have committed — for yourself and for me! Your association with an anti-Semitic chief expresses a foreignness to my whole way of life, which fills me ever again with ire or melancholy.... It is a matter of honor to me to be absolutely clean and unequivocal regarding anti-Semitism, namely opposed."[7] Of course, Elisabeth was not to be deterred, and I will write at a later point how, after your sad descent into dementia, she wrested control of your literary estate from your mother and distorted many of your writings.

It is crucial that we understand Hahshehm. In the Hebrew language, "Hahshehm" means, literally, "the Name." We will use this particular divine name instead of "God," for the word "God" is capitalized by some, not capitalized by others and is used in many different contexts. This will get us closer to understanding the secret of the Jews, and we will pursue the Jewish connection with Hahshehm in great depth.

Understanding the unique relationship of Judaism to time will also bring us closer to our quest. I headed this letter with the date on the Gregorian calendar and also the date on the Jewish calendar. Each Hebrew letter has a numerical representation. The date above is Yood-kheht in the month of Eeyahr. Yood-khet is eighteen, with yood representing ten, and khet representing eight. The year is 5765, indicating the time since the creation of the world; the letter tahf (ת) represents 400, sheen (ש) represents 300, sahmekh (ס) is 60, and hay (ה) is 5, adding up to 765. The five-thousand designation is assumed and is thus not represented in the written symbols. With this as an introduction, we will return, in a later communication, to the unique way that Jews live in time.

In the interest of demonstrating that the term "Judeo-Christian heritage" is a myth, we must carefully examine the difference between the culture of the Bayt Meedrahsh and Christianity. Making a flesh-and-blood man a divine figure was a singular and startling departure from Judaism. Then the Church entered the arena of world power politics. Initially, the persecution that the Jews had known for centuries before Christianity was visited on the early Christians. The tenure of any given pope was fragile in the extreme — every one of the first eighteen popes died a violent death. Between the death of Peter in 67 C.E. and the time of Constantine in the early fourth century, there were thirty-one popes.[8]

Despite facing the same physical dangers as all his predecessors, Pope Miltiades I kept the church free of political entanglements. You see, dear Nietzsche, this simple man could not allow his concept of what the Church should represent to be associated with worldly power, despite the emperor Constantine's vision-inspired conversion to Christianity. Not so his successor. When Miltiades died in 314, his deputy, Sylvester, joined in partnership with the irrepressible Constantine. He became the first pope so proclaimed by the "Holy Roman Emperor," and from that moment on, the leaders of Christianity eagerly entered into the secular, temporal world of power. Instead of being persecuted by the Romans along with the Jews, they, along with the Romans, became the persecutors of the Jews.

The first payment on the price of power politics soon came due when, in 325, Constantine called a meeting of bishops to agree on the central tenets of the Catholic Church. At this meeting in Nicea, the Church crafted the Nicene Creed. A master politician, Constantine prodded the council to create four patriarchates: in Rome, Alexandria, Antioch, and Jerusalem. At the time, the bishop of Rome was given primacy "because the apostles Peter and Paul had lived and died in Rome."[9] And yet, while the council was in session, the seeds of the split to come were planted when Constantine chose Byzantium as the "New Rome."

Not long after Constantine's death, a second council was called, this time in Byzantium. The coming crisis was advanced by the declaration that "the Bishop of Constantinople shall have precedence in honor after the Bishop of Rome because Constantinople is the New Rome."[10] The ultimate cause for the split, whether pretext or sincere doctrinal disagreement, was contained in the Latin word "*filioque*" — "and from the son." A major problem arose when the Church of Rome added the word unilaterally to the Nicene Creed. The intention was that the Holy Spirit proceeded from the Father and the Son as one entity, though the Greek Church preferred the construction that the Holy Spirit proceeded from the Father, *through* the Son.[11]

In 800, a common enemy forced an alliance between the colorful Emperor Charlemagne and Pope Leo III, plunging the Church inexorably deeper into world power politics. The Vikings had entered into the search for glory and riches in Europe. Also known as the Normans or Norsemen, these Scandinavians were hearty, lusty warriors. This threat from the north combined with the Arab threat from the south to trouble the sleep of Pope

Leo and Charlemagne. In crowning Charlemagne the Holy Roman emperor, Leo sought to combat these military threats and, at the same time, assert the principle that all power comes from God and thus is granted by God, through the Church, to temporal leaders and governments. The Roman Church's primary rival was the patriarchate of Constantinople, which was also the locus of the primary obstacle to Constantine's dream of world domination.

The twentieth-century Catholic scholar Malachi Martin laments this confluence of interests, writing, "Their alliance was inevitable.... It was one more fateful step downhill for Roman popes. They were now ready to abandon one half of Christianity (and the more ancient, the more flourishing part) for the sake of worldly domination."[12]

In 387, John Chrysostom, one of a long list of Jew haters canonized as saints by the Church, delivered himself of eight homilies against the Jews, including many passages such as this: "Nothing is more miserable than those people who never failed to attack their own salvation.... What is the source of this hardness? It comes from gluttony and drunkenness...although such beasts are unfit for work, they are fit for killing. And this is what happened to the Jews: while they were making themselves unfit for work, they grew fit for slaughter."[13]

In 414, the first in the long history of Christian mass murders of Jews took place in Alexandria. Many of the Jewish community were killed, and the survivors scattered.[14] In 466, Pope Leo I enthused, "God's providence previously brought the Roman Empire into existence so that many kingdoms should thus be confederated into a single empire.... Rome, you holy family! You chosen people! You priestly and royal city! You have become the capital of the world by being Peter's see."[15] Thus, as you, dear Nietzsche, knew so well, the church pilloried the Jews for considering themselves the chosen people, while at the same time usurping the title for itself.

The Christian Crusades were another chapter in the splitting of the Catholic Church. The first Crusade began in 1098, and the fourth Crusade continued into the thirteenth century. As Malachi Martin relates, "Antioch and Jerusalem, both under the jurisdiction of the Greek patriarch but held by Muslims, fell into crusader hands. The popes insisted that all Greek churchmen be replaced by Latins with Latin rites. The Greeks in Constantinople retaliated by massacring every Latin they could find within the city limits."[16]

In 1204, the fourth Crusade included a direct attack on Constantinople.

After taking the city, Crusaders went on a rampage, methodically raping, killing, robbing, and burning.[17] Not coincidentally, the Crusades were marked by an especially bloody and vicious attack on Europe's Jews; thousands were systematically massacred, and thousands more were forced to convert to Christianity.

The Holy Inquisition, beginning late in the fourteenth century, brought death to Jews all over Spain. The study of this period of Jewish peril, dear Nietzsche, is a reminder of one of the myriad ways in which history is distorted: the passing down, from generation to generation, of stories that become "history" in the absence of careful scholarship. Benzion Netanyahu is a twentieth-century scholar who spent many years researching the experience of the Jews in Spain. His findings illustrate mistakes in scholarship that are often glossed over, as well as the confusion caused by not distinguishing among Jews of varying affiliations in their faith.

As Netanyahu approached his studies of the Holy Inquisition, he held the traditional belief that "almost all the Marranos were crypto-Jews who followed the laws of Judaism, thereby arousing the ire of the Church, which could not tolerate such conduct within its ranks. Naturally I viewed the Marranos as moral heroes who courageously withstood the terrors of the Inquisition and adhered to their faith under grueling tortures, frequently even unto death."[18]

While Netanyahu was studying the life of the famous leader of Spanish Jewry in exile, Don Isaac Ahbrahvahnehl, his initial thesis was challenged by a large volume of documents demonstrating that by the year 1460, "most of the conversos were conscious assimilationists who wished to merge with the Christian society...while the number of clandestine Jews among them was rapidly dwindling to the vanishing point. In 1481, when the Inquisition was established, the Judaizers formed a small minority in both relative and absolute numbers. Inevitably, I came to doubt the common view concerning the reasons for the establishment of the Inquisition."[19]

Document after document refuted the thesis that Netanyahu had "inherited" from earlier scholars, and led him to ask himself a pertinent question: "If only a fraction of the Marranos were still Jewish and more and more of them kept becoming Christian, what sense was there in establishing the Inquisition?"[20] Exhaustive studies of documents from three major groups involved in the Inquisition — Jewish, Marrano, and Old Christian sources — helped him eventually solve this puzzle.

In the Jewish sources, an important issue was addressed: what to do with conversos who wanted to return to Judaism. In the first place, in the years leading up to the severe persecutions wrought by the Inquisition, there was minimal movement from Spain to the refuge of Muslim countries, where such a reentry into Judaism could take place. Secondly, the Jews considered the conversos voluntary and complete converts to Christianity. Many came from families that had been Christian for a number of generations. The position of most Spanish rabbis was that this was not a matter of readmission to Judaism, but of full-fledged Christians who wanted to convert.[21]

Don Isaac Ahbrahvahnehl stressed in his writings that the conversos were labeled as Jews against their will and were "burned...by the thousands." Thus, the Inquisition was also pursuing lifelong Christians.[22] Isaac Arama, a leading historian of the period, wrote, "Although they assimilated with those nations completely, they will find no peace among them; for the nations will always revile and beshame them, plot against them and falsely accuse them in matters of faith."[23]

Even before the Holy Inquisition, it was in Germanic Europe, in 1235, that the first blood libel took place. Jews were accused of ritual slaughter of Christian children — the beginning of a series of slanders that prompted the killing of thousands of Jews in the coming centuries. Frankfurt am Main was the site of a massacre of Jews in 1241, and in 1259 the color of the armbands that Jews in Mainz had been forced to wear for years was formally legislated to be yellow. Seven centuries later, dear Nietzsche, others of your country-men, who called themselves Nazis, forced the same-yellow armband on German Jews.

In the closing years of the thirteenth century, pogroms decimated over a hundred Jewish communities, including Nuremberg, Wurzberg, and Rothenburg. In only two years, from 1336 to 1337, over a hundred more Jewish communities from Alsace to Bavaria were ravaged by German hordes. And when the Jews were blamed for the Black Death from 1348 to 1350, another three hundred Jewish communities in Germany were destroyed.[24]

You saw little change in your contemporary Germans, Nietzsche. In *Twilight of the Idols*, you wrote, "One pays heavily for coming to power: power makes stupid. The Germans, once called the people of thinkers, do they still think at all today? The Germans are now bored with the spirit, the Germans now mistrust the spirit.... Deutschland, Deutschland über alles, I fear that was the end of German philosophy."[25]

In the sketch you wrote in 1888, intended as a preface for a new book, you spoke of "*The Will to Power*. A book for thinking, nothing else: it belongs to those to whom thinking is a delight, nothing else. That it is written in German is untimely, to say the least: I wish I had written it in French, so that it might not appear as a confirmation of any *reichsdeutschen* aspirations."[26]

And you well remember your dismay when you discovered that you were on the mailing list of the *Kreuzzeitung*, the official publication of the most venomous anti-Semitic group in Wilhelminian Germany. You wrote, "The thought frightens me that any people who are unauthorized and wrong-headed will cite me as an authority for their actions.... I know my fate; my name will be connected with the remembrance of something monstrous, a crisis, the like of which has never before occurred on earth."[27]

When I summon the courage, I will write to you, as promised, about your sister, Elisabeth, and her friend Adolph Hitler, who were the vessels through which your prophecy came true.

I do not write of the Jew hatred throughout history to complain. Indeed, in the long sweep of Jewish history, Jew hatred is no more of a problem for the Jew than hydrophobia is a problem for water — the problem lies with the one afflicted with the disease, a disease you so aptly named "*ressentiment*," as it applied to Jew hatred.[28] These atrocities help us understand the pressures faced by many Jews who abandoned their roots.

Who can blame them for opting out? The wonder is that they *all* did not opt out. What were the Jews of the Bayt Meedrahsh doing during all the many persecutions mentioned above? The short answer is that they were doing a great deal to assure that their centuries-old culture continued. What they did and how they did it is the longer answer, and we will return to it, dear Nietzsche.

Very truly yours,

Ben Moshe

# Letter Two

June 15, 2005                                          ח׳ בסיון תשס״ה

Dear Nietzsche,

The era in which you lived was an amazing time of intellectual ferment, and right in the middle of it, as you know so well, were many Jews. They were assimilating Jews, and they were of two very different minds. There were those who wanted out immediately — to be rid of their Jewish identity *now*. There were also those who wished to maintain their identity as Jews, yet who desperately wanted to distance themselves from the Jews of the Bayt Meedrahsh, the "old-fashioned" Jews who caused them embarrassment. And so they formed new institutions and tried to redefine Judaism.

One of your very good friends was Paul Rée. He died in 1901, one year after your death, and many of his charming letters are still extant. Through him you met Lou Andreas-Salomé, a remarkably intelligent woman. Both were intellectual companions whom you valued. In an 1882 letter, you wrote, "I wish to acquire a pupil in her [Lou] and, if my life should not last much longer, an heir and one who will further develop my thoughts. Incidentally, Rée should have married her; and I for my part, I have certainly urged him all I could. But the effort now seems to be in vain. At one final point he is an unshakable pessimist.... The idea of propagation of mankind seems intolerable to him. It goes against all his feelings to add to the number of the wretched. For my taste, he has too much pity at this point and too few hopes.[1]

This is one of many things you wrote that makes one wonder at the false image that some readers have of you as a pessimist, even a nihilist.

Paul Rée was completely ignorant of things Jewish, yet he was psychologically crippled by his Jewish background. Lou herself summed this up very well in a letter to a friend: "I, too, have frequently observed half-Jews who suffered because of their mish-mash situation. This dividedness in itself could hardly be termed pathological because it is just as normal as a limping person who has a long and a short leg. But to see someone limp with two healthy legs as did Rée! Being a Jew completely and finding in himself something deficient to identify himself with, something that despicably and contemptuously contradicts his own person — I never saw this in anyone else to the same degree.[2]

Another interesting friendship was the one you struck up with Helen Zimmern, who wrote a book about Schopenhauer and spent much time with you in order to understand your ideas, so that she could become a faithful translator of your works from German to English. Good to her word, after your death she published English translations of *Beyond Good and Evil* and *Human, All Too Human*. In 1888, you wrote about her to your friend Peter Gast, "Naturally a Jew: it's fantastic to see how greatly this race now holds Europe's 'intellect' in its hands (at length, today, she conversed with me about her race)."[3]

It seems it was natural for you to identify her as Jewish, yet she had been baptized into the Lutheran faith.[4] It was a sign of your times that Jews were designated as a "race," but I am sure you knew this was not the case. Much research, as well as common sense, refutes any idea of a "Jewish race,"[5] but I will share with you at a later time some fascinating data that now allows us to trace Jewish ancestry back to the time of Moses.

Now we come to a relationship that opened up for you, Nietzsche, the possibility of meeting a Jew raised in the culture of the Bayt Meedrahsh. When Professor Friedrich Ritschl recommended you for a position at Basel, you found not only a mentor in philology but also a warm family atmosphere. Ritschl's wife, Sophie Guttentag Ritschl, as you well knew, was born into a Jewish family but converted to Christianity. She was an especially close friend. More relevant to the focus of my letters to you is that in another of Professor Ritschl's protégés, Jacob Bernays, you came to know a Jew whose own father was an extremely erudite and respected rabbi of the Bayt Meedrahsh culture. Jacob's brother Michael converted to Christianity, perhaps to enhance his professorship at the University of Munich, but Jacob clung to his Jewish practices. Unfortunately, you apparently did not get close enough to him to develop an insight into this community of Jews.

We are left to wonder if your reluctance to make a friend of Bernays was based on his religious beliefs and practices. Jacob's cousin, Martha Bernays, married Sigmund Freud, the father of psychoanalysis, who, along with his disciples, discussed your writings and gave you great credit. Freud was a Viennese Jew, ten years younger than you, though perhaps you were familiar with his translation into German of John Stuart Mill's essays.[6]

Jacob Bernays's father, Rabbi Isaac Bernays, died rather young, so you had no chance to know him, but his most famous protégé, Rabbi Samson Raphael Hirsch, you could have known. Rabbi Hirsch was the leader of the German culture of the Bayt Meedrahsh in your time, and meeting him would have profoundly changed your understanding of the Jews, their past, and where they were headed. Of all the Jews you knew, none have Jewish descendants living today.

Johann Wolfgang von Goethe, as you know, was born in Frankfurt am Main in 1749. He was one of the true cultural giants in history. Many, including you, Nietzsche, admired him, not only for his writings but for his strength of will in overcoming illness that more than once threatened to curtail his illustrious career. Never aloof from his surroundings, he served in a variety of civic capacities.

In his youth, Goethe was put off by the conditions of poverty and crowding that he saw in Jewish ghettos. Later in life he had the grace to confess, "The aversion which I felt against them [the Jews] in my early youth was more of a timidity before the mysterious, the ungraceful. The scorn which used to stir in me was more a reflection of the Christian men and women around me."[7]

One of the ghettos Goethe may have seen was in Dessau, at the confluence of the Elbe and Mulde Rivers. About 150 Jewish families lived in the impoverished Dessau ghetto. There, in 1729, a Jew named Moses was born. According to Jewish custom, he was named Moses ben Mendel — Moses the son of Mendel. However, since Jews had been forced to take family names, they often chose the name of the place they were born. So Moses Dessau was the public name given to the son of Mendel Dessau, the director of a small Hebrew day school. The young Moses was taken early every morning to learn from the scholars of the ghetto where he was taught, in the uncomprehending words of a biographer, "to prattle mechanically the *Mishnah* and *Gemara* [the two components of the Talmud]."[8] The lives of Goethe and the Mendelssohn family were destined to become enmeshed.

Above all, young Moses loved learning. His rabbi moved to Berlin when he was only fourteen years old, and Moses moved with him. In German, "the son of Mendel" is rendered as "Mendelssohn," the name that Moses Dessau chose. Moses Mendelssohn, who would be the grandfather of the great musician Felix Mendelssohn, became a famous name in Jewish and non-Jewish German culture even before Goethe.

Mendelssohn was educated as a Jew of the Bayt Meedrahsh culture, and he personally never wavered in observance of *Hahlahkhah* — Jewish law. But, dear Nietzsche, he did not secure for his children the education he had received; thus, with hindsight, we see that his descendants' exit from Judaism was foreordained. Mendelssohn's oldest son, Joseph, remained observant of many of his father's traditions until his death, as did his son Alexander, first cousin to Felix Mendelssohn. But with Alexander's death in 1871, the year before the publication of your *Birth of Tragedy*, there was not left one single professing Jew of the Dessau-Mendelssohn family tree.

You probably read Moses Mendelssohn's *Phaedon*: Or, *The Immortality of the Soul*, "the most widely read book of its time."[9] The book's success led to Mendelssohn's nomination for membership in the Royal Academy of Sciences. But however educated and enlightened, Mendelssohn remained a Jew, and his name was eliminated from the list by Frederick the Great.[10]

Mendelssohn died as a Jew in 1786, but there were enormous pressures on his generation and those of his children and grandchildren to convert to Christianity. The year 1819 was the year of *Judensturm*, the time of the "Hep! Hep!" riots. These were in part a reaction to Jewish demands for more civil rights. Some scholars believe the term was an acronym taken from the Crusaders' cry "*Hierosolyma est perdita*," a Latin phrase meaning "Jerusalem is destroyed."

Moses Mendelssohn's second son, Abraham, was imbued by his father, and by his own sojourn in Paris, with the ideals of human reason and equality. Though not an observant Jew, he had no inclination to convert to Christianity. In Paris he met and married Leah Solomon, and when the newlyweds returned to Germany, Abraham went into business with his wife's brother, Jacob Bartholdy, who had converted to Christianity and changed his name.

Both Abraham's wife, Leah, and his brother-in-law kept pressure on Abraham to convert, with Jacob even suggesting that Abraham take his own adopted last name. Before taking the step himself, in 1816 Abraham had his four children baptized at the New Church in Berlin. His oldest child, Fanny, was ten years old; Felix, already a musical prodigy, was seven; Rebecca was four; and Paul was two.[11] It was not until six years later that Abraham and Leah were themselves converted, taking the hyphenated name Mendelssohn-Bartholdy and passing it on to their children.

Moses Mendelsohn's oldest daughter, Brendel, was intellectual and restless. Soon after converting to Catholicism and changing her first name to Dorothea, she started a cultural salon at her home. Two of her close friends were Rachel Levin and Henrietta Herz, Jews who branched out and started their own intellectual salons; in fact, Rachel Levin had two Berlin salons. It is so fascinating, Nietzsche, that these Jewish women were such great promoters of Goethe, who was a cult figure in their salons and met both women personally in European spas. Another of their Jewish intellectual circle was Marianne Meyer, who married and became Marianne von Eybenberg. Goethe fell in love with her, but she did not return his feelings.[12]

The match in Paris between Abraham Mendelssohn and Leah Solomon was made by Abraham's sister Henrietta, who had come to help him set up housekeeping. Following the example of her older sister, Dorothea, Henrietta opened a school for children of upper-class Parisians and also established a cultural salon in her home. After she was hired as tutor to the daughter of General Horace-François Sebastiani, a protégé of Napoleon, she followed her older sister out of Judaism by converting to Catholicism, the religion of her host family.[13]

One of the regular participants in the intellectual soirees hosted by Henrietta Herz was Carl Friedrich Zelter. Zelter was a composer of note and a confidant of Goethe, setting a number of Goethe's poems to music. It was this man whom Abraham Mendelssohn-Bartholdy selected to be the teacher of his child prodigy, Felix. This led to the touching relationship between the aging Goethe and the young, vibrant, brilliant pianist and composer Felix Mendelssohn. Zelter, writing to propose that he bring Felix with him to stay at Goethe's house, described Felix as his "best pupil," then added, "To be sure, he is the son of a Jew, but no Jew himself."[14] Both Goethe and Felix were delighted with their time together in Goethe's Weimar home. Originally meant to be a few days, the visit extended to more than two weeks.

Though Felix apparently never considered returning to Judaism, he questioned his father's wisdom in rejecting his heritage, and he refused to accept the calling cards his father had made for him, engraved with the name "Felix M. Bartholdy." The quarrel went on for some time, with Abraham writing to his famous son, "You cannot, you must not carry the name Mendelssohn. Felix Mendelssohn Bartholdy is too long; it is unsuited for daily use. You must go by the name Felix Bartholdy."[15] But Felix demurred.

The same factors in nineteenth-century Germany that influenced so many of the Mendelssohn family to convert to Christianity acted also on Heschel Marx, father of Karl Marx, and on Heinrich Heine, a poet whom you yourself admired, Nietzsche. Like many others, they converted from Judaism to Christianity for economic reasons. In *Ecce Homo*, you wrote, "The highest conception of the lyric poet, *Heinrich Heine* gave to me. I seek in vain in all the realms of millennia for an equally sweet and passionate music. He possessed that divine sarcasm without which I cannot imagine perfection."[16] Heine wrote about baptism as a Christian as "an entrance ticket into the community of European culture."[17]

We have seen that the Mendelssohns came from a strong family tree of Jews of the Bayt Meedrahsh. The background of the Marx family was even more remarkable. Karl Marx's father, Heschel, grew up in a family steeped in the culture of the Bayt Meedrahsh. His brother, Samuel Marx, was the chief rabbi of Trier. And this is just the end of this amazing line of rabbis, so back we go, Nietzsche! In addition to Karl Marx's uncle Samuel, the following served also, in their time, as the rabbis of Trier: Karl's grandfather, Meir HahLayvee Marx (died ca. 1804), his great-grandfather, Moses Lwow (died 1788), his great-great-grandfather, Joshua Heschel Lwow (died 1771), two of his great-great-great-grandfathers, Isaac Aaron Worms (died 1722) and Aaron Lwow (died 1712), and his great-great-great-great grandfather, Joseph Israel (died 1684).

Marx's great-great-great-grandmother, the wife of Aaron Lwow, was herself from a distinguished rabbinic background. Douglas M. Snyder tells us, "Her grandfather, Meir Wahl-Katzenellenbogen, was the rabbi of Brest-Litowsk. One of her great, great grandfathers, Joseph ben Gerson Cohen (died 1591) was a distinguished Jewish scholar in Cracow, Poland.

Another great, great grandfather of Aaron Lwow's wife, Samuel Juday Katzenellenbogen (died 1565) was head of the Talmudic High School of Padua in the 16th century."[18]

The above family line is all from Karl Marx's father's side. His mother, too, came from a distinguished rabbinic family, which included Rabbi Isaac Pressburg of Nijmegen. Marx's mother's baptism was clearly not a conversion of the heart. She kept in touch with her Jewish relatives, and eighteen years after her conversion in 1853, she wrote to her sister about the impending departure of her daughter and son-in-law to South Africa: "And it seems that the lot of the People of Israel is again being realized in me — that my children would be scattered throughout the world."[19]

Karl's father, Heschel Marx, became Heinrich Marx when he converted to the Lutheran Church. It was only later, when Karl was five, that he and the other children were converted. Despite the fact that his father, to whom Karl felt very close, remained a defender of the Jews, Karl displayed pronounced anti-Jewish sentiments (as quated already in my first letter): "Let us look for the secret of the Jew not in his religion, but let us look for the secret of religion in the actual Jew. What is the secular basis of Judaism? Practical need, self-interest. What is the worldly cult of the Jews? Schacher [swindler]. What is his worldly god? Money."

As one twentieth-century scholar put it, "For reasons perhaps explainable by the concept of self-hatred, Marx's detestation of Jews remained deeply rooted — a canker that neither time nor experience ever eradicated. In fact he never retracted his defamation of Jews, a fixation that found echoes in Socialist thought."[20]

Eliezer Berkovits, an extraordinary rabbi, thinker, and scholar of the twentieth-century culture of the Bayt Meedrahsh, explains that understanding Marx "reaches much deeper" than the conflict between atheism and religion: "The Jew as the witness to God's presence in history is a refutation of dialectical materialism.... As long as the Jew is around, he is a witness that God is around. And as long as God is around, any purely materialistic civilization can only be a passing phase in history."[21]

From a letter written after Marx's death by Friedrich Engels, Marx's collaborator in *The Communist Manifesto*, we see that Engels did not share Marx's disease of Jew hatred: "The anti-Semite presents the facts in an entirely false light. He doesn't even know the Jews he decries, otherwise he would be aware that, thanks to anti-Semitism in eastern Europe, and of the Spanish Inquisition in Turkey, there are here in England and in America thousands upon thousands of *Jewish proletarians*; and it is precisely these Jewish workers who are the worst exploited and the most poverty-stricken. In England during the past twelve months we have had *three* strikes by Jewish workers."[22]

Like others before him who tried to escape their Jewish backgrounds, Marx did not succeed. A Catholic Church official of the twentieth century, commenting on criticism by Jews of Pope Pius XII (much more about him in another letter, dear Nietzsche), said, "Jews who criticize Pius XII may be massive accomplices in the destruction of the Catholic Church.... *The Communist Manifesto* of Karl Marx and Friedrich Engels has Jewish origins, as well as the assertion that religion is the opiate of the masses."[23]

One German Jew of the nineteenth century who was greatly influenced by the writings of Moses Mendelssohn was Israel Jacobson, known as the father of the Reform movement. Here we are introduced to Jews who were descendants of Jews of the culture of the Bayt Meedrahsh but who desired to "modernize" Judaism and establish new movements. These Jews, unlike Rée and others known to you, Nietzsche, who were anxious to shed all vestiges of Jewish identity, wanted not to reject but to *change* Judaism. Israel Jacobson introduced organ music into synagogue worship and was the first to conduct services in the German language. When he moved to Berlin and began a Reform temple, the first to undergo the confirmation ceremony was his son Nahptahlee. For this pioneering family the process from assimilation to conversion was not long in asserting itself, with Nahptahlee later becoming Dr. Hermann Jacobson, a leader of Berlin's Catholic community. In fact, most of Israel Jacobson's children converted to Christianity.[24]

Another German Jewish leader of the Reform movement was Abraham Geiger, from a long family tree of Jews of the culture of the Bayt Meedrahsh. One of his principle teachers of Judaism was his older brother, Solomon Geiger, a scholar of classical Jewish sources. Abraham, too, was inspired by the Enlightenment and came to describe his circumcision, or *breet meelah*, as a "barbaric act of bloodletting." Another time, he declared, "The Talmud must go; the Bible, that collection of mostly so beautiful and exalted — perhaps the most exalted of human books — as a divine work must also go."[25]

Geiger's son Ludwig was the most prominent of a number of Jewish biographers of Goethe. He taught for a time at the College for the Science of Judaism, one of the educational institutions founded by his father, and fought anti-Semitism while diligently trying to define the common border between the German and Jewish cultures. Though his efforts were enthusiastic and determined, they ultimately failed.[26]

The forerunners of today's Conservative Judaism were also your contemporaries, Nietzsche. Zacharias Frankel, like Abraham Geiger a descendant of prominent rabbinic families, was chief rabbi of Dresden. He broke with the reformers over their resolution declaring the Hebrew language unnecessary for worship, and when he accepted the position of principal of the Jüdisch-Theologische Seminar of Breslau, he wrote in Hebrew his *Darkhei HaMeeshnah [Ways of the Meeshnah]: A Methodological Introduction to the Study of Meeshnah*.[27] His attempts to define his own issues of change in Judaism while remaining sensitive to traditional Judaism satisfied neither the reformers nor the traditional community.

A faculty member of Rabbi Frankel's Jüdisch-Theologische Seminar of Breslau was Heinrich Graetz. He died in Munich in 1891, and perhaps his name was known to you, Nietzsche. Graetz heartily welcomed Frankel's rejection of the reformers' elimination of Hebrew as the language of worship, and his *History of the Jews* was and remains an influential multivolume work that has been translated into many languages.

Graetz and Frankel, forerunners of the Conservative movement, as well as Hermann Jacobson and Abraham Geiger in the beginnings of the Reform movement, wanted only to "enlighten" Judaism, to introduce more "reason," to "improve" it. Hailing from a large family tree of Jews of the culture of the Bayt Meedrahsh, they certainly did not intend to destroy Judaism, that is, to "improve" it out of existence. Had they known that their children, grandchildren, and great-grandchildren would leave Judaism altogether, would they have acted differently? We cannot be certain. What we can say is that their "enlightened" vision for Judaism not only did not contribute to Judaism's place as the longest-lasting culture in recorded history, but was in fact antithetical to the survival of the Jewish people.

Yours,

Ben Moshe

# Letter Three

July 1, 2005          כ"ד בסיון תשס"ה

Dear Nietzsche,

I have mentioned your contemporary Sigmund Freud, born some ten years after you. Now, at the beginning of the twenty-first century, Freud's name still looms large among twentieth-century thinkers. He and the early circle of men around him were all assimilating Jews. Their original contribution was to refine unconscious mental processes into a coherent theory and develop treatment methods for those who could not use the knowledge revealed in your writings to "overcome" themselves. These patients, needing further help to overcome themselves, entered into psychoanalysis and into the analytic methods of individuals who split off from Freud's circle to develop their own separate identities.

Freud's circle drew much from your writings, and most of them gave you generous credit. In this letter, I write to you of those who were thankful to you throughout their lives, and of others who ran into the wall of *ressentiment* and wrote ugly things later in their lives.

There is much overlap between psychology and values, as you very well recognized. I now want to concentrate mostly on the psychology, with limited mention of values, because the issue of values is much larger — indeed, it will astound you to see in later communications just how much your value system and that of the culture of the Bayt Meedrahsh have in common. Given this concurrence of thought, it is not surprising that the basic psychology of the Bayt Meedrahsh and the basics of your own psychology are very close. Those who think clearly can comprehend them more

29

simply and more intuitively than they can the overly elaborate yet reductionistic systems of Freud and those schools that split off from Freud.

While an author of Freud's life and work claimed that "sublimation" was a word "coined by Freud," you acknowledged that the term was well established long before you used it. Between the first and second editions of *Human, All Too Human*, you brought "sublimation" from its less precise use into the understanding that Freud incorporated into his work, and today it is a term in general usage and understanding.[1]

Freud made sexual and aggressive drives the center of his understanding of human nature, as opposed to the "will to power," which was the primary drive in your system of thought. In your notes on the will to power you wrote: "Sexual stimulation in the ascent involves a tension which releases itself in the feeling of power; the will to rule — a mark of the most sensual men; the waning propensity of the sex impulse shows itself in the relenting of the thirst for power."[2]

Walter Kaufmann, who translated much of your work into English, explains that you "did not decide to reduce the will to power to a sexual libido: for sexuality is that very aspect of the basic drive which is canceled in sublimation and cannot, for that reason, be considered the essence of the drive."[3] In a key point in understanding one of your central objections to Christian "psychology," Kaufmann writes:

> Nietzsche believed that Christianity, instead of seeing that the sex drive could be sublimated, repudiated it. Some of Nietzsche's ideas that have generally been misconstrued are comprehensible only if this contrast of sublimation and emasculation is taken into account. It is, for example, a common misconception that Nietzsche admired Cesare Borgia and glorified him. Nietzsche found it ridiculous to consider a Cesare Borgia unhealthy in contrast to an emasculated man who is alleged to be healthy. When he was criticized on that point, Nietzsche clarified his point in another book three years later. He now explained that he did not favor "the abolition of all decent feelings" but that he was not sure "whether we have really become more moral." Perhaps we have just become emasculated and our failure to do evil is to be ascribed merely to our inability to do evil. Nietzsche believed that a man without impulses could not do the good or

create the beautiful any more than a castrated man could beget children. A man with strong impulses might be evil because he had not yet learned to sublimate his impulses, but if he should ever acquire self-control, he might achieve greatness.[4]

Another central concept that you depicted beautifully is what Freud came to call "denial." This is not a conscious denial but an automatic, unconscious action to relieve oneself from unacceptably painful thoughts and feelings. In this you clearly led the way. In one of your most succinct and brilliant formulations, you wrote, "'I have done that,' says my memory. 'I cannot have done that,' says my pride, and remains inexorable. Eventually memory yields."[5] You also phrased this struggle in this way: "The strength of a spirit might be measured according to how much of the 'truth' he would be able to stand — more clearly, to what degree it would need to be watered down, shrouded, sweetened, blunted, and falsified."[6] Rare indeed is the person who can look reality square in the eye, accept it, and adapt to it. The need for the psyche to construct a more agreeable, albeit fictional, world is widespread and powerful.

We have from the minutes of the Vienna Psychoanalytic Society documentation of the centrality that your thought played in the origins of psychoanalysis. While Freud denied having read your writings, from what he did know about you he was unstinting in his praise. From the minutes of the society's October 28, 1908, meeting, we read this: "There was discussion of Nietzsche's introspective capacities, and Freud suggested, 'The degree of introspection achieved by Nietzsche had never been achieved by anyone, nor is it likely ever to be reached again.'"[7] At the time of your death, Freud wrote to an intimate friend that he had "acquired a Nietzsche book," probably *Beyond Good and Evil*, in which he hoped "to find words that have remained unspoken with me, but I have as yet not opened the book."[8] Whether Freud later read your book, we do not know.

In his *Interpretation of Dreams*, Freud directly indicated some knowledge of your work: "We can guess how much to the point is Nietzsche's assertion that in dreams 'some primeval relic of humanity is at work which we can now scarcely reach any longer by a direct path'; and we may expect that the analysis of dreams will lead us to a knowledge of man's archaic heritage of what is psychologically innate in him."[9]

Alfred Adler was a member of Freud's inner circle. Like Goethe and your-self, Adler overcame daunting physical illness. The son of a Jewish grain merchant, he was, like Freud, born in Vienna. Freud was attracted by Adler's eager intellect and made him president of the Vienna Psychoanalytic Society. Adler also served as coeditor of the society's newsletter. At the April 1, 1908, meeting, Adler said: "Nietzsche is closest to our way of thinking.... In Nietz-sche's work, one finds almost on every page observations reminiscent of those we make in therapy, when the patient has come rather a long way and is capable of analyzing the undercurrents in his mind."[10]

Otto Rank was another Jewish, Viennese-born member of Freud's inner circle. He acknowledged his great debt to you over and over. At a desperate point in his life, he confessed, "For a long time, I had serious thoughts of suicide which, as Nietzsche says, 'helped me get past many a night and many a day.' Then in reaction came a tremendous love of life and creative joy, which swept me into activity." In a 1903 entry in what he called his "daybooks," he wrote, "To him I will set up a special memorial, for he was to me at once ideal leader and guide.... I virtually bathed in Nietzsche's genius, and got a charmed weather-tight and bulletproof skin that should protect me against attacks from without as I go along my way."[11]

Rank differed from Freud, in particular with the latter's emphasis on the primacy of sexual and aggression drives. Drawing from your concept of the will to power, Rank "thought of the ego not as a derivative of the drives or a byproduct of frustration and failed gratification as understood by Freud, but as a given primary self that strives to acquire and accomplish the building blocks necessary for its own growth and development."[12] Rank is represented by one writer as "often ambivalent about Nietzsche's overemphasis on the ideal person as amoral and morality as unnatural."[13] This, of course, is a misunderstanding of your thinking about morals. Many people have misun-derstood you, Nietzsche, in failing to realize that your attack on values is an attack on the gap between the life of values propounded by the church and the life actually lived, not a rejection of values per se. We will have much more to say about this in future communications.

Joseph Paneth, another Jew of your acquaintance, forged a direct connec-tion between you and Freud. Paneth's name is eternalized in his discovery of a special cell in the lining of the intestines: the Paneth cell. It was Paneth who sought you out for conversation, and he valued those meetings greatly. He described you in a personal letter to a friend: "uncommonly friendly, and without a trace of false pathos or the prophet-mongering I had suspected in his last book [Zarathustra].... In many questions of religion we shared the same viewpoints and skepticism."[14]

In another letter, Paneth wrote, "Nietzsche is possessed of many contradictions but is a thoroughly honest man, a man of moods and of an inspired prophetical nature."[15]

Paneth's connection with Freud developed in medical school. He thought highly of Freud, as he did of you, and at one important point in Freud's career, he made available the funds Freud needed to continue his studies.[16] Paneth shared with Freud the feeling of being handicapped by his Jewish background. Unfortunately, Paneth died of tuberculosis at the young age of thirty-three. In fact, he died in 1900 — the year of your own death.

Freud's father was a traditional Jew. On his son's thirty-fifth birthday, he gave him a copy of the Bible and wrote in Hebrew, "My dear son Shlomo [Freud's Hebrew name]...the spirit of the Lord began to move you and said to you: Go, read in My Book that I have written and there will be opened to you the sources of wisdom, of knowledge, of understanding. See the Book of books from which the wise men dug out their wisdom and the lawmakers learnt law and justice.... From your father, who loves you with unending love — Jacob, son of Rabbi Sch. Freud. In the capital city of Vienna 29 Nissan 5651, May 6, 1891."[17]

In the family Bible, Freud's father used the Hebrew date of Freud's *breet meelah* (ritual circumcision) as "the 8th day of the month of Iyar = May 15, 1856." He also recorded the name of the *mohel*, the one who performed the circumcision, and the *sahndahk*, the family member, esteemed rabbi, or close friend who is honored by being asked to hold the child during the circumcision.[18]

Another personal link between you and Freud was Jacob Bernays. I mentioned to you that he, your fellow student of Ritschl, was a first cousin of Freud's wife, Martha. Intellectually, the link was through Bernays's writings on catharsis. Bernays described the Dionysian rites as a cathartic process. You developed this further in *The Birth of Tragedy*.[19] Joseph Breuer, Freud's mentor, developed catharsis as a treatment modality, and this became central to Freud's method of free association, in which he instructed patients to talk about anything that came to mind, whether or not it seemed logical to them.

This free association was used as an entrée into the unconscious mind of the patient.

Note the similarities between what you wrote, Nietzsche, and what Breuer wrote about the repressed aspect of revenge. In *The Genealogy of Morals* you wrote of "the ressentiment of natures that are denied the true reaction, that of deeds, and compensate themselves with an imaginary revenge…the submerged hatred, the vengefulness of the impotent." In a footnote in his *Studies of Hysteria*, Breuer wrote, "The instinct for revenge which is so powerful in the natural man and is disguised rather than repressed by civilization, is nothing whatever but the excitation of a reflex that has not been released. To defend oneself against injury in a fight and, in doing so, to injure one's opponent is the adequate and preformed psychical reflex. If it has been carried out insufficiently or not at all, it is constantly released again by recollection, and the 'instinct of revenge comes into being.'"[20]

Freud came into his friendship with Breuer insecure about his Jewish identity. According to a close friend, "Freud was deeply self-conscious, and unsure of himself, and especially sensitive to social rejection. This insight illuminates the emotional intensity behind Freud's bitterness and embarrassment over provincial Jews [read *Jews of the culture of the Bayt Meedrahsh*], and behind the endeavor to separate himself…from them."[21]

Although Breuer was not a Jew of the culture of the Bayt Meedrahsh, he had a much stronger and healthier Jewish identity than did Freud and the Jews around him. In response to the way Jewish students were reacting to the anti-Semitism of the day, Breuer wrote to a Jewish fraternity, "Our epidermis has almost become too sensitive. I would wish that we Jews had a consciousness of our own value [which would make us] quiet and half indifferent to the judgment of others rather that this unwavering, hyper-sensitive point d'honneur."[22] A member of the volunteer Jewish burial society, *khevrah k'deeshah*, Breuer helped Freud become more comfortable as a Jew.

The value of Breuer's collegial "psychotherapy" is indicated by a letter Freud wrote to his wife, revealing that Breuer had "discovered that hidden under the surface of timidity there lay in me an extremely daring and fearless human being."[23]

Perhaps this latter trait is reflected in the fact that when a Jewish friend told Freud he was considering raising his son as a Christian, Freud replied, "If you do not let your son grow up as a Jew, you will deprive him of those sources of energy which cannot be replaced by anything else. He will have to struggle as a Jew, and you ought to develop in him all the energy he will need for that struggle. Do not deprive him of that advantage."[24]

Freud presented some of his earliest papers at the Vienna B'nai B'rith meetings. B'nai B'rith means "sons of the covenant" and remains today an active Jewish collegial, service-oriented organization. However, Freud did not pray as a Jew or celebrate any of the Jewish holidays. Martin Freud, his oldest son, recalled, "We were brought up without any traces of...or instruction in Jewish ritual." To the best of Martin's memory, none of the children ever attended synagogue.[25]

Otto Rank, who valued you so highly, dear Nietzsche, worked actively to shed his Jewish identification. He never used his family name, Rosenfeld, in his professional activity, and in 1903 he formally converted to Christianity. One can see his special *ressentiment* toward his contemporary Jews of the culture of the Bayt Meedrahsh in this fascinating statement, whose internal contradiction is obvious: "The observation of the laws in the Old Testament was very simple at the time of its inception... Today, it is utterly impossible to live in accordance to the viewpoints of that time. The last 'Jew' has been dead for a long time now; yet the descendants, with a mixture of obstinacy, arrogance, malice, self-conceit appropriate to their race, hold fast to their inherited laws."[26] And today, Nietzsche, in the twenty-first century, the descendants of those "dead for a long time now" continue to "hold fast to their inherited laws and prejudices," and many still call them arrogant and obstinate.

Ernst Jones was a non-Jewish colleague who joined Freud's widening circle and went on to write an authoritative biography of Freud. His experience of knowing only assimilating Jews was similar to yours, Nietzsche. He wrote, "Until this time, I had had no friends among Jews, and had met very few of them. In childhood I remember my grandmother telling me that Jews were people who kept pawnshops, a fact with hardly any meaning for me, and that they were obstinate people who kept apart from the rest.... In one important respect, however, my knowledge on this topic is singularly deficient. It has never been my fortune to know a Jew possessing any religious belief, let alone an orthodox one."[27]

A special case among Freud's followers was Carl Gustav Jung. Like you, the son of a minister, he was born in 1875 in Switzerland. His important years of study were in Basel and Zürich. He arrived at Basel more than fifteen years after you left. It was a paper he wrote in 1906 on dementia praecox (now known as schizophrenia) that brought him to Freud's attention. They worked very closely together for the next five years, and Freud saw in Jung a successor to himself. However, a formal break between them came in 1912 over Jung's *Psychology of the Unconscious*. Feeling that Freud's emphasis on libidinal drives was restrictive, Jung went on to found a psychological school of his own.

Early in his career, Jung, too, expressed his debt to you, Nietzsche, though his relationship to you and your works is often ambivalent. In his *Memories, Dreams, Reflections*, he wrote of his fear that "I might be forced to recognize that I too was another such strange bird.... Of course [Nietzsche] was a professor, had written whole long books and so had attained unimaginable heights, but, like me, he was a clergyman's son.... He spoke a polished High German, knew Latin and Greek, possibly French, Italian, and Spanish as well, whereas the only language I commanded with any certainly was the Waggis-Basel dialect. He, possessed of all these splendors, could well afford to be something of an eccentric, but I must not let myself find out how far I might be like him."[28]

Jung enjoyed a successful professional career and had every reason to be satisfied with his life and his accomplishments. However, he seems not to have studied your analysis of *ressentiment* closely enough to avoid the malady in his own psyche. This problem first surfaced vis-à-vis the Jews. Jung's five years in close association with Freud and his Jewish associates could have allowed for him, as for Jones, an appreciation for their introspection and psychological insights, but this was not to be.

I keep promising to write to you, Nietzsche, of your sister's activities after your death, and I will make good on my promise. For now, suffice it to say that the German leader whom she adored was the ultimate evil projection of the anti-Semitism you saw in Wagner and in your sister. This leader came to power in 1933, and his "Final Solution" to the "Jewish problem" was quickly put into motion. By 1934, Freud's work, that of his followers, and the music of Felix Mendelssohn had all been banned in Germany.

Jung, purporting to show that Freud's "Jewish psychology" had no relevance to the new German, wrote, "One cannot, of course, accept that Freud or Adler is a generally valid representative of European mankind.... The Jew as a relative nomad has never created, and presumably will never create, a cultural form of his own, for all his instincts and talents are dependent on a more or less civilized host people. The Jewish race possesses, in my experience, an unconscious that can bear only a very limited comparison with an Aryan one.... The Aryan unconscious has a higher potential than the Jewish.... He [Freud] did not know the Teutonic soul any more than his blind followers in Germany knew it. Has the mighty phenomenon of National Socialism not taught them to know better?"[29]

I hardly need to describe to you, Nietzsche, the "mighty phenomenon of National Socialism" that Jung extols. You wrote about nationalism in *The Gay Science*, over forty years before Hitler came to power: "The word 'German' is constantly being used nowadays to advocate nationalism and race hatred and to be able to take pleasure in the national scabies of the heart and blood poisoning that now leads the nations of Europe to delimit and barricade themselves against each other as if it were a matter of quarantine."[30] Six years later, having written much on the same theme in works after *The Gay Science*, you wrote in *The Twilight of the Idols*, "The Germans are now bored with the spirit, the Germans now mistrust the spirit.... Deutschland, Deutschland über alles, I fear that was the end of German philosophy."[31]

Over a five-year period in the mid-1930s, Jung conducted a series of seminars on Zarathustra that would make you cringe. Most of the seminars were about Jung and his work. The content of his remarks about Zarathustra are hardly relevant beyond their being symptomatic of Jung's *ressentiment*. This has not escaped the attention of twentieth-century commentators.

One scholar devoted an entire book to Jung's relationship with you. She comments rather sharply, "Jung's reception of Nietzsche's work and personality is peculiar because, on the one hand, Jung readily acknowledges his debt to Nietzsche's influence and the similarity of their ideas, but, on the other hand, he wildly misinterprets Nietzsche's ideas.... Furthermore, Jung's denigration of Nietzsche's personality and of his personal life in general is labored and unnecessary, and often diverts the reader from Jung's own argument."[32]

Jung's personal attacks on you are far worse than "labored and unnecessary" and only point out the depth of the *ressentiment* that motivated them. A few quotes will suffice: "Among my friends and acquaintances I knew of only two who openly declared themselves adherents of Nietzsche. Both were homosexuals; one of them ended by committing suicide, the other ran to seed as a misunderstood genius."[33] And "[Nietzsche was in reality] a neurotic, a poor devil who suffered from migraine and a bad digestion, and had such bad eyes that he could read very little and was forced to give up his academic career.... All that contributed to the most beautiful inferiority complex you can imagine."[34]

Neither of the scholars quoted above notes the obvious possibility that it was your pronounced disdain for the German national "spirit," and Jung's vigorous identification with it, that was likely a major reason for his *ressentiment* toward you.

Now for some challenges — here is a quote for you:

> Sensuality [has] an appeal to your senses, not that it should master and direct you, but that you should master and direct it, not that you should suppress or kill it.... For there is not a single natural tendency in man which is, in itself, either good or bad. If all good were sweet, and all evil were bitter, our whole virtue would be no more than the natural unfree following of that which attracted our senses, and the whole nobility of being a human being would be lost.[35]

Anyone reading this letter except you, Nietzsche, would certainly guess that you wrote it. *You* might even think you had written it, or might at least say, "I would be proud to have written it." I changed this quote slightly from Samson Raphael Hirsch's commentary on the biblical life of Cain and Abel to make the challenge a little more difficult. He actually wrote, "God has given sensuality an appeal to your senses..." To remind you, Rabbi Hirsch was your contemporary, the outstanding student of Rabbi Isaac Bernays, father of Jacob Bernays. You would have had much to talk with him about, but alas, you did not meet him, presumably because you assumed that the "religious" Jews you heard about were few in number, insignificant, and that *they* were the Jews who were disappearing from history.

Now, who wrote this? "The first preliminary schooling for spirituality: not to react at once to a stimulus, but to gain control of all the inhibiting, excluding instincts...the inability to resist a stimulus..."[36] You recognize this as your writing from *Twilight of the Idols*. You also wrote, "To sow the seeds of good spiritual works in the soil of the subdued passions is then the immediate urgent task."[37] Now, the unthinking reader of your works may be perplexed to find you writing about things "spiritual," just as he or she might react when

reading your writing about "gratitude." This is confusing material for someone who thinks of you as an antimoralist and a nihilist.

And the Tahlmood, the compilation of the Oral Law in Judaism, in speaking of the good and evil instincts in man, says that if one removes the *yehtzehr
hahrah* [evil impulse], "the whole world goes down," as this is part of man's
nature, and the goal is to strengthen the *yehtzehr hahtov* — the good
impulse.[38]

One of the aspects of Christianity to which you took the most vigorous
exception is expressed in your belief that Christianity repudiated unbridled
passions, especially sexuality, and failed to see that strength came from sublimating — overcoming — the negative aspects of these instincts. On this you
and Jewish thinking are in full agreement. Rabbi Hirsch addresses this issue
directly in his commentary on the biblical account of Adam and Eve: "But
what a miserable lie has been concocted from this historical account, a lie that
undermines all the moral future of mankind! We are referring to the dogma
of 'original sin' against which…it is the duty of the Jew to protest most vigorously, with every fiber of his being."[39]

In the *Tahlmood*, sexual impulses are not shameful and not a subject to be
avoided. The *Tahlmood* is full of instruction about sexual relations, so that
they may be properly expressed in a healthy, loving relationship between a
man and a woman. There is also recognition that sexual relations are often
expressed in unhealthy ways, and the *Tahlmood* explicitly deals with the
issues that arise around such behavior.

How does one overcome the *yehtzehr hahrah* (negative instincts)? The
answer is not to be found in reason alone. Eliezer Berkovits, an erudite rabbi
and thinker of the twentieth century whom I mentioned in a previous letter,
maintained, "Judaism does not accept the facile optimism of the Socratic-
humanistic tradition that all man needs for the good life is the intellectual
study of the essence of goodness. According to Judaism, man judged by his
own nature is not as hopeless a creature as Christian theology would have it;
neither is he as easily led to goodness as humanism imagines as possible.
There is, indeed, a great deal that man is able to do for his own redemption,
but much more is needed than the intellectual contemplation of the nature of
goodness."[40]

In explaining the essence of the struggle, Berkovits writes, "The motivat-
ing spring of all action being a desire, the ethical deed requires 'an appetite for

goodness.' Judaism assumes that such an inclination is indeed implanted in human nature. It is the *Yetzer Tov*, the good inclination, which, like its adversary, the *Yetzer Hara*, has its seat 'in the heart.' It is an emotional force, a desire for the good. It is present in all men, but — unfortunately — it is rather weak and helpless in the conflict with the other, self-centered and exclusively self-regarding urges and bio-physical needs of man. It is therefore necessary to foster the emotional force of the desire for the good, to increase its intensity and its hold over the emotional pattern of the human personality."[41]

Like you, Nietzsche, Rabbi Berkovits recognizes the importance of sublimation in the psychological battle for overcoming one's naked emotions in the culture of the Bayt Meedrahsh: "One may increase the intensity of the desire for the good by sublimating some of the egocentricity and self-seeking inclinations of human nature. But the sublimation of desires is brought about by inhibition.... Within the system of Judaism, the purpose of the method of inhibition is achieved by such 'ritual' laws as belong to the category of the *Mitsvot Lo Ta'aseh* or interdictory commandments. 'Thou shalt not do any kind of work on the Sabbath day' has obviously an inhibitory function too. The same is true of the numerous dietary laws and of many other 'purely religious' injunctions."[42]

In addition to sublimation, one requires action: "The only way of educating the bio-physical instrument of action is by making it perform and do. This task is fulfilled by the other group of 'ritual laws' which has its place in the category of *Mitsvot Asseh*, of commandments of positive injunction, prescribing certain religious performances."[43]

You, Nietzsche, had your own formula for "educating the biophysical instrument." You wrote in *The Dawn*, "Avoiding opportunities [for satisfaction] implanting regularity into the drive, engendering satiety and disgust with it and associating it with such ideas as that of disgust, evil consequences or offended pride, then dislocation of forces and finally a general weakening and exhaustion."[44]

You had a remarkable degree of self-discipline, and certain individuals can achieve the self-overcoming required for healthy spirituality without the psychotherapy developed by the various schools of psychology. But when we look to the health of an entire community — the culture of the Bayt Meedrahsh — we must look to education and ethical inspiration. Berkovits brilliantly outlined how this is accomplished.

Your concept of the will to power is at the center of your psychology and your values. The will to power over others is an unhealthy will to power, which needs to be overcome. In drafts for *The Birth of Tragedy*, you wrote of "power which is always evil," and seeing that Wagner had become corrupted by his success and sense of power, you wrote, "Who of you will renounce power, knowing and experiencing that power is evil?"[45] This also illustrates that when you wrote of "beyond good and evil," you were not proposing that there was no such thing as evil.

In the chapter in *Thus Spoke Zarathustra*, "On the Thousand and One Goals," you tie the will to power to "'overcoming': A tablet of the good hangs over every people. Behold, it is a tablet of their overcomings; behold, it is the voice of their will to power. Praiseworthy is whatever seems difficult to a people; whatever seems indispensable, and difficult is called good; and whatever liberates even out of the deepest need, the rarest, the most difficult — that they call holy."[46]

In *The Dawn* you contrasted the Jews to the Germans, saying of the Jews, "To honor father and mother and to follow their will to the root of one's soul — that was the tablet of [self-] overcoming that another people hung up over themselves and became powerful and eternal thereby." And of your countrymen: "Germans: 'To practice loyalty and, for the sake of loyalty, to risk honor and blood even for evil and dangerous things'"[47]

Thus, we see that your psychology was very much in tune with that which preceded it: the psychology of the Jewish Written and Oral Law. We will continue this theme much more extensively, dear Nietzsche, when we get to the realm of values. We are just getting started on this exciting adventure.

Ben Moshe

# Letter Four

July 1, 2005                                                כ"ה בסיון תשס"ה

Dear Nietzsche,

It is time to deal with your sister, Elisabeth, and how she conspired, as executor of your estate, to justify your premonition: "The thought frightens me that any people who are unauthorized and wrong-headed will cite me as an authority for their actions."[1] Those who want to appropriate or "misunderstand" your works for their own purposes find the perfect source in Elisabeth and those she recruited to do her will; on the other hand, those who want to understand your thought and values must study what Elisabeth did in its ugly intent to pervert your legacy.

It was in November 1883 that Elisabeth became engaged to Bernhard Förster. Less than six months later, you wrote to a friend, "I have broken radically with my sister: for heaven's sake, don't think of mediation or reconciliation. Otherwise I am as considerate as possible because I know what is to be said in defense of my sister."[2]

You had in common with Förster that you were teachers, sons of ministers, and admirers of Richard Wagner. However, the very reasons that led to your break from Wagner kept Förster strongly attached to him. Förster applauded Wagner's declaration to his royal patron, King Ludwig of Bavaria, that "the Jewish race is the born enemy of pure humanity and everything that is noble in it."[3] And Förster did not stop at mere declarations — he provoked fistfights with Jewish passengers on public transportation and addressed a petition to the German chancellor, Otto von Bismarck, requesting that he limit Jewish immigration from Eastern Europe.[4]

As you remember, Elisabeth and Förster married in 1885 and left the next year for Paraguay, where Förster founded a colony to promote his ideas. In 1889, at about the time when your nervous system disorder robbed you and the world of your fertile mind, Elisabeth lost her husband as well, when Förster killed himself.

Elisabeth worked in Germany to recruit clergymen for the colony in Paraguay, where she returned briefly in 1892. She was not warmly received, however. One of the colonists told the director of the colony, "I do not believe that she has been cured in Germany of her disease which borders on megalomania; on the contrary, her alleged successes concerning the clergymen, etc., have probably made her even more conceited and domineering."[5]

When your sister returned to Germany in 1893, she legally changed her name to Elisabeth Förster-Nietzsche. You will be happy to know that your loyal friends, the Overbecks, knowing of your contempt for her views and those of her late husband, continued to address her as Frau Förster.[6]

Elisabeth single-mindedly set about commandeering your literary works. She briefly considered engaging your friend Peter Gast to edit them, but she distrusted him. She wrote to him that *The Antichrist* was not to be published, saying, "We must tell nobody, but nobody, that we cannot publish it because of its content. Hence the following lie has occurred to me: A closer examination of the manuscript has shown that part of it is missing and before all existing manuscripts are reviewed, copied, and registered — a time-consuming procedure in view of the author's very difficult handwriting — any publication now is out of the question."[7]

Next Elisabeth set out to wrest legal control over all rights to your work from your mother. It was not pleasant — she even threatened to have your mother declared incompetent. When your mother became ill at the end of 1895, she gave up the fight and signed all rights over to Elisabeth.[8]

When Elisabeth edited your notes to publish, under your name, a book entitled *The Will to Power*, she left out your important caveat, which I mentioned in a different context in my first letter: "*The Will to Power*. A book for thinking, nothing else: it belongs to those to whom thinking is a delight, nothing else. That it is written in German is untimely to say the least. I wish I had written it in French so that it might not appear as a confirmation of any *reichsdeutschen* aspirations."[9]

I will not bore you with a long history of the twentieth century, Nietzsche, but it was an enormously bloody hundred years. Two major wars were ignited in Europe, spread beyond the European continent, and are now called World Wars I and II. Germany was at the center of both, and the Germans were on the losing side in both. In World War I, large numbers of German Jews served in the German army, with some thirty thousand decorated for their service. In the years before and during World War II, a German leader arose to solve "the Jewish problem" and set out to physically exterminate all the Jews of Europe. He and his accomplices succeeded in murdering six million Jews, among them one and a half million children.

This man Hitler was the embodiment of everything you despised in the German spirit. He was a cartoonish, almost laughable incarnation of the perversion of the will to power, the utter failure to overcome, the straight-from-central-casting antithesis of the *Übermensch*. Who would have anticipated that such a man could convince an entire nation to follow him? The answer is you, Nietzsche — you saw, long before he came to power, the sickness of the German spirit resonating with everything Hitler represented. Thus, it comes as no surprise that your sister, Elisabeth, was his enthusiastic supporter.

Many historians of the twentieth and twenty-first centuries still debate when the world became aware that Hitler posed a threat to the Jews in Germany and, ultimately, in all Europe. The debate stems from a combination of denial and faulty scholarship. To the leadership of American Jewry, looking on from afar at the Hitler phenomenon, there was no doubt about his intentions for the Jews of Germany. One American Jewish leader received the following report from a German Jew:

> We are having terrible day and nights. In the morning the bad news starts and during the night we cannot sleep expecting the worst. The papers only publish what the government permits. I cannot imagine that people abroad know how much the poor Jews have to suffer here. I cannot describe to you how desparate [sic] our situation is. If the foreign countries do not help us soon, we are lost.... How many poor Jews have already been tortured to death. They even cut "jakenkreuze" [swastikas] into their flesh. These are the real middle ages. Many Jews are in prison and it is doubtful if they ever leave it alive...."[10]

The recipient of the report, Stephen Wise, president of the American Jewish Congress, did not sit on the information. In a letter to a colleague, he wrote, "I am going through days and nights of hell, for I am mindful of our awful responsibility. But if you had seen the documents that we have seen, you would know that…silence is acquiescence."[11]

A few days later he wrote to the same colleague, trying to alert him to the ongoing danger: "I wonder whether many Jews realize that we are facing today…a Jewish upheaval which parallels, if it does not surpass in significance, the upheaval of 1881. … The trouble, Mack, is that none of us is quite alive to the fact that this may be the beginning of a world-wide movement against us, a world-wide conflagration, a world-wide undertaking against the Jews."[12]

Reports continued to pour out of Germany. This telegram is but one example:

> BERLIN NOT AMERICA NOT EVEN COUNTRIES BORDERING GERMANY CAN HAVE FULL PICTURE INSULTS TORTURES HOPE-LESSNESS WHICH JEWS UNDERGOING GERMANY. STOP.… EVERYTHING THAT WAS TRUE FIRST DAYS HITLER REVOLUTION IS STILL TRUE NOW EVEN DRASTICER [sIC]. STOP. JEWS STILL DISAPPEAR LATER FOUND IN MORGUES.… SUICIDES AMONG JEWS ASSUMING UNIMAGINABLE PROPORTION. STOP. TRAGEDY GREATER BECAUSE EVEN GERMANS ALL CLASSES FORMERLY ENEMIES OF HITLERISM ARE GRADUALLY ACCEPTING IT PATRI-OTICALLY THUS JEWS FIND THEIR FRIENDS OF LONG AGO CONVERTED ANTISEMITES ANXIOUS SEE JEWS OUTLAWED IN ORDER TO SHARE THEIR PROPERTIES BUSINESS JOBS.[13]

A month later another report reached American Jewish leaders, proclaiming, "The present situation of the Jews of Germany is deplorable beyond any words of mine to describe.… What you will decide to do is of course your own concern; all I can say, in conclusion, is that what you do should be done quickly. Either muffle your ears to the weeping and wailing of the children of Rachel, and harden your hearts to this cry of humanity itself and thus let the worst crime of our age proceed to its ordained end in the deliberate extinction of nearly a million men, women and children, or else come quickly and strongly to the rescue."[14]

All these reports, dear Nietzsche, were written the same year, 1933 — the *very first year* of Hitler's reign of terror. Before he was through, six and a half million Jews would be dead in the European theater of operations.

In that same year, 1933, your sister Elisabeth wrote to a friend, "Last Sunday, I had the great good fortune of a personal conversation with our wonderful chancellor. It was in the theater during a solemn performance of Tristan in honor of the fiftieth anniversary of Wagner's death. Hitler graciously visited me in my box.... We are drunk with enthusiasm because at the head of our government stands such a wonderful, indeed phenomenal, personality like our magnificent chancellor, Adolf Hitler. That is why the tremendous upheaval in Germany probably appears quite different to us than to people abroad. They cannot understand how we endure these vast transformations cheerfully. Well, the reason is that we have suddenly achieved the one Germany which for centuries our poets have depicted longingly in their poems and which we have all been waiting for: *Ein Volk, Ein Reich, Ein Führer.*" [15]

The full extent of her perversity as heir to your literary estate is neatly summed up in another letter, in which she wrote, "Believe me, Fritz would be enchanted by Hitler, who with incredible courage has taken upon himself the entire responsibility for his people."[16]

Despite the transparency, at least to anyone not thoroughly blinded by self-deception, of what Elisabeth was doing with your works, many were taken in — and still are to this day. Her sordidness is chronicled in many publications; indeed, an entire book, sardonically titled *Zarathustra's Sister*, was devoted to exposing her hoax. The author said this of her influence on German letters: "As the high priestess of the Nietzsche cult, 'Zarathustra's Sister' played an active part in the literary and political life of Germany from Bismarck to Hitler. So much so that on three occasions — in 1908, 1911, and 1923 — her name was proposed to the Swedish Academy for the Nobel Prize in literature. When she died in 1935, almost ninety years old, the German press eulogized her as an undaunted exponent of the true German spirit. Hitler personally attended her funeral and laid a wreath on her coffin."[17]

Abraham Lincoln, a United States president during your lifetime, left us with many memorable thoughts, perhaps the most often quoted being "You can fool all of the people some of the time; you can fool some of the people all of the time; but you cannot fool all of the people all of the time." Today, dear

Nietzsche, Elisabeth and the disease of the "German national" spirit are dead (at least in the *governance* of Germany), but your writings live on.

In that same period, the first half of the twentieth century, we must document the Catholic Church's continued pursuit of power, and the moral and ethical compromises this entailed. We must take an unblinking look at a chapter of history beginning in your time and continuing through the two World Wars. This was another of the many dark chapters chronicling the Catholic Church's behavior toward the Jews. Many have blamed the pope during World War II for his indifference to the murder of more than six million Jews; others feel he has been wrongly accused. A Catholic researcher, John Cornwell, deciphered the full story. His work is especially credible because he set out to defend Eugenio Pacelli — Pope Pius XII. "I was convinced," he said, "that if the full story was told, Pius XII's pontificate would be vindicated."[18]

Reassured by John Cornwell's intentions, the Vatican's archivists provided him with hitherto unseen documents. The results staggered him: "By the middle of 1997, nearing the end of my research, I found myself in a state I can only describe as moral shock. The material I had gathered, taking the more extensive view of Pacelli's life, amounted, not to an exoneration but to a wider indictment.... I found evidence, moreover, that from an early stage in his career Pacelli betrayed an undeniable antipathy toward the Jews, and that his diplomacy in Germany in the 1930s had resulted in the betrayal of Catholic political associations that might have challenged Hitler's regime and thwarted the Final Solution."[19]

Now, dear Nietzsche, in the twenty-first century, we are familiar with the notion of the infallibility of the pope — a strong central tenet of the Catholic Church in Rome. Yet, in your time, "the Catholic Church's authority was widely distributed through the great historical councils and countless webs of local discretion. As in a medieval cathedral, there were many thrusting spires of authority."[20] The story of the Pacelli family's loyal dedication to the papacy goes back to the early eighteenth century.

Pope Pius XII's grandfather, Marcantonio Pacelli, was a close adviser to Pope Pius IX, well known as Pio Nono (Spanish for "Pius IX"). Pio Nono became pope in 1846 and, only three years later, was humiliated by an Italian mob resentful of the power of the Church in Italy. On November 16, 1849, his summer palace was besieged, and Pio Nono, "disguised in a priest's simple cassock and a pair of large spectacles, fled to the seaside fortress of Gaeta within the safety of the neighboring kingdom of Naples."[21] At his side was Marcantonio Pacelli (the future pope's father). With a loan from the famous Jewish banking family Rothschild, and the backing of the French troops, Pio Nono was able to return to Rome a year later.

Though Pio Nono had abolished the Jewish ghetto at the beginning of his papacy, he gave in to the popular will, and Jews were forced back into ghettos in retribution for having backed those who fought for a united Italy. In 1858, the volatile pope found himself at the center of an episode that became a cause célèbre throughout the world. A six-year-old Jewish boy was kidnapped by papal police and forcibly educated as a Catholic. Despite pleas from the parents and condemnation of the episode from the United States, Emperor Napoleon III of France, and Emperor Franz Joseph of Austria, Pio Nono kept the child in a monastery for years, and ultimately he was ordained a priest. Pio Nono told the parents they could have the child back if they converted to Catholicism; it was his view that the well-known obstinacy of the Jews had caused the problem.[22]

In 1869, the final ignominy fell on Pio Nono when his French protectors pulled out of Rome to join in the Franco-Prussian war. The Italian revolutionary forces moved into the vacuum, and Rome was wrested from papal control, never to be returned. "All that remained to Pio Nono and his Curia, the cardinals who governed the former Papal States, were the 108.7 acres of the present-day Vatican City."[23]

In Germany, Bismarck instituted his own struggle against the Catholic Church with his *Kulturkampf*, systematically depriving the Church of powers previously taken for granted. This phenomenon spread throughout Europe, and it was in this atmosphere that Pacelli, the future Pope Pius XII, began studying for the priesthood.

When Pio Nono died in 1878, his successor was Leo XIII. I don't know, Nietzsche, how closely you followed these events. It was a time of rising anti-Jewish pronouncements from the Catholic intelligentsia. Between 1881 and 1992, *La Civiltà Cattolica* published a series of articles that included the medieval libel of Jews sacrificing Christian children at Passover time. This was cited as a Jewish law "binding on the conscience of all Hebrews." In order for the ritual to work, it was said, "The child must die in torment." The Jews were "the race that nauseates...an idle people who neither work nor produce anything; who live on the sweat of others."[24]

Pacelli, who would be the pope during the time of the Holocaust, was bright and ambitious. He was chosen as a close aide to Pietro Gasparri, undersecretary in the Department of Extraordinary Affairs. Gasparri would rise to cardinal secretary of state with Pacelli at his side, until Pacelli succeeded his mentor in that post in 1930.[25]

On the death of Leo XIII in 1903, Giuseppi Melchiorre Sarto became Pope Pius X. The following year, work was begun in secret on what would become the 1917 Code of Canon Law. Cornwell tells us, "The text, together with the Anti-Modernist Oath, became the means by which the Holy See was to establish and sustain the new, unequal, and unprecedented power of relationships that had arisen between the papacy and Church. Gasparri and Pacelli were its principle architects."[26]

Although well aware of the amoral doctrine of National Socialism, Pacelli and the Vatican deemed Communism the greater threat to the Church. The Church had already signed an accord with Mussolini in 1929. Drafted by Pacelli's brother along with Gasparri, the Lateran Treaty declared Catholicism the only religion recognized by Italy, and acknowledged the Vatican's right to impose in Italy the Code of Canon Law. The Catholic Popular party, similar to the German Catholic Center Party, was disbanded, and the Vatican instructed Catholics not to involve themselves in Italian politics.[27]

This development was not lost on Hitler, who had not yet ascended to power in Germany. He published an article declaring, "The fact that the Catholic Church has come to an agreement with Fascist Italy...proves beyond doubt that the Fascist world of ideas is closer to Christianity than those of Jewish liberalism or even atheistic Marxism to which the so-called Catholic Center Party sees itself so closely bound."[28] Hitler knew full well that the Vatican's Code of Canon Law — power centralized in Rome — was at odds with the German Catholic Center Party.

In the middle of the First World War, Pope Benedict XV, who acceded to the papacy with the death of Pius X in 1914, decided it was time for a peace initiative. The year was 1917; Russia was in the throes of revolution, and the United States had not yet entered the Great War. The person entrusted by the Vatican with approaching the Germans was none other than Pacelli. While in Germany as the pope's representative, he was approached by a rabbi seeking help with a shipment of *skhakh* — palm fronds, needed for the Jewish holiday of Sookoht. Pacelli's style of handling tasks decisively, as well as his attitude toward Jews, is apparent in his approach to this issue. He wrote to the Vatican, "To go along with this would be to give the Jews special assistance not within the scope of practical, arms-length, purely civil or natural rights common to all human beings, but in a positive and direct way to assist them in the exercise of their Jewish cult. I accordingly replied courteously to the aforementioned rabbi...that I had sent an urgent report to the Holy Father on the matter, but I foresaw that in consequence of the wartime delays in communication it was doubtful whether I should get an answer in time, and that the Holy Father would be delayed in explaining the matter in depth to the Italian government."[29]

In the 1919 German elections, the Catholic Center Party emerged with 91 seats, second to the Social Democrats' 163 seats. The Catholic party naturally was interested in maintaining its strong autonomy in Catholic affairs, putting it on a collision course with Pacelli, who was dedicated to centralizing power in Rome. Pacelli became a representative of the Vatican in Germany in 1925 and was still there in 1933, when Hitler came to power. Hitler's party replaced the Catholic Center Party as second to the Social Democrats in the elections of 1930.

In 1931, a Catholic Reichstag representative published a book entitled *Hitler and Rome*, which quickly became a best seller. Karl Trossman, the author, wrote that Hitler's party was a "brutal party that would do away with the rights of the people."[30] The following year, two Catholic journalists warned in an article, "National Socialism means enmity with neighboring countries, despotism in internal affairs, civil war, and international war. National Socialism means lies, hatred, fratricide and unbounded misery. Adolf Hitler preaches the law of lies. You who have fallen victim to the deceptions of one obsessed with despotism, wake up!"[31] The author saw what you, dear Nietzsche, had seen fifty years before — yet very few were listening.

Pacelli had his mind fixed on centralizing Catholic power in Rome. When Hitler came to power in 1933, he sought an agreement with the Vatican similar to the Lateran Treaty in Italy. Knowing that he could not pass the Enabling Act, giving the pope dictatorial powers, unless the Vatican directed the Catholic Center Party to support it, he negotiated with Pacelli through a sympathetic member of the Catholic party. The Vatican got the Enabling Act and a

Reich Concordat, making German Catholics subordinate to the Vatican in all matters, and the Catholic Center Party was disbanded.

A Catholic ex-chancellor of Germany, Heinrich Bruning, had no doubts about either the deal that was made or the men who made it: "Behind the agreement with Hitler stood not the Pope, but the Vatican bureaucracy and its leader, Pacelli. He visualized an authoritarian state and an authoritarian Church directed by the Vatican bureaucracy, the two to conclude an eternal league with one another. For that reason, Catholic parliamentary parties, like the Center in Germany, were inconvenient to Pacelli and his men and were dropped without regret in various countries."[32]

The situation of the Jews of Germany in 1933, when Hitler came to power, is described in the above-mentioned letters. In 1935, anti-Jewish laws were passed institutionalizing what had already been happening in practice. On November 8, 1939, incited by the killing of the third secretary of the German embassy in Paris, what came to be known as Kristallnacht broke out in Germany. Over seven thousand Jewish stores and homes were destroyed along with approximately two hundred fifty synagogues. More than thirty thousand Jews were rounded up and taken to concentration camps. The *New York Times* correspondent in Germany filed his story: "Beginning systematically in the early morning hours, in almost every town and city in the country, the wrecking, looting and burning continued all day. Huge but mostly silent crowds looked on and the police confined themselves to regulating traffic and making wholesale arrests of Jews 'for their own protection.'"[33]

The *London Daily Telegraph* carried the story of its Berlin correspondent: "Mob rule ruled in Berlin throughout the afternoon and evening and hordes of hooligans indulged in an orgy of destruction. I have seen several anti-Jewish outbreaks in Germany during the last five years, but never anything as nauseating as this. Racial hatred and hysteria seemed to have taken complete hold of otherwise decent people. I saw fashionably dressed women clapping their hands and screaming with glee, while respectable middle-class mothers held up their babies to see the 'fun.'"[34]

Less than four months later, following the death of Pius XI on February 10, 1939, Pacelli was elected Pope Pius XII. During the first week of his papacy, in a conference with his German cardinals, Pacelli showed them the letter he intended to send to Hitler as the new pope: "To the illustrious Herr Adolf Hitler, Führer and Chancellor of the German Reich! Here at the beginning of our pontificate, we wish to assure you that we remain devoted to the spiritual welfare of the German people entrusted to your leadership.... During the many years we spent in Germany, We did all in Our power to establish harmonious relations between Church and State. Now that the responsibilities of our pastoral function have increased our opportunities, how much more ardently do We pray to reach that goal. May the prosperity of the German people and their progress in every domain come with God's help, to fruition."[35]

Any debate whether Pacelli — Pope Pius XII — was anti-Jewish or could have done more to help Jews in World War II is moot, Nietzsche. Catholic attitudes toward Jews are for the self-examination of Catholics themselves. Pacelli's single-minded effort to restore the central power and authority of the pope, which had been lost to secular governments and local Catholic councils, speaks loudly to the fictitious nature of a "Judeo-Christian ethic." Catholic hierarchical culture and the culture of the Bayt Meedrahsh cannot be more different, one seeking power and authority at the inevitable expense of compromising moral and ethical imperatives, and the other isolating itself from such temptations so that ethical and moral imperatives remain at the very center of education and daily pursuits.

How, dear Nietzsche, did the persecutions in Europe in your time and on into the twentieth century influence displaced Jewry? Here we must not focus solely on Europe. Before the two World Wars, major persecutions of Jews took place in the domain of the Russian czars. This led to widespread emigration to the United States, the *goldena medina* (golden country) seen as a new land of opportunity. These dislocations and those of the World Wars posed a major challenge for Jewish life. The Russian czars and the Germans of the nineteenth and twentieth centuries were only the latest manifestations of Jew hatred, *ressentiment* spreading across thousands of years of history. Once safe in the United States, what would the Jews do? Would the persecutions and dislocations cause an increase in the flow of Jews from the culture of the Bayt Meedrahsh into the stream of assimilation? Would Jews perceive that in the hoped-for safety of the United States they would be able to preserve and advance the culture of the Bayt Meedrahsh?

Now, at the beginning of the twenty-first century, with over a century of Jewish experience in the United States since your time, Nietzsche, that country's environment has in fact turned out to be safer and more nurturing for

Jews than any similar span of time anywhere else in the world. In the chronically hostile surroundings of Europe and the Middle East, we can understand the historical desire of Jews to assimilate into the surrounding cultures, to be like "all peoples," to stop being different, to escape persecution and death. Hence the question: "Left alone," to their own devices, what are American Jews doing?

Jews have historically married other Jews. Among intermarried couples, the chances of children being raised as Jews in those homes decrease significantly. In the 1940s in the United States, intermarriage rates of Jews with non-Jews were below 10 percent. The figure rose to 10 percent in the early 1960s, prompting a major magazine article entitled "The Vanishing American Jew."[36]

In a demographic study in the mid-1970s, the intermarriage rate had risen to 49 percent, with a steady decline in conversions of non-Jewish spouses to Judaism.[37] In 1989, sociologists reported that barring a change in this trend, there would be a drop from 5.7 million Jews in the United States in 1985 to 5.4 million in 2000.[38] This was a very accurate projection — the figure from the actual 2000 survey is a little lower than the projected 5.4 million.

The only thing standing in the way of general acceptance by Jews of the mass of accumulated data is a phenomenon that you, Nietzsche, describe aptly. I have mentioned it already, but it is a quality so much at the core of human behavior that it is worth stressing over and over again: man has an almost infinite ability to fool himself in order to construct a world where he can comfortably live.

In 1990, Jonathan Sarna, then a professor of American Jewish history at the Reform Hebrew Union College in Cincinnati, released data from his study of converts among the leadership of Reform congregations. His conclusions were less than sanguine: "Frighteningly, about 80 percent of converts or those married to converts...would not, by their own admission, feel too badly if their children married non-Jews.... In the Reform leadership study, more than 50 percent of the converts responding — leaders I remind you — would not even be bothered a great deal if their children converted to Christianity."

Sarna warned of the implications of denial: "Let us make no mistake; the data we now have at hand should serve as a dire warning.... We will be accountable to posterity if, knowing what we now know, we close our eyes and do nothing."[39] This data was followed by the 1990 National Jewish Population Study, the most comprehensive study of United States Jews ever undertaken. That study was commissioned by the Council of Jewish Federations, the national body of the largest group of lay Jewish leaders in the United States.

The data revealed what was called a "core" of 5.5 million Jews. Of these, more than a million classified themselves as having been born Jewish but with no affiliation to any religious group. The intermarriage rate now topped one half. Except among Jews from the culture of the Bayt Meedrahsh, birth rates had dropped below replacement levels.

Providing more detail about marriages, the survey reported, "Since 1985 twice as many mixed couples (born Jew with Gentile spouse) have been created as Jewish couples (Jewish with Jewish spouse)." Outside the culture of the Bayt Meedrahsh, the only Jewish women whose birth rates were above replacement levels were those in the no-longer-childbearing age group of fifty-five to sixty-four years. Birthrates among younger couples had dropped off dramatically.

Perhaps the most discouraging data came from the findings about children. Included in the survey were 1.9 million children under the age of eighteen. Fewer than half of all children in the survey were being raised with Judaism as their religion. Among children of mixed marriages, the results were dramatic: of the 664,000 children under age eighteen who were living with a Jewish and a non-Jewish parent, 45 percent were being raised in another religion, 30 percent were being raised without any religion, and only 25 percent were being raised as Jews.[40]

The conclusion of the major demographer involved in the study was straightforward: "The new data show the substantive debate is over. To our deep regret, the pessimists, or rather the realists were proven to be right."[41]

When the national convention of this group was convened in 1997, the keynote speaker was a rabbi of the Jewish Conservative movement. He made only oblique mention of the 1990 survey data, repeatedly glorifying "what is called secular." He confidently pronounced the demise of "rabbinic Judaism," another term for the culture of the Bayt Meedrahsh. He explained to a packed hall of over four thousand Jewish leaders from throughout the United States: "When I say that rabbinic Judaism has died, I don't want you to think that means that Judaism doesn't have anything to teach us. Just like for rabbinic Judaism, biblical Judaism died, biblical Judaism was the womb out of which rabbinic Judaism was born, so too for the next Judaisms that are coming, and we don't know what they are..."

Taking another shot at the Jews of the culture of the Bayt Meedrahsh, this leader pronounced *Shahbaht* (Sabbath) observance a false value: "Shabbos (*Shahbaht* — Sabbath) is easy; it's a fake. It's a giant fantasy..."[42]

These responses are reminiscent of Otto Rank's observations about the "old," "outmoded" Jews of his time that I mentioned to you in a previous letter. Rank and this leader just mentioned shared a feeling of *ressentiment* vis-à-vis the stubbornly generative Jewish culture of the Bayt Meedrahsh.

This study stunned the Jewish world, at least for a time. In keeping with the need to construct a world "comfortable" and in keeping with one's cherished preconceived notions, many Jewish leaders, to use your words, "watered down, shrouded, sweetened, blunted, and falsified."

Now that it is clear — to all who can see, at any rate — that assimilating Jews are not the generative Jews responsible for thousands of years of unbroken cultural continuity, we will turn in the next letter to those who are responsible.

Very truly yours,

Ben Moshe

# Letter Five

August 24, 2005                                    י״ט באב תשס״ה

Dear Nietzsche,

When I first studied your works, I wondered just how familiar you were with Jewish texts. You wrote often and favorably of the "Old Testament," yet this was almost always in the context of your antipathy toward the Christian testament. It is now clear to me that your knowledge of the Five Books of Moses — the Torah — was minimal. You were familiar with the more "exciting" parts of the Five Books, which is to say *B'raysheet* — Genesis — and most of *Sh'moht* — Exodus. These were, to you, sagas of admirable people, whose type is no longer to be found.

At the end of Exodus, the people of Israel are at Mount Khorev, also called Sinai. Moses ascends the mountain to receive the Torah, the incident of the Golden Calf occurs, and Moses ascends once more after breaking the tablets. This ruins the "story" for you, and your response is sharp. You concluded that "Yahweh," the "god of justice" of whom you approved, was somehow replaced: "The concept of God becomes a tool in the hands of priestly agitators, who now interpret all happiness as a reward, all unhappiness as punishment for disobeying God, as 'sin.'"[1]

There are major errors here, Nietzsche, errors that we must deal with. The history is flawed, and this faulty view of history only fueled what must be called your obsession with Christianity. Your errors, dear Nietzsche, flow from three primary sources:

(1) Your buying into Wellhausen's concept of "priestly Judaism"

57

(2) Your construction that Christianity grew out of "priestly Judaism"

(3) Your unawareness of the enduring culture of the Bayt Meedrahsh

All this left you with a view that Christianity was "mankind." I put this last word in quotation marks because it is from your writing, in *Ecce Homo*: "The Christian has hitherto been the 'moral being,' a curiosity without equal — and, as a 'moral being,' more absurd, more mendacious, vain, frivolous, harmful to himself than even the greatest despiser of mankind could have allowed himself to dream.... It is not error as error which horrifies me at the sight of this.... It is the lack of nature, it is the utterly ghastly fact that anti-nature itself has received the highest honors as morality, and has hung over mankind as a law, as categorical imperative!... To blunder to this extent, *not* as an individual, *not* as a people, but as mankind!"[2]

It is clear that Christianity on the European continent was in your time, and is today, a dominant force. However, it was not "mankind." Had you known of the strong, vital culture of the Bayt Meedrahsh in Europe in the 1800s, you would have found a counterpoint to the way you viewed Christianity.

The appointing of the priests that you cite from the last part of Exodus took place in the desert. The priests had no decision-making role among the Israelites. The "legislative body" was Moses and the seventy elders whom his father-in-law, Jethro, advised him to appoint. The priests were subject to very stringent rules of behavior laid out in the same Five Books of Moses, from which you quote, and were subject to removal from their spiritual office for violation of those rules.

Your statement that "the priest formulated once and for all, down to the large and small taxes he was to be paid (not to forget the tastiest pieces of meat, for the priest is a steak eater)" is erroneous; the reason they were *given* tithes of food was so they would be preoccupied solely with things spiritual, not things material. It is made clear at the very point in the Torah from which you quote that when the Israelites enter the Promised Land, the tribe of Levi, from which came the priests, would be the only one of all the tribes of Israel that would *not* own any of the land. They would be scattered among the territories given to the other tribes, to be spiritual guides. They did not in the desert, and would not in the Promised Land, have any lawmaking or law-enforcing role.

You were very much influenced by Julius Wellhausen and his biblical criticism. It is ironic that you adopted the term "priestly Judaism," for this was a phrase often used by Protestant writers in your time, and you had little love for Protestant theology.[3] We need not attack Wellhausen's misconceptions, but had you sat with the scholars of the culture of the Bayt Meedrahsh, you would have had an opportunity to compare the ideas of a then "modern" scholar with those of Jewish scholars from a culture that had survived thousands of years by virtue of a life lived in accordance with the precepts of the Torah. For Wellhausen, the Torah was a text; for the Jews of the culture of the Bayt Meedrahsh, it is nothing less than a divine guide by which a moral, ethical life is lived.

Had you sat with Rabbi Samson Raphael Hirsch, he would have told you what he wrote about the priests in his commentary on Leviticus. It is clear that he was aware of the misconception under which you and Wellhausen labored. Hirsch wrote, "Nowhere in all the millennia of Jewish history do we see a priest exercising a significant influence on the development of his community by virtue of his priestly office. By far the overwhelming majority of the men who have had an impact on the life of the Jewish nation as its leaders and teachers were not priests."[4]

For the Jew of the culture of the Bayt Meedrahsh, the Written Law and the Oral Law were given by Hahshehm. We will see that the continuity and evolution of the law does not derive from a fundamentalist clinging to the literal meaning of every chapter and verse. Such an interpretation would spell dissolution rather than the thousands of years of continuity that have marked the culture of the Bayt Meedrahsh.

Let us begin to get a sense of the culture of the Bayt Meedrahsh through literature. You describe beautifully your sense of inspiration in *Ecce Homo*, in the chapter on Zarathustra: "The concept of revelation, in the sense that something suddenly, with unspeakable certainty and subtlety, becomes visible, audible, something that shakes and overturns one to the depths, simply describes the fact.... Everything is in the highest degree involuntary but takes place as in a tempest of a feeling of freedom, of absoluteness, of power, of divinity.... This is my experience of inspiration; I do not doubt that one has to go back thousands of years to find anyone who could say to me 'it is mine also.'"[5]

You also asked, "What language will such a spirit speak when he speaks with himself alone? The language of the dithyramb. I am the inventor of the dithyramb."[6] Now let us indeed go back thousands of years before your Zarathustra to find one whose spirit expressed itself in a dithyramb you apparently did not know of, though you came close to emulating it. This ancient dithyramb was written in Hebrew, and I will juxtapose it to a selection from *Thus Spoke Zarathustra*. Only a serious student of your work could say with confidence which is yours:

1) Wisdom cries aloud in the street; she utters her voice in the squares; she cries in the chief place on concourse, at the entrances of the gates; in the city she utters her words, saying, How long, you simple ones, will you love being simple? And how long, O scorners, will you delight in scoffing, and fools hate knowledge? Turn at my reproof: behold, I will pour out my spirit to you, I will make known to you my words. Because I have called, and you refused; I have stretched out my hand, and no man regarded; but you have set at naught all my counsel, and would none of my reproof: I will also laugh at your calamity; I will mock when your fear comes upon you; when your fear comes like a storm and your calamity comes like a tempest; when distress and anguish come upon you. Then shall they call upon me, but I will not answer; they shall seek me early, but they will not find me; for they hated knowledge...[7]

2) But why do I speak where nobody has my ears? And so let me shout it into all the winds: You are becoming smaller and smaller, you small people! You are crumbling, you comfortable ones. You will yet perish of your many small virtues, of your many small abstentions, of your many small resignations. Too considerate, too yielding is your soul.... And when you receive it is like stealing, you small men of virtue.... But why do I speak where nobody has my ears? It is still an hour too early for me here. I am my own precursor among this people, my own cock's crow through dark lanes. But their hour will come! And mine will come too!...[8]

The first dithyramb, Nietzsche, is from the first chapter of Proverbs; the second, from your own *Thus Spoke Zarathustra*. King Solomon, the author of Proverbs, would doubtless tell you that his inspiration came from Hahshehm.

While many who are only faintly familiar with your work "know" that you pronounced God dead, they do not know what that means in the context of your works. In *The Gay Science*, you wrote, "Have you not heard of the madman who lit a lantern in the bright morning hours, ran to the market place, and cries incessantly: 'I seek God!'... The madman jumped into their midst and pierced them with his eyes. 'Whither is God?' he cried. 'I will tell you. *We have killed him* — you and I. All of us are his murderers.'"[9]

What did it mean to you that "God is dead"? To careful readers, this is clearly not a triumphant expression of atheism. In *The Gay Science*, you wrote, "The meaning of our cheerfulness — the greatest recent event — that 'God is dead,' that the belief in the Christian god has become unbelievable — is already beginning to cast its first shadows over Europe."[10] And in *The Antichrist*, you were yet clearer: "That we find no God...is not what differentiates *us*, but that we experience what has been revered as God, not as "godlike" but as miserable.... If one were to *prove* this God of the Christians to us, we should be even less able to believe in him."[11]

If a Church sets out with a vision of ethics and morals and then, weary of persecution at the hand of the Romans, enters into an alliance with its oppressors and becomes occupied with worldly power and riches, then we have reason to question the power and influence of a godhead who commands ethical and moral behavior but whose followers do not adhere to those commands. So you pronounced dead the "Christian God." Given that you did not know the culture of the Bayt Meedrahsh, you did not know there was a culture whose people are very much influenced by their Creator — Hahshehm. You did not know that despite centuries of persecution, this culture has refused to sell out to worldly powers and continues to live according to Hahshehm's commandments.

We will spend a great deal of time discussing Hahshehm and his commandments. For now, let us return to King Solomon to demonstrate the continuity of the culture of the Bayt Meedrahsh. Solomon, despite his position, was commanded by the Torah, the word of Hahshehm, to write a copy of the Torah — the Five Books of Moses — in his own hand and carry it into battle. All this was a thousand years before the time of Jesus. More than a king, Solomon was a philosopher and writer par excellence. We have just read his dithyramb; now we turn to his haunting piece of philosophy and a literary jewel called *Kohelet* — Ecclesiastes. This masterpiece has earned for its author the accusation, from careless readers, of nihilism, just as your writing, dear Nietzsche, earned for you the same accusation from similarly careless readers.

Millions upon millions of readers have thrilled to these lines:

> To everything there is a season,
> A time to be born and a time to die,
> A time to plant and a time to uproot what is planted,
> A time to kill and a time to heal,
> A time to wreck and a time to build,
> A time to weep and a time to laugh,
> A time to wail and a time to dance,
> A time to scatter stones and a time to gather stones...

Thus I perceived that there is nothing better for man than to rejoice and do good in his life. Indeed every man who eats and drinks and finds satisfaction in all his labor — this is a gift of Hahshehm."[12]

Also from the prolific pen of Solomon flowed an extraordinary work called, in Hebrew, *Sheer Hahsheereem,* or in English, "The Song of Songs." One of the greatest of the Tahlmoodic sages, Rabbi Ahkeevah, said, "The entire world is not as worthy as the day when the Song of Songs was given to Israel, for all the scriptural writings are holy, but the Song of Songs is the Holy of Holies."[13] The Song of Songs, like every other part of the Jewish canonized works, is read and studied in depth, along with many commentaries about the text, by members of the culture of the Bayt Meedrahsh. These lines are from chapter four of *Sheer Hahsheereem:*

> Thy lips are like a thread of scarlet, and thy mouth is comely;
> Thy temples are like a piece of pomegranate split open behind thy veil.
> Thy neck is like the tower of David built with turrets,
> Wherein there hang a thousand shields,
> All the armor of the mighty men.
> Thy two breasts are like two fawns that are twins of a gazelle,
> Which feed among the lilies.
> Until the day breathe, and shadows flee away, I will get me to
> The mountain of myrrh, and to the hill of frankincense.[14]

Not only are there clear sexual allusions in the Songs of Songs, but the interpretation of the sages is that this is a metaphor of the relationship between
Hahshehm and the people of Israel. This is hardly a culture in need of a
godhead born of a virgin!

King Solomon came from quite a literary family. His father, King David,
wrote most of the one hundred fifty Psalms, of which William Gladstone, a
British prime minister during your lifetime, Nietzsche, said, "All the wonders
of the Greek civilization heaped together are less wonderful than is the single
Book of Psalms."[15] How many times have the inspired words of the Psalms
been set to music by composers of all eras!

We move forward from the time of King Solomon, ultimately arriving at
your time, with the continuity of the Jews of the Bayt Meedrahsh. In the first
century of the Common Era, we encounter the Sadducees. The Sadducees
were mostly priests who sold out to the Romans, conspiring with the Romans
against their own people. At the point that they rejected the Oral Law, they
separated themselves from the Jews of the culture of the Bayt Meedrahsh,
who followed a tradition that was already, at that point in history, thousands
of years old.

With the destruction of the Second Temple in the year 70, the dispersion
of the Jewish people began. The Sadducees were in the process of disappearing from history. Paul, as well as the other writers of the gospels, took nothing
from the Sadducees. Unlike the Sadducees, they did not honor the Written
Law — the Torah — and reject the Oral Law; instead they created their own
gospels that rejected the laws of both the written and the oral traditions of the
Jews.

Few people know that the first Jewish Christians adhered strictly to the
tenets of Jewish law, both the Torah and the Oral Law. They were, in fact,
from the family of Jesus. Mostly farmers and merchants, they cared nothing
for worldly power and relished their own obscurity. These were the *desponysi*,
a Greek term which means "belonging to the master." They included Mary
and Jesus' brothers, James, Joseph, Simon, and Jude. We know of three blood-
lines from Jesus' own family. Joachim and Ann were Jesus' maternal grandparents; Elizabeth was the first cousin of Jesus' mother, Mary; another first
cousin of Mary was Cleophas, whose wife was also Mary's first cousin. From
these relatives came the *desponysi*. The blood descendants of Joseph, Mary's

husband, did not qualify, since only persons in bloodline with Jesus through his mother were *desponysi*.[16]

In addition to the Christians who were born Jewish and adhered strictly to Jewish laws and tradition, there were also proselytes. Such men were the first to join Christianity as a result of the preaching of Paul and his followers.

These tensions led to a formal council in the year 49, at which Peter and Paul's insistence that non-Jewish converts need not be circumcised to become Christians and that only Jewish converts need be bound by the Torah carried the day. This decision set the stage for the spread of Christianity.[17] The numbers of strictly practicing Jewish Christians gradually dwindled, and by the early fifth century of the Common Era they were beyond recognition. They had been punctilious in following both the Written and the Oral Law. After Jesus' death, the acceptance of Jesus as the messiah by the Jewish Christians completely separated them from the culture of the Bayt Meedrahsh.

The term "Pharisee" is also widely misunderstood. Christian hostility toward Judaism has fostered the mistaken notion that the "Pharisees" were the enemies of Jesus. The term "Pharisee" does not appear in Jewish sources as a general designation for the sages, except when used by those who opposed them — the Sadducees.[18]

Scholars have pointed out, dear Nietzsche, that your comments about "priestly Judaism" must be understood in the context of your revulsion at Christianity — that you wanted to taunt the Christians that their origins were from the very Jews that they hated. This is correct as far as it goes. But previous writers have not recognized the fundamental misconceptions just mentioned. This is curious, because there is ample academic scholarship documenting them.

Certain confounding generalizations have bedeviled our attempts to understand the secret of the Jews' survival as a culture essentially unchanged throughout thousands of years of history. The first generalization that gets in our way is the lumping together of many different schools of thought, tradition, and belief under the label "Jew" or "Judaism." To get past this hurdle, we must examine closely the many names attached to Jews: Sadducees, Essenes, Karaites, Samaritans, Reform Jews, Conservative Jews, Reconstructionist Jews, cultural humanist Jews, and others. The first four mentioned above deviated from the culture of the Bayt Meedrahsh centuries ago and ceased to be part of the Jewish people.

Today we still have a large number of Diaspora Jews who belong to movements that are in a rapidly assimilating process, as demographic data over more than fifty years amply demonstrates. They are in the process of disappearing, but thanks to the fallacious notion — tacitly assumed though seldom examined — that the time in which one lives and the life that one is now living are somehow the "real world" and will continue forever, they are blinded to the painful facts that document the deterioration of their communities. Nor could the Sadducees, Essenes, Karaites, or Samaritans foresee their inevitable disappearance when they were at the height of their cultural dominance.

The second generalization blocking our attempts to get at the secret of Jewish survival is the myth of "the Judeo-Christian ethic." First of all, we must thrust aside the word "religion." Just as speaking of "the Judeo-Christian ethic" conjures false parallels, so, too, calling Judaism "one of the three great religions" confuses rather than elucidates. What invariably happens is that all involved nod their heads sagely as if they understood one another, all the while obeying an unspoken agreement *not* to think.

In eschewing the term "religion," we have likewise eliminated the term "Judaism" from our discourse. At the time of the revelation on Sinai and at the time of the compilation of the *Tahlmood*, there was no Hebrew word for "religion." And indeed, there still isn't — the word now used for "religion" is *daht*, a word meaning "decree, law."

It is not easy to find in the spiritual realm even superficial areas that "all Jews" have in common or that "all Christians" have in common, let alone areas that Jews *and* Christians have in common. One may be tempted to say, "All Jews and all Christians attend a house of worship." Well, almost all — some who identify themselves as Jews or Christians never do, and many do so only on rare occasions. Can we even say, "All Christians and all Jews believe in God"? Again the answer is a resounding no.

In Jewish law — *hahlahkhah* — a child born to a Jewish mother is considered Jewish. Some members of the culture of the Bayt Meedrahsh say to a Reform or Conservative Jew something like this: "If your mother is Jewish, then you are Jewish; it is just that the law you adhere to is not that given to Moses." The Reform and Conservative Jews are insulted by this and say that their religion is indeed Judaism, that they have a right to make their own interpretation of Judaism and worship as they wish. Conversations of this type are numerous, heated, and useless.

It is crucial to stress the central principle that all Jews (those born of a Jewish mother, or those who undergo a conversion sanctioned by Jewish law to join the Jewish people) feel a responsibility for one another, and that this responsibility is taken very seriously. Reform, Conservative, and even totally nonobservant Jews are not shunned and considered non-Jews by members of the culture of the Bayt Meedrahsh. Their disappearance over time is a natural function of what *they* do and do not do until the time comes when their descendants, searching for spirituality and not finding it in the choices they see as available to them, choose some form of Christianity or shun any association with a "formal religion" altogether. Thus, by their own choice, they cease to identify themselves as Jews.

Therefore, dear Nietzsche, you can understand the wisdom in avoiding this multiplicity of terms and discerning between Jews of the culture of the Bayt Meedrahsh and assimilating Jews. Among the Jews of the culture of the Bayt Meedrahsh, we will find that many values and practices *are* held in common by all Jews of this culture — and have been over thousands of years. This will get us closer to understanding the secret of the Jews.

Returning to your fellow writer, King Solomon, he built the First Temple in the middle of the tenth century before the Common Era, and it was destroyed in 586 B.C.E. This led to the Babylonian exile, which lasted approximately seventy years. A minority of the expelled Jews returned, and under the leadership of Ezra and Nehemiah the Temple was rebuilt, initiating what is called the Second Temple Period.

Ezra was a major figure in the continuity of the culture of the Bayt Meedrahsh. We will find, dear Nietzsche, that whenever hostile forces threatened to obliterate this culture, men of enormous stature rose to the occasion. The first chapter of *Peerkay Ahvoht* — Sayings of the Fathers — a tractate of the *Tahlmood* (Oral Law), delineates the reception and passing down of the Torah: "Moshe [Moses] received the Torah from Sinai and handed it on to Joshua, and Joshua to the Elders, and the Elders to the Prophets, and the Prophets handed it on to the men of the Great Assembly."[19] You would have loved the Sayings of the Fathers, Nietzsche, because, along with King Solomon's proverbs, they are a rich source of aphorisms — a literary form that you used with great skill.

Ezra is often referred to as "Ezra the Scribe." The Hebrew word for "scribe" is "*sofer*." Today a *sofer* writes Torahs, copying them line by line; likewise, he pens the contents of the *t'feeleen*, the phylacteries that Jewish men of the culture of the Bayt Meedrahsh lay on every morning except Shahbaht — the Sabbath — during their prayers. We will return to this when we discuss a day in the life of a Jew of the culture of the Bayt Meedrahsh.

Ezra was not a scribe in the modern sense. The *sohfreem* (plural of "*sofer*") were interpreters of the Torah. They were freelance individuals, not a formal body; in that sense they were analogous to rabbis today. Ezra is accorded the highest honor by the *Tahlmood*, in which he is compared to Moses: "It has been taught: Rabbi Yosi said: Had Moses not preceded him, Ezra would have been worthy of receiving the Torah for Israel."[20]

In an important work of the twentieth century, Moshe Koppel, a professor of mathematics and a knowledgeable Jew of the culture of the Bayt Meedrahsh, traces the development of *hahlahkhah* — Jewish law — using paradigms of mathematical logic along with much insightful historical interpretation. He points out, "Ezra's achievements in terms of the progressive formulation of Halakhah are clear; whereas the prophets interpreted the idea of what God requires in the abstract, Ezra made the written Torah the basis for all future interpretations. From then on, interpretation was required not of the ideas of the Torah, but of its text.…[21] This is not to say that the text did not exist earlier, simply that the text (along with the existing body of Oral Law) became the sole basis of future interpretations."[22]

In addition to being an important interpreter of the law, Ezra was also the head of the *Ahnshay hah-K'nehseht hah-G'dohlah* — Men of the Great Assembly. Included in this esteemed body were Haggai, Zechariah, and Malachi — the last of the prophets. Mordechai of the Purim story, well known to almost all Jews, is also thought to have been a member, as is Nehemiah, architect of the rebuilding of the Temple after the Babylonian exile.

The Men of the Great Assembly instituted the central prayer of the Jewish worship service — the *Ahmeedah* (literally, "standing"), or *Sh'moneh Ehsreh* (literally, "eighteen"). Regular prayer three times a day took the place of the sacrifices that ceased with the destruction of the Temple. The Men of the Great Assembly instituted other changes as well, making it easier for a people who had lost much of its learning as a result of the Babylonian exile to participate and reengage with Torah learning.

Mohsheh (Moses), who received the written and oral tradition from Hahshehm on Mount Sinai, was denied the right to cross the Jordan into the Promised Land and passed the law on to his successor, Yehohshooah bin Noon (Joshua). Joshua spearheaded the conquest of the Promised Land, then passed his learning and leadership responsibilities on to his successor, Kahlayv ben Yehphooneh (Caleb). Joshua and Caleb had been the only two of the twelve spies sent by Moses to spy out the land of Canaan who returned with praise for the land.

Thus, we will see, dear Nietzsche, that throughout history, when Jews were knowledgeable about Torah, with learning and intuition, they were able to provide reliably for continuity. However, when Torah was lost in times when the culture of the Bayt Meedrahsh was under great stress, formalization was necessary. Koppel brings the apt analogy of language: "The rules of grammar are not taught to children and then transmitted to the next generation. Instead the language is spoken. In this sense Hahlahkhah is like a spoken language, passed down from generation to generation, not necessarily by anyone teaching 'These are the rules,' but rather by the unspoken transmission of rules that are implicit in practice. Nevertheless, grammatical rules must sometimes be made explicit in order to introduce stability to the process by which language grows and develops in its transmission from one generation to another."[23]

The passing down of the Oral Law from generation to generation is indispensable to understanding the secret of the Jews. One of the youngest of the 120 members of the Men of the Great Assembly was Shimon the Righteous, the high priest after Ezra. Here again, Nietzsche, it is important to emphasize that while the high priest, if worthy, could be included among the assemblies of the great men of a generation, the priests themselves never constituted a lawmaking or enforcement body.

The generations that passed down the Oral Law are meticulously documented by Rabbi Moses ben Maimon, better known as Maimonides. In tracing the generations of the Oral Law after Ezra and the Men of the Great Assembly, Maimonides meticulously documents the leaders of each era who passed down the law to their successors. These were the leaders of the culture of the Bayt Meedrahsh until the times of the Common Era. Hillel the Elder and Shahmai were the fifth and last of five generations of *zoogoht* (pairs) of leaders of their generations. Hillel and Shahmai were esteemed colleagues, and differences of opinion between them were settled by majority rule.

Ezra served the culture of the Bayt Meedrahsh after the fall of the First Temple, and Hillel also served at a crucial time for the Jews. Koppel writes, "Just as at the time of Ezra the basis for interpretation shifted from the ideas of the Torah to its text, so, at the time of Hillel, the interpretative basis began to shift from the Torah's text to the substantial body of formalized Oral Law that had already resulted from the earlier interpretation of the text."[24] The terrible persecutions under the Romans led to a significant decrease in learning: "In ancient times, when the Torah was forgotten from Israel, Ezra came up from Babylon and established it. It was again forgotten, and Hillel the Babylonian established it."[25]

In *Human, All Too Human*, you wrote, Nietzsche, about attributes that, though you did not know it, characterized Hillel and his students: "Modesty. — There is true modesty (that is, the recognition that we are not the work of ourselves); and it well becomes the great mind because it is precisely he who can grasp the idea of his complete unaccountability (also for the good he creates). One hates the immodesty of the great man, not to the extent that it comes from a sensation of his own strength, but because through it he evidences a desire to experience this strength by wounding others, treating them in a domineering way and seeing how far they will put up with it."[26]

In the same work, again without knowing it, you wrote of the sages of the culture of the Bayt Meedrahsh: "Quiet fruitfulness. — The born aristocrats of the spirit are not too zealous; their creations appear and fall from the tree on a quiet autumn evening unprecipitately, in due time, not quickly pushed aside by something new. The desire to create continually is vulgar and betrays jealousy, envy, ambition. If one is something one does not need to make anything — and one nonetheless does very much. There exists above the 'productive' man a yet higher species."[27]

The idea of passing along great ideas was well known to you: "Acknowledging heirs. — He who has founded something great in a selfless attitude of mind takes pains to rear heirs for himself. To see an opponent in every possible heir of one's work and to live in a state of self-defense against them is a sign of a tyrannical and ignoble nature."[28] The Jewish sages received rather than "founded something great," and they took great pains to pass along the received tradition.

You were suspicious of democracies, Nietzsche, believing they encourage mediocrity. The leadership of the Men of the Great Assembly, as well as the leadership throughout the thousands of years of history of the culture of the Bayt Meedrahsh, has always been determined by superior intellectual and moral characteristics — a true meritocracy.

Observers innocent of the content or process of decision making in the culture of the Bayt Meedrahsh typically pose either of two contradictory criticisms: (1) the *hahlahkhah* (Torah law) is a rigid set of legalistic rules leaving no room for individual differences; or (2) rules are just made up as the necessity arises. Neither of these observations is correct, the former being an entirely uninformed statement, and the latter an understandable (though incorrect) observation by interested observers who are not aware of the process of hahlahkhic development.

The covenant between Hahshehm and the people of Israel is and was ever a covenant of partnership. This is well illustrated by a parable about a rabbi at the time of a flood in his city. Perched on his roof as the water climbed above the first floor of his house, he saw a man in a rowboat approaching, who told him to climb down into the boat. The rabbi responded, "I am fine. Just be sure all my congregants are cared for." Some time later, as the water crested at the roofline, the rescuer returned. "Rabbi, all your congregants have been moved to safety; please come with me." The rabbi replied that the man should double-check that all citizens of the town had been evacuated. With the water at the rabbi's ankles, the man in the boat beseeched him, "Everyone is safe, rabbi; please, *please* come with me." The rabbi replied, "Hahshehm will provide for me." He was engulfed by the flood waters and drowned.

When the rabbi arrived in heaven and was given an audience with Hahshehm, he complained, "Master of the universe, all my life I kept your commandments. I studied Torah and tended to my people. Why, oh why, did you let me drown?" Hahshehm said to the man, "Rabbi, three times I sent the boat."

The study of the Written and Oral Law leads man to an understanding of Hahshehm's will, but only by seeing himself as an active partner in the covenant can the Jew understand that he is not simply a passive receiver of rigid laws and miracles. Jewish law — *hahlahkhah* — is a covenantal partnership that was built in to Hahshehm's instructions to Moses on Mount Sinai. The belief in Hahshehm's omniscience and the belief that man has a role in perfecting the world form one of the antinomies that are part of Jewish life; members of the culture of the Bayt Meedrahsh who study Jewish texts for hours each day grapple with these texts and their differing interpretations, to try to discern the will of Hahshehm.

Emanuel Rackman, educator and *tahlmeed khakhahm* — Torah scholar — of the current era, expounds on this issue: "Implicit in almost every discussion is a balancing of the conflicting values and interests which the law seeks to advance. And if the Halakhah is to be viable and at the same time conserve its nature and spirit, we must reckon with the opposing values where such antinomies exist. An equilibrium among them must be achieved by us as objective halakhic experts rather than as extremists propounding only one of the antithetical values."[29]

These issues, dear Nietzsche, are nothing new. The rabbis of the time of the *Tahlmood* grappled with them on many occasions. The incident of Akhnai's oven illustrates this very well; it also illustrates that the content of the issues under discussion in the *Tahlmood* is often secondary to the process of decision making. In the example of Akhnai's oven, the issue is ostensibly whether the oven's composition is ritually clean or unclean:

> Rabbi Eliezer declared it clean, and the Sages declared it unclean; and this was the oven of Akhnai.... On that day Rabbi Eliezer brought forward every imaginable argument, but they did not accept them. Said he to them: "If the Hahlahkhah agrees with me, let this carob tree prove it!" Thereupon the carob tree was torn a hundred cubits out of its place — others affirm, four hundred cubits. "No proof can be brought from a carob tree," they retorted. Again he said to them: "If the Halakhah agrees with me, let the stream of water prove it!" Whereupon the stream of water flowed backwards. "No proof can be brought from a stream of water," they rejoined. Again he urged: "If the Halakhah agrees with me, let the walls of the schoolhouse prove it," whereupon the walls inclined to fall. But Rabbi Joshua rebuked them saying: "When scholars are engaged in a hahlahkhic dispute, what have ye to interfere?" Hence they did not fall, in honor of Rabbi Joshua, nor did they resume the upright, in honor of Rabbi Eliezer; and they are still standing thus inclined. Again he said to them: "If the Halakhah agrees with me, let it be proved from Heaven!" Whereupon

a Heavenly Voice cried out: "Why do ye dispute with Rabbi Eliezer, seeing that in all matters the Halakhah agrees with him!" But Rabbi Joshua arose and exclaimed: "It is not in Heaven. What did he mean by this?" Said Rabbi Jeremiah: "That the Torah had already been given at Mount Sinai; we pay no attention to a Heavenly Voice, because Thou hast long since written in the Torah at Mount Sinai, 'After the majority must one incline.'"[30]

The issue of the majority in Jewish life is mentioned in many Jewish texts. Koppel cites the following: "Rabbi Yanai said: The Torah that God gave to Moshe (Moses) included forty-nine arguments in favor of [declaring a given object] clean, and forty-nine arguments in favor of [declaring a given object] unclean. [Moshe] said to Him: What should be done? Hashem said to him: If those who rule 'unclean' are the majority, it is unclean; if those who rule 'clean' are the majority, it is clean."[31] Thus, we see that while the leaders of the culture of the Bayt Meedrahsh are chosen in the context of a meritocracy, the democratic principles of debate, doubt, opposition, and majority rule are very much a part of the process.

Now, dear Nietzsche, we have documented the continuity of the culture of the Bayt Meedrahsh from the time of the giving of the Torah on Mount Sinai to the time of the destruction of the Second Temple in 70 C.E. At this time, Jesus is dead, and the Sadducees are passing from history. The Jewish Christians, loyal to the Written and Oral Law, are quietly studying and shepherding in the Promised Land, a land the triumphant Romans renamed Philistia. When next I write to you, we will document the continuation of the culture of the Bayt Meedrahsh right up to your time in the eighteenth century.

Ben Moshe

# Letter Six

Oct 13, 2005

י' תשרי תשס"ו

Dear Nietzsche,

His name was Rabbi Yohkhahnahn ben Zahkai, and he was destined to play a pivotal role in the Bayt Meedrahsh culture's transition away from its traditional nucleus in the Jerusalem Temple to new and far-flung centers of learning imposed by life in the Diaspora — the dispersion of Jews to all parts of the world. One of the great rabbi Hillel's many students, he was learned in all areas of the Written and Oral Law, including the Kahbahlah — the esoteric wisdom of the Torah.

A story in the *Tahlmood* relates that Rabbi Yohkhahnahn ben Zahkai was riding on a donkey being driven from behind by his disciple, Rabbi Ehlee'ayzehr ben Ahrahkh. His pupil asked him to teach him a chapter from the Work of the Mehrkahvah — "Chariot" (a Tahlmoodic term for the esoteric tradition). Rabbi ben Zahkai answered, "My son, have I not instructed you that the Work of the Chariot is not to be taught even to one person unless he is a sage and able to draw inferences on his own?" Rabbi Ehlee'ayzehr entreated, "Master, then permit me to say something before you that you already taught me." Rabbi Yohkhahnahn ben Zahkai gave his permission and descended from the donkey and wrapped himself in his cloak. When Ehlee'ayzehr ben Ahrahkh asked why he had done so, his master replied, "While you are expounding the Work of the Chariot, the Divine Presence might be with us, and the Ministering Angels might accompany us — is it proper that I should continue riding an ass?"[1]

I mention this story, Nietzsche, to emphasize that the Kahbahlistic

73

tradition — the hidden wisdom of the Torah — is an integral part of Torah study for those so engaged; "Jewish mysticism," a misleading term often used for Kahbahlah, is not something learned by a separate sect of Jews. Like the *Tahlmood*, the Kahbahlah is interpretation and elucidation of the Torah — the five books of Moses. In Tahlmoodic literature it is often referred to as "the Work of the Chariot." Rabbi Ehlee'ayzehr ben Ahrahkh, who asked to be taught the secrets of the Chariot, went on to become one of the masters of that literature and passed it on to chosen others. We will meet this aspect of Torah learning again.

The three-year siege of Jerusalem by Vespasian, a general of the mighty Roman Empire, convinced Rabbi Yohkhahnahn ben Zahkai that resistance was useless and that he must plan for the future of the culture of the Bayt Meedrahsh in an entirely different way. However, those committed to holding out against the Romans refused to allow any Jew to leave the besieged city. Taking the advice of his nephew, Ahbah Seekrah, the rabbi feigned illness, allowing only a few students access to his room. After a short time, his students brought the sad "news" that Yohkhahnahn ben Zahkai was dead. Since burial had to be outside the city, he was placed in a coffin and carried out.

Once outside the walls of Jerusalem, Yohkhahnahn ben Zahkai arose from the coffin and approached Vespasian. He asked that he be allowed to set up a center of Jewish learning in the city of Yahvneh. Yahvneh was on the western coast of *Ehrehtz Yeesrah'ehl* — the land of Israel — just south of the port of Yahfoh (Jaffa). Jewish life existed there even before the destruction of the Temple, but once Rabbi Yohkhahnahn ben Zahkai reestablished the Sanhedrin in Yahvneh, it became the center of Jewish life.

To understand the secret of the Jews, it is essential to see that adaptation to new "realities" has nothing to do with "modernization." In the culture of the Bayt Meedrahsh, there is no concept of "keeping up with the times." The sole focus is doing Hahshehm's Will, and Hahshehm's Will is contained in the Torah given to Moses on Mount Sinai. Understanding what constitutes Hahshehm's Will means understanding the Torah; the *Tahlmood* (Oral Law) is an in-depth examination of Hahshehm's will, as are the Kahbahlah and many other texts studied by the Jews of the culture of the Bayt Meedrahsh.

Since every era considers itself modern, only to be superseded by another "modern" era, it becomes clear that any definition of "modern" contains an inescapably ephemeral quality. The culture of the Bayt Meedrahsh, dear Nietzsche, is eternal, not ephemeral. One does Hahshehm's Will despite the times, as opposed to keeping up with the times despite Hahshehm's Will.

So when Rabbi Yohkhahnahn ben Zahkai left the walled city of Jerusalem and negotiated with Vespasian, his sole intention was the continuity of the culture of the Bayt Meedrahsh, the perpetuation of the study of Torah — the perpetuation of a culture dedicated to carrying out Hahshehm's Will. Your emphasis, Nietzsche, on the will to power was right on the mark. The overcoming of the *Übermensch* is, as you made clear, the overcoming of the destructive will to power, of the need to dominate others. We will see that the values you wrote about repeatedly are the values contained in the Torah.

The fall of Jerusalem and the Second Temple (the First Temple having been destroyed by the Babylonians in the year 586 B.C.E.) meant that the Temple would no longer be the center of study and worship. It meant the end of the priesthood. The rise of Christianity was coincident in time, but Christianity, it must be said again, did not evolve from the Sadducees — the priests who aided the Romans against the Jews of the culture of the Bayt Meedrahsh. The culture of the Bayt Meedrahsh continued without the Temple and without the priests because the Temple and the priesthood were only a means to an end: the carrying out of Hahshehm's Will.

Because of the loss of the Temple and the banishment from Jerusalem, there was deep concern that the *khakhameem* (wise men, Torah scholars) would disperse and that learning would diminish. It was greatly feared that the Oral Law, handed down verbally from generation to generation for thousands of years, would be lost; thus, the momentous decision to write down and redact the Oral Law.

The *Tahlmood* is comprised of the *Meeshnah* and the *G'mahrah*. The scholars of the Bayt Meedrahsh during the period of the *Meeshnah* are known as *Tahnah'eem*. The word "*Meeshnah*" (משנה in Hebrew) comes from the Aramaic root שנה, which means "teach, learn, repeat." The final redaction of the *Meeshnah* was accomplished by approximately 200 C.E.

The period of the *G'mahrah* followed the end of period of the *Meeshnah* (250 C.E.) to the year 500 C.E. The scholars of this period are known as *Ahmorah'eem*. The word "*G'mahrah*" is derived from the Aramaic root גמר, which means "to finish, to complete." The generations of the *Tahnah'eem* and the *Ahmorah'eem* are meticulously documented in the *Tahlmood*.[2]

In its specific use, the word "Torah" refers to the scroll of the Five Books of Moses, the basis of all study in the culture of the Bayt Meedrahsh. More generally, "Torah" means "teaching and studying Torah." In the culture of the Bayt Meedrahsh, Torah, in the broader sense of "the teachings," incorporates the study of the Written and the Oral Law and all the elucidating texts that surround them. Although the Oral Law and Written Law teach the positive and negative commandments, there is much more to Torah than mere laws.

The giants of the *Tahlmood* appear in page after page as living members of the culture of the Bayt Meedrahsh. When the head of a Torah academy, or *rohsh y'sheevah*, enters a classroom and gives a lesson in the *Tahlmood* in the twenty-first century, the *Tahnah'eem* and *Ahmorah'eem* come to life through him. This is part of the timelessness of the world of the Bayt Meedrahsh. Rabbi Ahkeevah, for example, is as much a Jew of the culture of the Bayt Meedrahsh in the twenty-first century as he was in the first century.

Rabbi Ahkeevah is a figure of giant proportions in the *Tahlmood*. He grew to adulthood as an *ahm hah'ahretz* — an unlearned man. In the Babylonian *Tahlmood* it is written, "Our rabbis taught: Let a man always sell all he has and marry the daughter of a scholar. If he does not find the daughter of a scholar, let him marry the daughter of [one of] the great men of the generation.... Let him marry the daughter of an elementary teacher, but let him not marry the daughter of an *am hah'ahretz*."[3]

At the time of Vespasian's siege of Jerusalem, one of the wealthiest men in Jerusalem was Kahlvah Sahvoo'ah. One of his shepherds was an *ahm hah'ahretz* named Ahkeevah. Because of Ahkeevah's gentleness, Rahkhel, Kahlvah Sahvoo'ah's daughter, fell in love with him. She told Ahkeevah that she would marry him if he agreed to go and learn, to become a scholar. They were betrothed in secret, and Ahkeevah went off at age forty to learn Torah. When Kahlvah Sahvoo'ah found out about the engagement, he drove his daughter out of his house and took a vow that she would have no share in his estate.

Ahkeevah studied twelve years in an academy and returned home a learned man with twelve thousand disciples. He heard a man asking Rachel how long she would continue in "living widowhood." She replied: "If he would listen to me, he would spend another twelve years." So Ahkeevah went off to study another twelve years and returned with twenty-four thousand disciples. When Rachel's father heard that a great man had entered the city, he decided to go to him, not knowing it was Ahkeevah, and to ask if he could invalidate his own vow not to leave his daughter any part of his estate.

Ahkeevah asked whether he would have made the vow had he known that the man to whom his daughter was betrothed was a great man. Kahlvah Sahvoo'ah replied that he would not have done so had he known that the man was familiar with even the simplest *hahlahkhah* — Jewish law. Rabbi Ahkeevah then revealed his identity, whereupon Kahlvah Sahvoo'ah bowed before him and gave to Ahkeevah one half of his wealth.[4]

Many of the giants of the *Tahlmood* came from distinguished families. Rabbi Ahkeevah's background is proof that this was not a requirement; knowledge of Torah and its elucidating texts, along with high moral character, were the primary characteristics of a Tahlmoodic scholar. Not only had Rabbi Ahkeevah been an *ahm hah'ahretz* — a commoner — but he was also descended from a convert to Judaism.

Rabbi Yohkhahnahn ben Zahkai was mentioned above as the leader of the Jewish community after he was surreptitiously carried out of the walled city in a coffin. Also cited was the story of one of his disciples, who asked to be taught about the secrets of the *Mehrkahvah*, the esoteric tradition. One of the greatest of the rabbi's disciples was Rabbi Yehohshoo'ah ben Khahnahnyah. Like Rabbi Yohkhahnahn ben Zahkai, he was a prominent scholar in the oral tradition at the time of the *Meeshnah*, who had received the mysteries of the *Mehrkahvah*, or Chariot (the esoteric teachings), from his mentor. Rabbi Yehohshoo'ah's greatest student was Rabbi Ahkeevah.

Some sources even attribute authorship of the *Sayfehr Y'tzeerah* to Rabbi Ahkeevah.[5] The *Sayfehr Y'tzeerah* is the oldest work of the Kahbahlah. Many of the prominent rabbis of the *Tahlmood* were also privileged to receive the esoteric wisdom; however, not all the prominent Tahlmoodic scholars, or all the scholars who came after them, received these Kahbahlistic teachings. Some sources trace the source of the *Sayfehr Y'tzeerah* all the way back to Abraham; others believe that Abraham had knowledge of the mystical secrets but did not write the text.

"The highest faculty in man is will." Though you might indeed have written such a thing, Nietzsche, this comes from an exposition of the ancient text of the *Sayfehr Y'tzeerah*. "If one were to attempt to describe God, it would be tempting to say that He is pure Will...; this is also the highest of all human faculties."[6] Among the highest characteristics in the Kahbahlistic tradition are *khokhmah* and *beenah*. *Khokhmah* is "pure nonverbal thought.... It is very difficult to experience pure, nonverbal thought. *Beenah* is 'understanding,' which involves verbal thought. Understanding consists of the normal reverie, where the person thinks out things so as to understand and organize the thoughts."[7]

Aryeh Kaplan, an outstanding twentieth-century scholar of Torah and Kahbahlah, provides a practical way to differentiate between *khokhmah* and *beenah*: "Try for a moment to stop thinking. You remain completely conscious, but there are no verbal thoughts in your mind. If you are an average person, you may be able to maintain such a state for a few seconds, but immediately your mind begins to verbalize the experience. 'I am not thinking of anything.' But as soon as you do this, of course, you actually are thinking of something."[8]

Rabbi Adin Steinsaltz explains that intellect (*khokhmah*) is "the basic essence of the soul's power to understand.... It is the soul's intrinsic ability to attain holistic intellectual understanding. Comprehension by the intellect (as opposed to that by thought) is the totality of whole entities, and to a certain degree, of things-in-themselves. At this level, the concepts and words of thought are not manifest. When, however, thought emerges from this general state of potentiality and enters the instrument of thought — the brain — there is a transformation from potential content to actual content, a translation of the abstract capacity for comprehension into words and concepts which, in turn, are expressed in the alphabet of thought.... Thought, a physiological-mental activity, serves as a performing instrument, carrying out the directives of the intellect."[9]

Whereas the *Meeshnah* [*Meeshnah* + *G'mahrah* = *Tahlmood*, or Oral Law] has references to the occult wisdom, the Kahbahlah is not a prominent part of the text. The final redactor of the *Meeshnah* was Rabbi Yehhoodah ben Gahmlee'ehl II. In his name we see a source of confusion for those who do not study the *Tahlmood* in depth, because many of the scholars of the *Tahlmood* period had the same first name; for example, there are several rabbis named "Yehhoodah." Thus, there is reference to his father. "*Ben*" means "son of," and this is how Jews have been known throughout history. There were no "last" names until these were forced on Jews.

So the redactor of the *Meeshnah* was Yehhoodah ben Gahmlee'ehl II, from among many sages named Gahmlee'ehl. The confusion is lessened by the fact that Yehhoodah ben Gahmlee'ehl II was known by other names and titles. He was Rabbi Yehhoodah the Prince, or the *Nahsee* (president of the Sanhedrin). His highest appellation was simply "*Rehbee*," often translated as "our holy teacher." He was a direct descendant of Hillel, who, together with Shahmai, made up the last of the pairs of scholars mentioned in previous letters. They passed down the laws and traditions set down by the Men of the Great Assembly.

From the time of Moses, who wrote down the Torah, which he received on Mount Sinai, to the time of *Rehbee*, no one had written a work from which the Oral Law was publicly taught. Rather, in each generation, the scholars wrote down, for private use, notes on the traditions that each heard from his teachers, and each passed these on to his disciples.

Rabbi Yehhoodah the *Nahsee*, also known as *Rehbee,* brought together all the notes and memories of all of the scholars of his generation and assembled them in the *Meeshnah*. He taught this body of knowledge in the academies, and it became known and accepted.

The *Meeshnah* and the *G'mahrah* after it cover the full range of issues dealt with in current jurisprudence, philosophy, and, in fact, all other endeavors of the mind. They are divided into six major tractates, or "orders." In Hebrew the words are שׁשׁה סדרים (Six Orders), for which the acronym is שׁ"ס (*Shahss*).[10] The Six Orders are:

1. *Z'rah'eem* (seeds) — includes eleven tractates, including *B'rahkhoht* (Blessings), and deals with setting aside quantities of food and crops for the poor and the priests
2. *Moh'ed* (festivals) — includes *Shahbaht* (the Sabbath) and all the holy days and festivals
3. *Nahsheem* (women) — primarily deals with engagement, marriage, and divorce
4. *N'zeekeen* (damages) — expounds on civil and criminal law, including property law, business law, labor law, partnerships, and capital and other types of punishment
5. *Kohdahsheem* (sacred things) — contains laws pertaining to the sacrifices during the time of the Temple
6. *Tahahroht* (purity) — deals with laws of ritual purity and impurity,

ritual baths, menstruation, nocturnal emissions, and gonorrheal
discharges

There are also a number of so-called minor tractates — shorter tractates that
deal with important subjects. As you can see, Nietzsche, nothing is excluded.
Sexual issues, being an important part of human relationships, are dealt with
in great detail. Among Jews of the culture of the Bayt Meedrahsh, studying
*Shahss* is an everyday, lifetime pursuit.

Following the period of the *Meeshnah*, the *Ahmorah'eem* saw the need for
greater clarity and more detailed explication. The *Meeshnah* is written in
concise rabbinic Hebrew; it assumes a great depth and scope of prior knowledge. The *G'mahrah* was compiled in Aramaic, at the time the spoken and
written language of many peoples, both Jewish and non-Jewish.

It is impossible to imagine the continuation of the culture of the Bayt
Meedrahsh without *Shahss* — the oral tradition. Here, Nietzsche, are the
comments of only a few twenty-first-century scholars of the Bayt Meedrahsh:

> The Talmud…has all the characteristics of a living dialogue. Fresh-
> ness, vivid spontaneity, and acute awareness of every subject perme-
> ate every argument and discussion. The spirit of life breathes on
> every single page."[11]

> Anybody can learn formal rules without internalizing the language,
> but one insider can identify another by the way he or she speaks the
> language. The nuances of a subtly evolving spoken language distin-
> guish the native speaker from the outsider, who grasps only the
> formal structure. Oral Law, the spoken language of the Jewish
> people, is what separates the Jewish people from other nations.[12]

> In some instances the oral tradition represented the common law of
> the people. In other instances, it represented new interpretation. In
> the main, it was a method, a process, whereby revelation was kept
> viable — and progressive.[13]

> The Torah ["Torah" in the broader sense, including the written and
> the oral traditions] is eternal because it has a Word for each genera-
> tion. Every day the Torah should seem as new to you as if it had been
> given on that day, says the Midrash. One can find the Word that has

been waiting for this hour to be revealed only if one faces the challenge of each new situation in the history of the generations of Israel
and attempts to deal with it in intellectual and ethical honesty.[14]

Your contemporary whom I have mentioned so often, Rabbi Samson Raphael
Hirsch, wrote, "The Written Law announces itself as dependent on the Oral
Law." Rabbi Hirsch's rich prose lyrically describes the importance of the Oral
Law: "It is that part of Divine Revelation which was entrusted by God to Oral
Tradition that has made the mental eye of the Jew keen to survey and judge
even the smallest manifestations of human life in their relation to truth and
justice and duty; to equity and love; to guilt and innocence; to what is permitted and what is not. It is just through its oral character, and its accessibility to
all, that it has sunk so deeply into the collective and individual mind of the
Jew, and has given mental nourishment to a whole nation for over 3,500
years."[15]

Someone who has not studied your work in depth, Nietzsche, might think
that the following quote comes from Jewish literature: "Undervalued effect of
grammar-school teaching. — The value of the grammar school is seldom
sought in the things that are actually learned and safely brought home there,
but in those that are taught, but which the pupil acquires only with reluctance.... But herein lies the value that usually goes unrecognized — that these
teachers speak the abstract language of higher culture, ponderous and hard to
understand but nonetheless a higher gymnastics for the head; that concepts,
technical terms, methods, allusions continually occur in their language such
as young people almost never hear in the conversation of their relations or in
the street. If the pupils merely listen, their intellect will be involuntarily
prepared for a scientific mode of thinking. It is not possible for them to
emerge from this discipline as a pure child of nature quite untouched by the
power of abstraction."[16]

You, of course, recognize this as coming from your *Human, All Too
Human*. It is a testament to teaching classics, if only to inculcate abstract
thinking, and highly developed abstract thinking is part of the secret of the
culture of the Bayt Meedrahsh. The classics of the culture of the Bayt
Meedrahsh are the Torah and *Tahlmood*. Here are two more quotes: "Education ought to compel to virtue, as well as it can, and according to the nature of
the pupil: virtue itself, as the sunshine and summer air of the soul, may then

perform its own work on the soul and bestow maturity and sweetness upon it."[17] And what if the students have "the good fortune to receive an upbringing which offered finest teachers, models and methods"?[18]

These latter quotes, too, could fool almost anyone but you. They also come from *Human, All Too Human*, though they speak directly to the actual process of education in the Bayt Meedrahsh.

If a group of teenage students anywhere in the developed world were shown a list of classic philosophers, no doubt some of the students would recognize a name here and there, but only a very few would be able to tell you anything meaningful about those thinkers and their writings. And moving up to college-age students would increase the percentage only slightly, because the classic philosophers belong to cultures long since dead.

But the sages of the *Tahlmood* (*Meeshnah* and *G'mahrah*) redaction period are alive to all who study these texts, as I mentioned above. Far from becoming more and more removed from each subsequent generation of the culture of the Bayt Meedrahsh, these sages become ever more important. The oral transmission of the law from the revelation on Mount Sinai meant that as time progressed, those passing down the law from generation to generation were further and further removed from the time of the incomparable spiritual height achieved in the desert. Thus, each generation had to study ever more diligently simply to minimize the level of spirituality lost over time.

There is a widely held notion that as time passes, civilizations progress. You rejected this idea in more than one of your works. At the beginning of *The Antichrist*, you wrote, "Mankind does not represent a development toward something better or stronger or higher in the sense accepted today. 'Progress' is merely a modern idea, that is, a false idea. The European of today is vastly inferior to the European of the Renaissance: further development is altogether not according to any necessity in the direction of elevation."[19] It is possible to add definitively that the European of the twenty-first century is inferior yet to the European of your day.

Expounding on ancient texts, Nietzsche, was the discipline that you left behind in favor of philosophy, and you had something to say to philologists: "A remark for philologists. — That some books are so valuable and so royal that whole generations of scholars are well employed in their labors to preserve these books in a state that is pure and intelligible — philology exists in order to fortify this faith again and again."[20]

For the culture of the Bayt Meedrahsh, the "books" are the Torah and the *Tahlmood*. They are more than "valuable and royal"; they are sacred, holy. The expounders of the texts of the Bayt Meedrahsh are held in esteem quite beyond the imagination of anyone outside this culture. These commentators did not live in time as the rest of the world knows it, but are alive today to hundreds of thousands of Jews within the culture of the Bayt Meedrahsh who study their works.

Forgive me for burdening you with a long list, but there is a point: All the names on this list are instantly recognizable to all Jews of the culture of the Bayt Meedrahsh from the age of high school on, and even to many younger students — and all of them easily meet your criteria for *Übermenschen*:

Sah'ahdee'ah Gah'ohn, 882-942; Rabbi Shlohmoh Yeetzkhahkee (*Rahshee*) 1040-1105; Jacob ben Meh'eer Tahm, known as *Rahbaynoo Tam*, 1100-1171; Rabbi Samuel ben Meh'eer (*Rahshbahm*), 1080-1158; Rabbi Mohsheh ben Maimon (Maimonides, *Rahmbahm*), 1135-1204; Rabbi Yeetzkhahk Ahlfahsee (the *Reef*), 1013-1103; Rabbi Yehhoodah HahLayvee, 1075-1141; Rabbi Ahvrahhahm ibn Ezra, 1070-1140; Rabbi Moses ben Nahkhmahn (Nahkhmahnehdees, *Rahmbahn*), 1194-1270; Rabbi Kheezkeeyah ben Mahnoakh (*Kheezkoonee*), mid-thirteenth century; Rahv Sh'muel Ehlee'ayzehr Hahlayvee Ayedels (the *Mah'harshah*), 1555-1631; Don Isaac Ahbrahvahnehl, 1437-1508; Ovahdee'ah ben Jacob S'forno (the *S'forno*), 1475-1550; Rabbi Joseph Kahro, 1488-1575; Rabbi Yeetzkhahk Looreeah (*Hah Ahree*), 1534-1572; Rabbi Mohsheh Cordovero (*Rahmahk*), 1522-70; Rabbi Yeh'hoodah Loew, (the *Mah'hahrahl* of Prague), 1525-1609; Rabbi Elijah ben Solomon Zalman (the Vilna *Gah'ohn*, the *Grah*), 1720-1797; Rabbi Shnay'oor Zahlmahn (the *Alter Rebbe*), 1745-1812; Rabbi Khahyeem Volozhiner, 1749-1821; Rabbi Mohsheh Sohfehr (the *Khahtahm Sohfehr*), 1762-1839, Rabbi Menahkhem Mendel Schneerson (the *Tzehmakh Tzehdehk*) 1789-1866; Rabbi Yehhoodah Layb Alter (the *Tz'faht Ehmeht*), 1847-1905.

This is a long list, but it is far from complete. It is important to say again that all the names on this list are instantly recognizable to *all* Jews of the culture of the Bayt Meedrahsh. These leaders not only contributed major works to the study of the Bayt Meedrahsh but were giants as teachers of Torah and *Tahlmood* — the basic "curriculum" of the Bayt Meedrahsh. Many also were well read in science and philosophy and wrote treatises on these subjects. We will not discuss them all but will move through the centuries to demonstrate the ongoing vibrancy of their culture, a culture hidden from your eyes, the eyes of most of your philosophical predecessors, and indeed the eyes of most of the world, both in your time and today.

The period following the redaction of the *Meeshnah* and *G'mahrah* is often designated as the period of the *G'ohneem* (singular: *Gah'ohn*). These were the heads of the academies where students studied *Tahlmood* just as they do today in the twenty-first century. The word *Gah'ohn* has come into vernacular use meaning "genius."

Rabbi Sah'ahdee'ah Gah'ohn (882–942) was born in Egypt but moved to Tiberias, where he headed the prestigious Academy of Soorah. After his tenure as a respected teacher and head of the Jewish community in Babylonia, Rabbi Sah'ahdee'ah Gah'ohn returned to Egypt and dedicated himself to learning and writing. Like many Jewish sages before and after him, he was very learned in Greek philosophy. He did not regard philosophical inquiry as dangerous to belief in Hahshehm. In his major work, *Ehmoonoht-D'oht*, (Belief-Opinion), he brings proofs that the universe was created *ex nihilo* — out of nothing — that the Creator is one, that man has a soul, that the Torah was given to the Jewish people by God on Mount Sinai, and that man has the freedom to choose between good and evil.

I told you, Nietzsche, that every name on the long list above is known to all members of the culture of the Bayt Meedrahsh. It is equally true that the vast majority of assimilating Jews are *not* familiar with the works of these Jewish scholars. The one name most likely at least to be recognized is *Rahshee*. This is an acronym for Rabbi Shlohmoh Yeetzkhahkee, but to millions he is simply Rahshee.

It is not possible to exaggerate Rahshee's importance. Born in Lyon, France, in 1040, he was head of his own Torah academy by age twenty-five. He wrote volumes of clarification and commentary on the Torah and the *Tahlmood* and dedicated himself to presenting the simple meaning of the text in a way that a schoolchild can understand. Every Jew of the culture of the Bayt Meedrahsh studies Torah and *Tahlmood with* Rahshee's commentary.

There are over two hundred works of super commentary on Rahshee's exegeses. That is an accomplishment unmatched in the history of the exposition of important rabbinic texts.

In all standard editions of the *Tahlmood*, Rahshee's commentary accompanies every page. His mastery of the ocean of Jewish literature speaks to the power of the scholarly generations that passed the oral tradition down for centuries. It was as if Rahshee sat with the sages of the *Tahlmood*, who lived and worked five to ten centuries before him. He is "living" proof that Jews of the culture of the Bayt Meedrahsh live outside time as the rest of the world understands it. He is the past, present, and future of understanding Torah in the broadest sense of the term.

From France we move to Spain. Yehhoodah HahLayvee, an immensely learned Jew with a love for poetry and philosophy, was born in Toledo, Spain, in 1075. His chosen profession was medicine, but his great loves were poetry and philosophy. His most famous work was *The Koozahree — Proof in the Defense of the Despised Faith*. This book has retained its popularity and is studied regularly even today. Although he considered reason fundamental to man's intellect, "he has remained the solitary figure among Jewish philosophers of religion who succeeded in recognizing the independence of the religious realm, combining with this a healthy respect for the faculty of reason in its own domain.... Revelation and reason do not conflict in Halevi's philosophy; but neither has reason a chance to absorb revelation, nor need revelation defame the intellectual faculty of man — or denigrate human nature — in order to reach its own validity."[21]

I don't know if you were familiar with Hahlayvee's work, Nietzsche, but Immanuel Kant called him "the most Jewish of Jewish philosophers."[22] He set out to live in *Ehrehtz Yeesrah'ehl* — the land of Israel — but accounts differ on whether he died before reaching the Holy Land.

One of the most recognizable names in the culture of the Bayt Meedrahsh is Moses Maimonides, known as the *Rahmbahm*, an acronym for Rabbi Moses ben Maimon. He came from an illustrious line of Jewish scholars who could trace their ancestry back to Rabbi Yehhoodah HahNahsee, the compiler of the *Meeshnah*. Born in 1135 in Córdova, Spain, he was forced, together with his family, to flee from persecution by the Almohads, a Muslim dynasty that ruled Spain and Morocco for more than a century. He lived in *Ehrehtz Yeesrah'ehl* for a short time, but the Holy Land was then under

Christian control and had only a tiny Jewish community. The Rahmbahm moved on to Egypt, where the death of his brother, who had supported him in his scholarly work, obliged him to take up medicine. He became renowned as the physician of Saladin, one of the most famous Muslim leaders. The Rahmbahm's prodigious literary output includes many treatises on medicine as well as on Jewish law.

The Rahmbahm is best known in the non-Jewish world as a philosopher and the author of *The Guide of the Perplexed* (In Hebrew, *Moreh Nehvookheem*). Like Rabbi Sah'ahdee'ah Gah'ohn before him, he reached out to assimilating Jews imbued with "reason" to demonstrate to them that there was no conflict between reason and belief in Hahshehm.

However, the Rahmbahm's codification of the *Tahlmood, Meeshneh Torah*, was his most important creation — a monumental achievement that preoccupied him for over ten years. Fearful that knowledge of the *Tahlmood* was rapidly decreasing and would one day cease entirely, he compiled, in clear Hebrew, a comprehensive codification of all the complicated subjects in the *Tahlmood*. Whereas any given subject is scattered among many tractates of the *Tahlmood*, the Rahmbahm systematically arranged each area of law into logical order. His concerns, however, have not been borne out — Jews continue to study *Tahlmood* in increasing numbers and use the Rahmbahm's writings as a highly valued supplementary work.

Since it is a given that every twenty-first-century *tahlmeed khakhahm*, or scholar, of the culture of the Bayt Meedrahsh has in-depth knowledge of the *Tahlmood*, it is equally understood that the scholar has studied Rahmbahm in depth and can quote without hesitation many of his rulings. The Rahmbahm's codification of *hahlahkhah* — Jewish law — extends even beyond his monumental *Meeshneh Torah*. He also systematically listed 613 commandments, found in the Torah, describing each in detail, and wrote many other treatises on *hahlahkhah*.

Ten years before Maimonides' death in 1204, one of his most illustrious successors in the culture of the Bayt Meedrahsh was born. Just as Rabbi Moses ben Maimon became known as Maimahn'dees (Maimonides) and "the Rahmbahm," so did Rabbi Moses ben Nahkhmahn become known as Nakhmahn'dees (Nachmanides) and also as the *Rahmbah<u>n</u>*. They had much in common, each being an accomplished scholar steeped in Torah, *Tahlmood*, and all the accompanying Jewish texts of the sages. They were both physicians of note; however, whereas the Rahmbahm is known as a rationalist, the Rahmbahn is steeped in the tradition of the Kahbahlah.

Nachmanides had harsh words for Aristotle, referring to him as "the chief of the philosophers, may his name be erased." Nachmanides charged that "he [Aristotle] has denied things that many had seen, and truths that we have realized, and that have become known to the world."[23] On the connection between body and soul, the Rahmbahn wrote, "Their research has failed to reveal the connection between soul and body. And we have already stated that it is forbidden to reason and rationalize in matters such as the wondrous mysteries of God's creations. The philosophers don't understand their body, let alone the soul, about which they are totally ignorant."[24]

This was far from a sweeping rejection of reason and rational thinking. In his *Shah'ahr Hahgehmool*, the Rahmbahn writes concerning divine justice: "And if you'll ask us: Since there exists something hidden in justice why should you burden us and command us to learn those arguments and the kabalistic allusions mentioned earlier, when we ultimately should depend fully on the rightness of Divine Justice? This is the argument of fools and disputers of wisdom…. It is the obligation of every individual who worships out of love and awe, to explore with his mind the righteousness of Justice and to ascertain the truth of the law as deeply as possible. This is the way of the wise men, to understand and to fathom the truth of the Creator's law, to recognize what is hidden, and especially the kabalistic hint, until there are no doubts left in his mind."[25]

The holiness of the land of Israel, dear Nietzsche, is central to the Jews of the culture of the Bayt Meedrahsh. There is a clear Tahlmoodic citation: "Dwelling in the land of Israel is of equal importance as the observance of the whole Torah."[26] It is also central to tradition that there are 613 commandments in the Torah — the Five Books of Moses. However, more than 613 statements in the Torah could be included. Thus, not all lists are the same. Maimonides' treatise on the commandments is considered eminently authoritative, as is the *Sayfehr Hah-Kheenookh*, from a later period. Nachmanides' rendering differs somewhat from Maimonides', and there are editions of the Rahmbahm's work on the subject that include the comments of the Rahmbahn.

Though the Rahmbahm did not explicitly count the mandate to live in the land of Israel among the 613 commandments, it is clear that he accepted its centrality to Jewish life. For the Rahmbahn, the charge to live in Israel comes as the fourth commandment in his rendering of the 613 commandments. We will trace the movement of Jews of the Bayt Meedrahsh to the land of Israel in more depth in another letter.

Moving to a different part of Europe, Nietzsche, may I present Rabbi Judah Loew, also known as the *Mah'hahrahl* of Prague, or simply the *Mah'hahrahl*, who taught and wrote in the sixteenth century. His vast erudition included Torah, *Tahlmood*, philosophy, and science. He wrote extensive commentary on Rahshee's Torah exegesis, and his writings are part of the library of every teacher in the culture of the Bayt Meedrahsh.

One of the surest signs that we are dealing with men whom you would have accepted as *Übermenschen*, dear Nietzsche, had you but known them, is that in describing their erudition and personal qualities, one quickly runs out of superlatives. One exemplar in this long line of Torah giants, and perhaps the most influential of all Jewish leaders of the culture of the Bayt Meedrahsh from the 1700s onward, is the *Gah'ohn* of Vilna, known by the acronym "the *Grah*."

Ehleeyahoo (Elijah) ben Solomon Zahlmahn was recognized as a genius from early childhood. He had mastered the Torah by age six, and the entire *Tahlmood* by his early teenage years. He spent many years in a room closed to the outside, engaged in solitary study. As I must emphasize over and over, Nietzsche, your *Übermensch* is not only a thinker of the highest caliber, he has "overcome" himself — conquered the impulse to project his power outside, so that instead of using the will to power to control others, he has harnessed it to overcome the primary, unchecked instincts, thus allowing him to elevate learning to the upper echelon of priorities.

Rabbi Ehleeyahoo was the first to have the appellation "*Gah'ohn*" attached to his name since the era of *Sah'ahdee'ah Gah'ohn*, when "*Gah'ohn*" was a title. In the case of the Vilna Gah'ohn, this was a sign of the enormous respect accorded him by the culture of the Bayt Meedrahsh. Rabbi Ehleeyahoo was a child prodigy who gave a public discourse at the age of seven. As a young man, he moved from one community to another in the guise of a beggar. When he returned to Vilna, he could not hide his vast knowledge and was soon renowned as a great *tzahdeek* (righteous man) and Torah scholar.

You wrote, dear Nietzsche, in *Human, All Too Human*, "Shunning the light. — The good deed shuns the light just as fearfully as does the bad deed:

the latter fears that detection will bring pain (in the form of punishment), the former fears that detection will bring loss of pleasure (namely that pure pleasure in oneself that ceases immediately vanity is satisfied)."[27] Here you described not only the Vilna Gah'ohn but all the sages of the culture of the Bayt Meedrahsh.

The Vilna Gah'ohn's diligence in learning was incomparable. He slept only a few hours each night and displayed an encyclopedic breadth of knowledge. Not only was he learned in Torah, *Tahlmood*, and Kahbahlah, he also considered secular knowledge a vital adjunct to Torah study. Among his literary achievements were works on science and grammar.

The Gah'ohn's kindness was legendary. Despite extremely limited means, he always gave 20 percent of his income to charity, so that no needy Jew went unattended by this giant of his generation.

The chief aim of all the great *m'forsheem* — commentators — in writing treatises was to make the sources more accessible to those of their generation who were leaving the culture of the Bayt Meedrahsh. That is to say, the phenomenon of assimilation has been part of Jewish life throughout the ages.

During the Vilna Gah'ohn's time, a new phenomenon arose, which he feared might take Jews out of the culture of the Bayt Meedrahsh altogether. This new threat was known as *Khahseedism*, and when next I write, we will see whether history vindicated the Vilna Gah'ohn's concerns.

Yours, as always,

Ben Moshe

# Letter Seven

December 4, 2005          ג' בכסלו תשס"ו

Dear Nietzsche,

The Vilna Gah'ohn was an intellectual giant and a peerless scholar, and his students followed his methods. Many of the impoverished Jews in Europe of his day — the eighteenth century — worked long hours and had little time for study. Hardly able to consider themselves scholars, they thus began to question whether they were "good" Jews. Enter into this depressed socioeconomic and spiritual environment a remarkable man, Rabbi Israel Bahl Shehm Tov, known to all as the *Bahl Shehm Tov* — "master of the good name" — or simply by the acronym "*Behsht.*"

Young Israel, born in 1698 in Okop, a small village on the Polish-Russian border, was orphaned at a young age and was cared for by his community. It quickly became apparent that this youth, who spent much time wandering in the forests, was very spiritual. He sought out teachers who spoke to his soul, many of them students of the Kahbahlah, a body of knowledge well guarded and taught to a chosen few in each generation. After Israel's first wife died prematurely, he remarried and spent some years in secluded study in the Carpathian Mountains before settling in the city of Tluste. He lived simply, but his modesty could not hide his erudition and charismatic personality.

The Bahl Shehm Tov attracted many students, to whom he taught the esoteric wisdom of the Kahbahlah. He taught that prayer and yearning for Hahshehm could bring great spiritual elevation, which meant that a simple man without erudition was holy and valued in the eyes of the Creator. The Bahl Shehm Tov and his followers became known as *Khahseedeem*, or "pious

91

ones." The Bahl Shehm Tov was a master storyteller, and his stories fill volumes that are read to this day.

The Vilna Gah'ohn himself was thoroughly versed in the Kahbahlah, but he feared that the emphasis on emotion and prayer would diminish the importance of Torah study, and that Khahseedism would thus lead Jews away from the values of the culture of the Bayt Meedrahsh. He was immovable in his opposition and moved to excommunicate the Khahseedeem.

However, the Khahseedic masters, who were learned in all aspects of Jewish holy texts, developed close personal relationships with their followers, teaching with great patience those who had not the time, or perhaps the aptitude, for scholarly pursuit. There was no compromise with observance of the commandments, no intent to begin a new "branch" of Jewish observance. For the Khahseedeem, as for all Jews of the culture of the Bayt Meedrahsh, the Written and Oral Law were and are the word of Hahshehm, given to Moses on Mount Sinai.

For these reasons, Nietzsche, Khahseedism has flourished and spread within the culture of the Bayt Meedrahsh. This monumental development was a part of Jewish life in your time, and it is a great misfortune that you were not aware of this intellectual and spiritual ferment within the Jewish world.

Great and lasting dynasties flowed from both the Vilna Gah'ohn and the Bahl Shehm Tov. Rabbi Shnay'oor Zahlmahn of Liadi, one of the most prominent Torah giants of the eighteenth century, was a descendant of Rabbi Judah Loew, the Mah'hahrahl of Prague. His immense talent for learning was recognized in his early years, and his father took him to study with a famous teacher, Rabbi Issahkhar Behr of Kobilnik, in the Russian city of Lubavitch. There Shnay'oor Zahlmahn was thoroughly grounded in all the Jewish texts, though his thirst for learning led him also to study on his own all the available information in science and mathematics.

When Rabbi Issahkhar Behr felt that his young student had nothing more to learn from him, Shnay'oor Zahlmahn traveled to Vilna and to Mezeritch, centers of learning of the Lithuanian tradition of the Vilna Gah'ohn and the rapidly growing Khahseedic movement. Feeling that he had attained great depth in *Tahlmood*, he wanted to learn how to pray with more profound *kahvahnah* — spiritual intent — the better to serve Hahshehm. Therefore, he went to study with Rahv Dov Behr, known as the *Mahgeed* of Mezeritch, the heir to the tradition and teachings of the Bahl Shehm Tov.

After his studies with the Mahgeed of Mezeritch, Rabbi Shnay'oor Zahlmahn became a Khahseedic master in his own right and had many disciples. He developed his own unique spiritual and psychological approach to serving Hahshehm, based largely on esoteric wisdom. He was the first in a line of seven Khabahd Khahseedic rebbes (rabbis) and is thus known as the Alter Rebbe (elder rabbi). He is also known as the *Bahl HahTahnyah* (Master of the *Tahnyah*) for his multivolume work called the *Tahnyah* — an Aramaic word meaning "it has been taught." The Alter Rebbe labored more than twenty years on this masterwork, and it is studied every day now, in the twenty-first century, by tens of thousands of people all over the world.

After the Alter Rebbe's death, the mantle fell to his son, Rabbi Dov Behr (the Mittler Rebbe), who moved to the city of Lubavitch — now the terms "Loobahvitcher" and "Khabahd Khahseed" have become synonymous. Rabbi Menahkhem Mendel Schneerson, known as the Tzehmakh Tzehdehk, followed Dov Behr at the helm of Khahbahd. The Tzehmakh Tzehdehk's leadership extended into your lifetime, Nietzsche. He often visited Vilna, where his teachings were well received. He went a long way toward healing the rift with Lithuanian Jewry stemming from the burning of Khahseedic books during the time of the Vilna Gah'ohn.

Many other Khahseedic dynasties grew up, each generally associated with the city of its founding rebbe. The Lubavitch movement's seventh rebbe was another Menahkhem Mendel Schneerson. Born in 1902, he went on to become one of the most dynamic and inspiring leaders of twentieth-century Jewry; his depth of knowledge and spirituality were known to non-Jews throughout the world. When the Hitler war machine forced him and many other Jews out of Europe, Rabbi Schneerson came to the United States in 1940.

"The Rebbe," as he is known to Jews throughout the world, vigorously developed the outreach program of his predecessor. Over four thousand Khahbahd *shlookheem* (representatives) live in communities all over the world. Unlike many other outreach programs where representatives come and go after a brief stint, the Khahbahd *shlookheem* stay in their community and raise their children there. Their mandate is to remain there until the coming of the *M'shee'ahkh* (Messiah), whereupon all Jews will move to the land of Israel. The Rebbe died in 1992, and though there is no successor to the leadership of Khabahd, his work is faithfully carried on by representatives all over the world.

Returning to the Vilna Gah'ohn, who vigorously opposed the spread of Khahseedism, we can also follow his disciples through the centuries to another great rabbi in the United States, a contemporary of Rabbi Menahkhem Mendel Schneerson in the twentieth century.

From 1569 to 1712, Poland and Lithuania were part of a commonwealth. Lithuanian Jewry, headed in the eighteenth century by the Vilna Gah'ohn, was an amalgam of Turkish, Syrian, Mesopotamian, Russian, and Western European Jews. Here again, dear Nietzsche, we see the phenomenon of Jews of the culture of the Bayt Meedrahsh moving from one part of the world to another to continue worshiping, learning, and teaching as did their forefathers. Those Jews who converted to Christianity or tried to assimilate quietly into the persecuting culture were more or less successful in saving their lives and those of their families — at least for the time being — but at the cost of their very identity as Jews.

From the Vilna Gah'ohn came a succession of brilliant Torah scholars who made Lithuania the center of the culture of the Bayt Meedrahsh for over a century. The Gah'ohn's most gifted student was Rahv Khahyeem of Volozhin, who continued his mentor's method, favoring systematic study of the *Tahlmood* text, coming to conclusions through logical reasoning instead of through the time-honored tradition of *peelpool* — detailed debate over each discussion among the sages of the *G'mahrah*. He was the founder of the Volozhiner Y'sheevah, the premier center of Torah study for almost a century and the model for many of the y'sheevoht (plural of "y'sheevah") that exist today.

From Rahv Khahyeem through Rahv Ehlee'ayzehr Yeetzkhahk, we arrive at the period of leadership of Rahv Nahftahlee Yehhoodah Berlin — the Nehtzeev — and the era of the first rabbis of the Soloveitchik family, a family with an especially honored place in the culture of the Bayt Meedrahsh for over a century and a half. The Nehtzeev, who was born in 1817 and died in 1893, was older than you, Nietzsche, but very much your contemporary. He joined with Rabbi Samson Raphael Hirsch of Germany and many others in opposing the activities of the Reformers, whom we discussed in an earlier letter.

When Rahv Joseph Behr Soloveitchik's son, Rahv Khahyeem

Soloveitchik, married the granddaughter of the Nehtzeev, two families of enormous knowledge and energy were united. To this sampling of Lithuanian Jewry in your time and after we must add the names of Rahv Israel Meh'eer Hahkohen — the Khahfetz Khahyeem — and Rahv Israel Leepkeen of Salant. What is to most people merely a bewildering list of unknown rabbis is part of the secret of the Jews. These men, as teachers, models of Torah scholarship, and authors of important works, are known and revered by all members of the culture of the Bayt Meedrahsh — they are alive today as part of a timeless culture more than five thousand years old.[1]

In the decade of the 1930s, Rabbi Joseph Dov Soloveitchik and Rabbi Menahkhem Mendel Schneerson met while pursuing secular studies at Berlin University. Rabbi Soloveitchik was destined to become, in America, "the Rav" to the culture of the Bayt Meedrahsh that traces its roots back through Lithuanian Jewry. They are often referred to as *Leetahyeem* (Jews of Lithuania) or Litvaks. Rabbi Schneerson was destined to become, in America, "the Rebbe" to Khahbahd/Lubavitch Khahseedeem. The two men had great respect for each other. The Rav had been tutored in his early learning by a Lubavitch *melahmed* — teacher. On more than one occasion he went out of his way to emphasize to his followers what this meant to him: "What do I know about Habad? I know quite a bit, since as a child I had a melamed who was a Habad hasid. Instead of teaching me Gemara, he taught me hasidut [Khahseedic thought]. Even today, I still know sections of the *Tanya* by heart.... It was my father who taught me Gemara and enabled me to master the rabbinic idiom. Nevertheless, if not for my Habad melamed, I would today be lacking in an entire dimension of knowledge. Many of my derashot are based upon the knowledge imparted to me by that melamed. Those who enjoy my derashot owe him a thank-you."[2]

In a lecture about the future of Jewish education, Rav Soloveitchik spoke again of his *melahmed:* "The melamed inspired me with his descriptions of the Kingship of God.... The melamed had studied in the Yeshiva in Lubavitch, and his method of speech uplifted and transformed me. At the time I was too young to truly comprehend many of his teachings. Only later did I understand and appreciate the lectures in their full depth. He taught me how to pray with emotion and ecstasy, and gave me an appreciation for the High Holy Day prayers.... This is the basic message of Habad. Do something mundane and simple, but do it with divine inspiration and meaning!"[3]

Rav Soloveitchik was the spiritual leader of thousands of graduates of Yeshiva University for many decades. For many years, the director of this university, located in New York, was Rabbi Samuel Belkin, a dynamic leader who guided this primary training ground for American Jewish young people through a period of enormous change. The dislocations from Europe in the early 1900s and after World War I put great pressure on the new Americans to preserve the traditions of the culture of the Bayt Meedrahsh. The need to provide for their families forced many to work on Shahbaht, and once this line was crossed, there was significant assimilation.[4]

In the y'sheevoht, most of the rabbis were Eastern European immigrants, as were many of the students. The language of instruction was Yiddish. As the inevitable "Americanization" took place, the discipline within many congregations broke down. The rise of the Conservative and Reform movements took a toll, as did the traumatic effects of the Second World War. However, beginning in the 1960s, things began to change. The emphasis on social adaptation and general education for new immigrant families having largely been met, the synagogues returned their focus to central values of the Bayt Meedrahsh. As studies highlighted the growing assimilation of American Jews, there was withdrawal into neighborhoods and synagogues of like-minded people. Jews were reminded once again of the need to be "a people apart."

This trend was well documented in the mid-1970s in an important study of the culture of the Bayt Meedrahsh in America, carried out by William Helmreich. Helmreich documented this return to the generative culture of the Bayt Meedrahsh.[5] Here, Nietzsche, we begin to take a deeper look at what goes on inside the educational institutions of this culture.

The trend of assimilation of American Jewry continued at an increasing pace after World War II and the Nazis' extermination of over six million Jews. The culture of the Bayt Meedrahsh was hit very hard by the Nazis; advanced y'sheevoht that had trained many generations of leaders ceased to exist after hundreds of thousands of *tahlmeeday khahkhahmeem* — Torah scholars — went to their deaths. Those fortunate enough to escape the inferno and arrive in the United States found a place to rebuild Torah institutions.

A *y'sheevah k'tahnah* is an educational institution for elementary-age children, a *m'seevtah* is a high school y'sheevah, and a *y'sheevah g'dolah* is for post-high school students. Many of the higher-level y'sheevoht are connected to a *m'seevtah.* A y'sheevah serves not only for training rabbis. Many of the students go on to study law, medicine, accounting, and other fields. This does not contradict the goals of the y'sheevoht; their primary role is to teach the Torah values that have characterized the continuity of this culture for thousands of years. A high value is attached to learning Torah *leeshmah* — for its own sake — and Helmreich's study demonstrated that this had indeed been happening.

In surveying social contacts of the graduates of the particular y'sheevah that was the focus of his study, Helmreich was struck by "the relative lack of contact with non-observant Jews. It is in itself an indication of how important the religious way of life is to this population, and how determined they are to maintain it."[6] When respondents were asked to characterize their four closest friends as observant, nonobservant, or not religious, 84 percent were characterized as "observant."[7]

As for the children of these y'sheevah graduates, "ninety-seven percent reported that their children would attend a y'sheevah day school or were already enrolled in one…. Ninety-two percent *disagreed* with the statement: 'For a son, a good secular education is more important than a religious one.'"[8]

An important ingredient of y'sheevah study for the descendants of the Lithuanian y'sheevoht is *moosahr* — values. Partly in response to the *hahskahlah* — the Jewish enlightenment — and partly in response to the successful spread of the Khahseedic movement, Rabbi Israel Salanter began this aspect of education in the late 1880s. Helmreich tells us, "Rabbi Salanter was concerned that, without ethical behavior and spiritual warmth, study of the Talmud would become motivated by vanity and that adherence to the laws would turn into an unfeeling, mechanical process. The *moosahr* movement's overall goal was a spiritual uplifting of man in his relations with God and with his fellow man…. Students read on a daily basis ethical works. The constant repetition of ethical principles was required so that they could become ingrained in the lives of the students."[9]

To study the Torah and *Tahlmood* is to study the will of Hahshehm, and whereas young children of the culture of the Bayt Meedrahsh absorb these values at home, Rabbi Salanter introduced the regular study of *moosahr* into y'sheevah life as a direct method of reinforcing the same Torah values that a child imbibes at home. This is the equivalent of the students in a Khahseedic y'sheevah learning *khahseedoot* — the ethical and moral philosophy of

Khahseedism. So, dear Nietzsche, you might ask, what *are* the values in the culture of the Bayt Meedrahsh? That is such an important discussion, we must leave it for a later missive.

What we have convincingly proved is that the culture of the Bayt Meedrahsh has a remarkable, even unique, continuity — a continuity unaffected by historical events, unaffected by time. Although we need no scientific method to confirm this well-documented history, advances in science have done just that. You took an active interest in science, Nietzsche, and this will fascinate you.

It has been found that DNA, a protein found in the nuclei of all cells, transmits genetic traits and information down through the generations. While initial research began during your lifetime, the structure and role of DNA did not come into focus until the 1940s. The cells of all organisms, from the simplest bacteria to human beings, contain this life code known as DNA. "The human genome — the total DNA makeup of a human being — consists of over three billion nucleotides, mostly packaged in the 23 pairs of chromosomes residing in the nucleus of each of the body's cells."[10] Equally important for our discussion here, "the genome contains the genetic history of our species and its predecessors since the dawn of life."[11]

In the late 1990s, the fertile mind of Dr. Karl Skorecki was working one Shahbaht as he looked around his synagogue in Toronto, Ontario. When the Torah was read, as is traditional, a *Kohein* — a Jewish man tracing his descent from Aaron the priest — was called to say the blessings for the first reading of the Torah portion. On that Saturday morning, the *Kohein* was a Sephardic Jew. The Sephardeem are Jews whose ancestors came from North Africa and Spain; Spain, in Hebrew, is "Sepharahd."

The *Kohein* who caught Dr. Skorecki's attention was of Moroccan extraction; however, his parents were born in Eastern Europe, making him of mixed Sephardic and Ahshkenahzic Jewish background. Ahshkenahz was a grandson of Noah, and the location of his descendants has traditionally become associated with the Germanic and Slavic areas of Europe; hence the term "Ahshkenahzee" or "Ahshkenahzic Jew." Dr. Skorecki looked at the Sephardic *Kohein*, whose skin, eye, and hair color were much darker than his own. Could he, Skorecki, and this Sephardee both be descendants of Aaron, the older brother of Moses?

Dr. Skorecki thought, if the *Kohahneem* are all descendants of Aaron, they should have a common set of genetic markers (called a haplotype).[12] The Sephardic and Ahshkenahzic Jews, though scattered through different parts of the world for many centuries, have, through the continuity of the culture of the Bayt Meedrahsh, retained remarkably similar practices of Jewish legal and ritual observance. It is well known that Jews are not a race. Throughout the centuries, surely, through intermarriage, rape, and instances of non-Jews taking upon themselves Jewish law and tradition, there would be no common genetic pool. The DNA holds the story!

Only about 10 percent of the DNA actually codes the genetic makeup of an individual. The rest, sometimes called "junk" DNA, carries the most information about past generations. Since all individuals have remarkable similarity in their genetic code, it is the variations that provide crucial information. Mutations — rare changes in the DNA code that create modifications in the embryonic individual — can cause deformities and many serious diseases. But here, dear Nietzsche, is the crucial point: mutations in the noncoding DNA — the "junk" DNA — do not affect the human being at all; rather, they are silent mutations carried in the DNA.

The rate of mutations over time provides scientists with what is called the coalescence time, or, as Rabbi Yaakov Kleiman explains, "the approximate date of the Most Common Ancestor of a sample group."[13] The male, or Y, chromosome is unique. Basic genetics informs us that the mother carries two X chromosomes, and the father carries one X and one Y chromosome. Recombination — the forming of new DNA sequences — occurs naturally in all but the Y chromosome. Therefore, each son receives exactly the same Y chromosome as his father (and as his male ancestors thousands of years back).

Except for determining male gender, the Y chromosome is made up of the noncoding, "junk" DNA. Although the mutations that occur in the junk DNA do not affect the individual, it is the pattern of these mutations over time that creates a chromosomal "family tree."

It was this information that was fueling Dr. Skorecki's imagination in Toronto on that fateful Shahbaht, and he transformed his vision into a study that stunned the scientific world. The results, dear Nietzsche, were published in the January 2, 1997, edition of *Nature*, one of the most prestigious of all scientific journals. Samples of DNA were taken from 188 Jewish males via scrapings of cheek cells. The men indicated whether they were *Kohahneem* or members of one of the other two groupings: *Layvees* or *Israelites*. The analysis of the Y chromosome of *Kohahneem* versus non-*Kohahneem* was highly significant. One particular chromosome was found in 98.5 percent of the *Kohahneem*, though in a much lower percentage of other Jews.[14]

In a follow-up study, the range of Y chromosome markers was expanded, and a particular sequence of six different markers on the chromosome was found in 97 of the 106 *Kohahneem* in the study. Rabbi Kleiman explains, "The chances of these findings occurring at random are less than one in 10,000."[15] A molecular geneticist at Oxford University remarked, "It looks like this chromosomal type was a constituent of the ancestral Hebrew population. It was incredibly exciting to find something that could be tracing paternally-inherited traits over (one hundred) generations, three or four thousand years of history."[16] Professor Skorecki's conclusions at the end of the article in *Nature* were clear:

> The oral tradition of the priesthood has a DNA or genetic counter-part. The scientific information confirms that the majority of contemporary Jewish males who identify themselves as Kohanim are descended from a common male ancestor who founded a patrilineal dynasty consistent with the tradition of the Jewish priesthood. It is almost equivalent to finding a remnant of the garb of the first priest's family, as if you went to the Sinai and found some remnant of Aharon's [Aaron's] anointment ceremony.[17]

One scientist involved in the research pointed out that while this was a groundbreaking study, there were limitations to its implications: the study *had not* proved "that the Bible is correct."[18] The Jewish people are not a race, and these distinguishing patterns can be found in many non-Jews. The importance is the unusually high statistically significant percentage of *Kohahneem* carrying the distinguishing patterns.

These common patterns have been verified across Sephardic-Ahshkenahzic lines. One study involved six Jewish populations in geographically far-flung countries. There were clear differences in genetic makeup between the Jews in any given location and the non-Jews they lived among. However, the widely scattered Jewish groups had the "lowest ratio of genetic-to-geographic distance of all groups in the study. This means that, despite being highly geographically scattered, Jews are, nonetheless genetically very closely related and unique in the world. These facts are compatible with a model of recent dispersal and subsequent isolation during and after the Diaspora" — the dispersion of Jews from the land of Israel to many distant parts of the globe.[19]

Thus, science confirms the Jewish experience. The repetition of the experience of Jews of the culture of the Bayt Meedrahsh, generation after generation, does not support a concept of linear history with a gradual improvement in man and the human condition. It supports an existence beyond time and space. This timeless recurrence of life events is poetically expressed by King Solomon in *Kohehlet* — Ecclesiastes:

> *One generation passes away, and another generation comes;*
> *And the earth abides forever.*
> *The sun also rises, and the sun goes down,*
> *And hastens to his place where he arises.*
> *The wind goes towards the South,*
> *And turns about to the North;*
> *It turns about continually in its circuit,*
> *And the wind returns again to its circuits...*
> *That which has been is that which shall be,*
> *And that which has been done is that which shall be done,*
> *And there is nothing new under the sun.*[20]

Just as King Solomon wrote dithyrambs, so did you, dear Nietzsche, and just as King Solomon wrote aphorisms, so, too, did you. And also like King Solomon, you had an abiding fascination with the cycles of time. Because you were unfamiliar with Ecclesiastes, you traced this concept back only to Heraclitus, writing, "The doctrine of the 'eternal recurrence,' i.e., of the unconditional and infinitely repeated circular course of all things might in the end have been taught by Heraclitus. At least the Stoics, who inherited almost all their principles from Heraclitus, show traces of it."[21] While your doctrine of eternal recurrence referred to very long cycles, we will see that both for very long cycles and for shorter ones as well, the culture of the Bayt Meedrahsh uniquely illustrates this timelessness.

From what we have learned so far about the culture of the Bayt Meedrahsh, imagine putting your inspired question to a Jew of that culture at any time that we have reviewed:

What if, some day or night, a demon were to steal after you into your loneliest loneliness and say to you: "This life, as you now live it and have lived it, you will have to live once more and innumerable times more; and there will be nothing new in it, but every pain and every joy and every thought and sigh…must return to you — all in the same succession and sequence — even this spider and this moonlight between the trees, and even this moment and I myself. The eternal hourglass of existence is turned over again and again — and you with it, speck of dust!" Would you not throw yourself down and gnash your teeth and curse the demon who spoke thus? Or have you once experienced a tremendous moment when you would have answered him: "You are a god, and never have I heard anything more divine!" If this thought were to gain possession of you, it would change you as you are, or perhaps crush you. The question in each and every thing, "Do you want this once more and innumerable times more?" would lie upon your actions as the greatest weight. Or, how well disposed would you have to become to yourself and to life to crave nothing more fervently than this ultimate eternal confirmation and seal?[22]

Your concept of the eternal recurrence is clearly tied to your motto of *amor fati* — loving one's fate, accepting life as it is. You wrote, "For the new year. — I still live, I still think: I still have to live, for I still have to think…. I want to learn more and more to see as beautiful what is necessary in things; then I shall be one of those who make things beautiful. *Amor fati*: let that be my love henceforth!"[23]

The Jew of the Bayt Meedrahsh would welcome with a cheerful smile your challenging question quoted above and would answer: "Yes, yes." Every morning, in the first of his three daily devotions, he says: "*Ahshraynoo, mah tov khelkaynoo, mah nah'eem gorahlaynoo, oo'mah yahfeh yerooshahtaynoo!* We are blessed! How good is our lot, and how pleasant our fate, and how beautiful is our heritage!"

The timelessness of the Jew of the culture of the Bayt Meedrahsh reflects the complete identification of that culture with Hahshehm — with God. As I explained in an earlier letter, the Hebrew name "Hahshehm" is preferable to "God" because many groups use the latter term. Only by going into depth to understand the relationship of the Jew to Hahshehm can we come to appreciate the uniqueness of the relationship between the Jew of the culture of the Bayt Meedrahsh and Hahshehm, and it will be clear how your procla-mation "God is dead," conditioned by your perception of the lack of "godli-ness" in Christian Europe, has no application to Hahshehm. So I will write soon to explore the most central tenet of the Jews of the culture of the Bayt Meedrahsh.

Very truly yours,

Ben Moshe

# Letter Eight

December 11, 2005                                                    י' בכסלו תשס"ו

Dear Nietzsche,

In understanding Hahshehm and his relationship to the people of Israel, let us begin with the central tenet of the Jews: *"Sh'mah Yeesrah'ehl Hahshehm Ehlokaynoo, Hahshehm Ehkhahd!* — Hear O Israel, the Lord is Hahshehm, the Lord is one!" This expression of the oneness of Hahshehm is on the lips of every Jew of the culture of the Bayt Meedrahsh at least twice a day, in the morning prayers and in the evening prayers. Martyred Jews over the centuries have gone to their deaths with these words on their lips.

The first two of the Ten Commandments are (1) "I am Hahshehm, your Lord, Who brought you out of the land of Egypt, out of the house of bondage"; and (2) "You shall have no other gods before Me."

The Torah opens with "In the beginning *Ehloheem* created the heavens and the earth." The name *"Ehloheem"* is one of Hahshehm's many names, used in specific contexts in the Torah to denote His different roles in the world. Hahshehm has no shape, no form, no human emotions or qualities of any kind. Drawing from many sources in the Torah, Maimonides — the Rahmbahm — writes in his *Meeshneh Torah*, "Behold, it is explicitly stated in the Torah and [the works of] the prophets that the Holy One, blessed be He, is not [confined to] a body or physical form, as [Deuteronomy 4:39] states: 'Because God, your Lord, is the Lord in the heavens above and the earth below,' and a body cannot exist in two places [simultaneously]. Also, [Deuteronomy 4:15] states: 'For you did not see any image,' and [Isaiah 40:25] states:

105

'To whom can you liken Me, with whom will I be equal.' Were He [confined] to a body, He would resemble other bodies."[1]

Yet, there are many anthropomorphisms in the Torah. How can human beings, especially children, relate to a formless God? The Rahmbahm explains: "If so, what is the meaning of the expressions employed by the Torah: 'Below His feet' [Exodus 24:10], 'Written by the finger of God' [Exodus 31:18], 'God's hand [Exodus 9:3], God's eyes' [Genesis 38:7], 'God's ears' [Numbers 11:1], and the like? All these [expressions were used] to relate to human thought processes which know only corporeal imagery, because the Torah speaks in the language of man. They are only descriptive terms as [apparent from Deuteronomy 32:41]: 'I will sharpen My lightning sword.' Does He have a sword? Does He need a sword to kill? Rather, this is metaphoric imagery. [Similarly] all [such expressions] are metaphoric imagery."[2]

Hahshehm is the creator of all things. You, Nietzsche, the spiritual philosopher, wrote, "In the beginning — to glorify the origin — that is the metaphysical aftershoot that breaks out when we meditate on history and makes us believe that what stands at the beginning of all things is also what is most valuable and essential."[3]

How do Jews know that Hahshehm exists? Your contemporary, Rabbi Samson Raphael Hirsch, summed it up very well: "Our knowledge of God is based on the evidence of our national community, and there is no need for us to arrive at a belief in the existence of God from the observation of nature and history; the reverse is true. With our knowledge of God we look at nature and history.... Our knowledge of God is not founded upon philosophical speculation or the observation of nature and history; nor is it founded upon the inner voice of our conscience, but on the empirical evidence of historical experience — the Exodus from Egypt and the revelation at Mt. Sinai. These extraordinary happenings took place in the presence of the entire Jewish people and are part of its national consciousness forever after."[4]

Rabbi Hirsch also rephrased Descartes' famous "*cogito ergo sum*" from "I think; therefore, I am" into "I am thought about; therefore, I am — my existence depends upon the thought of a Supreme Being Who thinks of me."[5] What is common to everything cited is that Hahshehm chose not to exist in a vacuum. The Jew of the culture of the Bayt Meedrahsh came to "know" Hahshehm through the encounter with him.

One contemporary rabbinic scholar, Eliezer Berkovits, cites the components of the encounter:

> God chose Abraham and his seed to give them a land and a law. The covenant — reconfirmed several times in the lives of the patriarchs and in the wilderness en route from Egypt to Canaan — is forever binding on us. Three basic dogmas of Jewish theology derive from the covenant. First, God is personal — He intervenes in the lives of individuals and nations. Second, He chose a particular people. Third, He and His people are forever bound by the provisions of the Torah. Any interpretation of Judaism which does not involve commitment to these three facts as historical occurrences deviates so far from the preponderant weight of the tradition as to constitute a new faith.... Jews may conceive of God differently. Their philosophies and theologies may be hewn from different sources. But all must believe that God is aware of individuals and nations whose Creator, rather than whose creature, He is. He does permit the exercise of free will so that He is not the sole author of history. Man also writes many a chapter of his own biography, as well as substantial parts of the annals of his people. But God, who is personal, knows what is happening, participates in events, and is the ultimate judge of all that is done.[6]

Rabbi Berkovits points out that the Torah, while insisting on Hahshehm's incorporeality, "...also stresses, and with hardly less fervor, the importance of the sense impressions of 'the stand at Sinai.' The full story is told by means of the paradox that the invisible God revealed Himself to the senses of man.... The Living God is God invisible and yet encountered; it is God, unlike the metaphysical deity, in active relationship with the world."[7]

These tensions and seeming paradoxes are inherent in an understanding of Hahshehm, who is far above the intelligence and understanding of man. The Jew of the culture of the Bayt Meedrahsh lives with these antinomies and anthropopathisms; he has no need to demand that they "make sense." The great difficulty experienced by non-Jews in understanding and relating to this relationship between Hahshehm and the Jews of the Bayt Meedrahsh appears over and over again; they speak or write of Hahshehm as a "stern, harsh God." Hahshehm does not have such feelings, Nietzsche; it is man, because of his inability to relate to one so far superior, so far above him, who requires his own language to try to comprehend the incorporeal Creator of the universe. Jews of the culture of the Bayt Meedrahsh, on the other hand, do not experience Hahshehm as stern or harsh.

Jews of the culture of the Bayt Meedrahsh accept that they are nothing compared to Hahshehm. So how can they not be depressed by this understanding? How can they have any shred of a positive self-image? "God elevates man to 'fellowship' with Himself. Meeting the other, in the image of the paradigm of all encounters, is an act of creative fellowship through caring involvements. It is the essence of the religious way of life. It is the concept of *imitatio dei*."[8]

Those without knowledge of Jewish sources think that the concept of *imitatio dei* was introduced by Plato. However, the *Tahlmood* and the almost two thousand years of written and oral tradition that preceded the redaction of the *Tahlmood* have inculcated in the Jews of the culture of the Bayt Meedrahsh that man is created in the image of Hahshehm. Since "image" cannot refer to a physical image, it must be the *attributes* of Hahshehm that man experiences through the encounter.

At the end of my last letter to you, Nietzsche, I quoted an excerpt from the morning prayers: "*Ahshraynoo, mah tov khelkaynoo, mah nah'eem gorahlaynoo, oo'mah yahfeh yerooshahtaynoo!* — We are blessed! How good is our lot, and how pleasant our fate, and how beautiful is our heritage!" Now let us take a look at that short quote in its full context. In the first paragraph we see the enormous gap between man and Hahshehm — a gap so seemingly unbridgeable as to foster despair:

> Master of all worlds! Not in the merit of our righteousness do we cast our supplications before You, but in the merit of Your abundant mercy. What are we? What is our life? What is our kindness? What is our righteousness? What is our salvation? What is our strength? What is our might? What can we say before You, Hahshehm our God, and the God of our forefathers? Are not all of our heroes like nothing before you, the famous as if they had never existed, the wise as if devoid of wisdom and the perceptive as if devoid of intelligence? For most of their deeds are desolate and the days of their lives empty before You. The preeminence of man over beast is nonexistent, for all is vanity.[9]

The recognition of man's nothingness appears to lead to a dead end. What is the way out? The passage continues, saying, in essence, "Wait a minute": "...we are Your people, members of Your covenant, children of Abraham, Your beloved, to whom You took an oath on Mount Moriah, the offspring of Isaac, his only son who was bound atop the altar; the community of Jacob...whom — because of the love with which You adored him and the joy with which You delighted in him — You named Israel."[10]

One could justifiably claim that Abraham, Isaac, and Jacob did not have easy lives, yet the perception of Hahshehm's love derives from being happy with one's lot — your own *amor fati*, Nietzsche. Given that perception, the passage draws a conclusion: "Therefore, we are obligated to thank You, praise You, glorify You, bless, sanctify, and offer praise and thanks to Your Name. We are blessed, fortunate — how good is our portion, how pleasant our lot, how beautiful our heritage! We are fortunate, for we come and stay late [in the Bayt Meedrahsh, the study hall], evening and morning, and proclaim twice a day: Hear O Israel, the Lord is our God, the Lord is One."[11]

Then, in a classic statement of Hahshehm's existence beyond time and space, the text continues: "It was You before the world was created, it is You since the world was created, it is You in this world, and it is You in the world to come. Sanctify Your Name through those who sanctify Your Name and sanctify Your Name in the universe. Through Your understanding way, You exalt and raise our pride. Blessed are You, Hahshehm, Who sanctify Your Name among the multitudes."[12]

Your *Übermensch*, Nietzsche, is one who "overcomes." At a very early age, a child in the culture of the Bayt Meedrahsh is taught that he is created in the image of Hahshehm, that Hahshehm loves him, and what Hahshehm expects from him. As for "sin," a word with which you had great difficulty, this is not something that preoccupies the Jewish child. Rabbi Adin Steinsaltz (also known as Adin Even-Israel) elaborates: "Since sin is defined, from a hahlahkhic and a theological point of view, as the negation of mitzvah, where positive commandments are concerned it consists of abstention and where negative commandments are concerned it consists of action. In every case, that is to say, it is conceived as the negation of something else and not as an independent entity in its own right."[13]

Hahshehm told Adam and Eve that because they disobeyed His word, they would die. They lived many more years, so what does that say about

Hahshehm's omnipotence? The answer: nothing. Hahshehm lives outside time. The meaning is that man would now face death. No child in the culture of the Bayt Meedrahsh is taught "fire and brimstone" or that Hahshehm will strike him down if he does wrong. The *yeeraht shahmahyeem* — fear and awe of heaven that is a central awareness in the culture of the Bayt Meedrahsh — has nothing to do with fear of punishment for one's sins.

Again we turn to Eliezer Berkovits. In describing the trembling and awe of the people of Israel before Hahshehm at the giving of the Ten Commandments, he writes, "The peril that emanates from 'contact' with the Divine Presence has nothing to do either with the sinfulness of man or with the judgment of the Almighty. It is something quite 'natural,' almost 'physical.' Man is threatened and affirmed at the same time. Through the peril that confronts him, he is bound to recognize his nothingness before God; yet, in the divine affirmation, the highest conceivable dignity is bestowed on him: he is allowed into 'fellowship' with God."[14]

Is this beginning to sound familiar, Nietzsche? Consider the following from your *Zarathustra*: "O heaven above me, pure and deep! You abyss of light! Seeing you, I tremble with godlike desires. To throw myself into your height, that is my depth. To hide in your purity, that is my innocence.... And when I wandered alone, for whom did my soul hunger at night, on false paths? And when I climbed mountains, whom did I always seek on the mountains, if not you? And all my wandering and mountain climbing were sheer necessity and a help in my helplessness: what I want with all my will is to fly, to fly up into you."[15]

What a beautiful description of the encounter! And King David wrote, "One thing, I asked of Hahshehm, that shall I seek: Would that I dwell in the House of Hahshehm all the days of my life, to behold the sweetness of Hahshehm and to study/contemplate in His Sanctuary."[16] Yet the inspired Zarathustra is drawn back to reason: "God is a conjecture; but I desire that your conjectures should be limited by what is thinkable.... If there were gods, how could I endure not to be a god! Hence there are no gods."[17] Zarathustra did not understand that precisely because man is corporeal and "limited by what is thinkable," he cannot be anything but man and cannot, through his reason, even begin to comprehend Hahshehm.

Zarathustra could benefit from Eliezer Berkovits: "Reason as such may neither command nor has it the power to induce action.... Reason may tell the difference between right and wrong; perhaps even the difference between good and evil. It cannot, however, provide the obligation for doing good and eschewing evil. The source of all obligation is will, and the motivation of a will is a desire. Reason knows no desire, though man may desire to be reasonable.... There is nothing in the laws of logic to obligate man to logical thinking, should he prefer foolishness to wisdom."[18]

The difference between the laws of a secular society and the laws of the culture of the Bayt Meedrahsh is clear: "A secular society need not be less exacting in demands of obedience to its laws than a community governed by a divine law. Mercy and justice are the things in which God delights. But a law instituted by a relative authority admits of compromises for the sake of expediency; the law of absolute authority will not be overruled by such consideration. All secular ethics lack the quality of absolute obligations. They are as changeable as the desires and the wills that institute them; the law of God alone is as eternal as His Will."[19]

Zarathustra has an encounter with a higher force, though he cannot call that force "God," with a capital "G." Again your reaction against Christianity rears its head. It is precisely Christianity that corporealized the godhead by calling divine a man who walked on this earth. Zarathustra, too, was a mortal, so why not aspire to be a god? Jesus lived and died in time and space. Hahshehm is found in the encounter and lives outside time and space. He was not born and does not die. He created the universe from nothing and revealed himself at Sinai.

Hahshehm created the world and continues the act of creation every day. Jews see themselves as Hahshehm's partner in *teekoon ohlahm* — perfecting the world. All Jews, past, present, and future, stand at Sinai; that is to say, the experience was outside time — it was, is, and will be the revelation of Hahshehm and his will. This may sound "un-reason-able" to some, but as we will see in a future letter, scientists — many of them avowed atheists — have had a revelation of their own, as their ever-increasing body of evidence supports the long-scoffed-at notion that the world was created *ex nihilo* — from nothing. Hahshehm made a pact with a man named Abram thousands of years ago and changed the man's name to Abraham. Thus, Hahshehm chose an *individual*, not a "people" or a "nation," but he promised Abraham that his descendants would be a great nation. It is possible to look at this interaction in another way: Was Abraham chosen, or did he choose?

There is a classic question concerning Abraham's chosenness — why was he chosen? The relevant section in Torah begins: "And God said to Abram, 'Go...' There is no preamble, no reason given for that choice. In the case of others — Noah, for example — a reason is given; Noah was exceptionally righteous, as the verse clearly states: "Noah was a righteous man..." But why did God speak to Abraham? Why is no reason given?... The *Sfat Emet* [renowned Khahseedic commentator] says: the Torah here is not saying that Abraham was chosen at all. God was speaking to all men, but Abraham was the only one who heard. God was not speaking to him, He was speaking to anyone who listened, and Abraham was listening. The Torah is simply taking up the story of the one who heard. And of course, God is still speaking to everyone; the question is only who is listening.[20]

It was at Mount Sinai that the pact was made with the "people of Israel." The Five Books of Moses, the Torah, were written down by Moses, and the Oral Law was given to Moses; the covenant was passed down from generation to generation. This required teachers and pupils, lawmakers and law enforcers. In short, it required a community, a culture.

The member of the culture of the Bayt Meedrahsh studies and prays, striving to understand Hahshehm's will and to "draw close to" Hahshehm, to "cling to" Hahshehm. What these terms mean is simply that the Jew strives to know the values Hahshehm expects and to *live* those values. Each individual has his or her own balance of intellectual life and spiritual life. Intellectually one can learn and be guided by the values taught in the Torah and be inspired by the culture that he is a part of. Those with a propensity for more internal, spiritual pursuits are able to study deeply, in addition to the Torah, the Kahbahlah.

Yet, one is warned that he may not see Hahshehm's face and live. Since Hahshehm has no "face" or any other human characteristics, this language and many other such metaphors in the Torah and the *Tahlmood* tell us, over and over again, that there is a limit to how much we can know, can comprehend, Hahshehm. The intense desire to leave behind the difficulties, deceits, and materialism of this corporeal world and live in peace at a "higher" level is expressed throughout the Torah, the *Tahlmood*, and innumerable commentaries on these works. You, Nietzsche, used the word "higher" more than once in exactly the same context, such as when Zarathustra expressed his fervent desire "to fly up into you."

Yet the Jew's task is here on earth, and there are dangers in drawing too close to Hahshehm. If one draws as close as is permitted, he achieves a wonderful level of inner peace and understanding of Hahshehm's will; but he may stay in that suspended place only temporarily before he returns to this world to partner with Hahshehm in *teekoon ohlahm* — perfecting the world. One cannot "cross over." The *Tahlmood* teaches that four of our sages entered the "orchard," a metaphor for Hahshehm's garden or even his presence. One died, one became demented, and one became an apostate. Only the revered Rabbi Ahkeevah survived to return and to continue teaching Hahshehm's will to his pupils.[21]

Even in silent prayer and individual study, the Jew, by definition, is part of a community; some use the term "nation." One can pray alone, but the highest level of prayer is in the synagogue, and there are certain prayers in the culture of the Bayt Meedrahsh that can only be said in a *meenyahn* — a gathering of at least ten men aged thirteen and over. One may not recite *Kahdeesh* in the honor of a deceased family member except in a *meenyahn*. The *Kahdeesh* prayer contains no mention of death. It is a glorification of Hahshehm's name, connecting the remembered loved one to the past and the future — to the timelessness of Hahshehm and the culture of the Bayt Meedrahsh.

"The branch of a nation that preserves itself best is the one in which most men have, as a consequence of sharing habitual and undiscussable principles, that is to say common belief, a living sense of community. Here good, sound custom grows strong, here the subordination of the individual is learned and firmness imparted to character as a gift of birth and subsequently augmented.... Only when there is securely founded and guaranteed long duration is a steady evolution and ennobling inoculation at all possible."[22]

Though you did not know of the culture of the Bayt Meedrahsh, Nietzsche, you wrote those words. And though you did not find around you many of the individual and community values that you wrote about, they existed in your time, in a culture that escaped your attention — the culture of the Bayt Meedrahsh.

The covenant between Hahshehm and the people of Israel was forged in the experience of the Exodus from Egypt and the wanderings in the desert that led to the giving of the Torah at Mount Sinai. The unity of Hahshehm, the deliverance from slavery and Egypt, and the giving of the Torah are central concepts in understanding Jews of the culture of the Bayt Meedrahsh.

We mentioned at the start of this letter the earliest prayer that a child is taught, the same prayer that a pious Jew fervently wishes to be his last utterance before he dies: "*Sh'mah Yeesrah'ehl Hahshehm Ehlohaynoo, Hahshehm Ehkhahd!* — Hear O Israel, the Lord is our God, the Lord is One!" This prayer has three paragraphs, the last of which ends with "I am Hahshehm, your Lord, who brought you out of the land of Egypt, to be your Lord. I am Hahshehm your Lord."[23] We also cited the first of the Ten Commandments: "I am Hahshehm, your Lord, Who brought you out of the land of Egypt, out of the house of bondage." On Friday night, the beginning of Shahbaht (the Sabbath), this holy day is blessed by the recitation of the *Keedoosh* — the sanctification of the Shahbaht over a cup of wine. Here, too, is raised the memory of *y'tzeeyaht Meetzrahyeem* — the Exodus from Egypt.

These are only three of the many places where this central bonding experience is mentioned. Just as the Jew of the culture of the Bayt Meedrahsh needs no "proof" of the existence of Hahshehm, so, too, does he feel no need for proof of the Exodus and the giving of the Torah. The people of Israel experienced these events, and these experiences have been passed down from generation to generation. Does it matter that some dismiss these and other testimonies from the Torah as mere fables? For some people, their spirituality is reinforced by "reason-able" documented archeological findings and other scientific research that supports the reality of the Exodus from Egypt.

One of the important aspects of the Torah in describing the Exodus is the sheer amount of geographical detail given. This is not something found in myths and fables. Moreover, the details allow contemporary scientists to attempt to examine whether such geographical sites existed on ancient maps and whether such places exist today. One contemporary scientist, Colin Humphreys, has done a great deal of "detective" work to identify site names from biblical accounts of the Exodus, and as we shall see, he has come up with some remarkable results.[24]

The Torah provides the following account of the scene at the Jordan River when the children of Israel crossed: "Now the Jordan is in flood all during the harvest. Yet as soon as the priests who carried the ark reached the Jordan and their feet touched the water's edge, the water from upstream stopped flowing. It piled up in a heap a great distance away, at a town called Adam in the vicinity of Zarethan, while the water flowing down to the sea of the Arabah [Dead Sea] was completely cut off. So the people crossed over opposite Jericho."[25]

In the original Hebrew text of the Bible, the place for the crossing over the Jordan was given as "adm," spelled with the Hebrew letters *aleph*, *daled*, *mem*. Thus, the name would be something like "Ahdahm." And so Humphreys, aware that over centuries, names on maps can and do change, tried eliminating the vowel placeholder *aleph* and searched for the basic consonants "dm." There is a town in Jordan today called Damiya, situated only seventeen miles north of where the Jordan River is closest to Jericho. In the 1989 Bartholomew World Travel Map including Israel and Jordan, this town is listed as Damiya (Adamah), strongly suggesting that this site is the ancient "Adam" from the book of Joshua.[26]

So, Nietzsche, what about the cessation of the river's flow, which allowed the Israelites to cross the Jordan? In 1927 there was a powerful earthquake in the area of Jericho. A professor of geophysics studied this event and found that the earthquake was the result of what is now known as the Jericho fault, which runs north-south beneath the Jordan River. This same scientist found that mudslides, caused by earthquakes, had temporarily stopped the flow of the Jordan River on many occasions: "Adam is now Damia [Damiya], the site of the 1927 mud slides which cut off the flow of the Jordan. Such cut-offs, lasting typically one to two days, have also been recorded in 1906, 1834, 1546, 1534, 1267, and 1160. The stoppage of the Jordan is so typical of earthquakes in this region that little doubt can be left as to the reality of such events in Joshua's time as well."[27]

The belief that Hahshehm created a miracle that allowed the children of Israel to cross the Jordan is not debunked by the scientific account. Since Hahshehm created the world, and all nature is his handiwork, the event, as well as its impeccable timing, is seen as the work of Hahshehm.

Humphreys reports similar research into the route of the Exodus. Again the Bible is specific, devoting thirty-eight verses to documenting the route.[28] The first stop was at Rameses. We know from Exodus 1:11 — "And they built Pithom and Rameses as store cities for Pharaoh" — that there was a city called

Rameses, though it does not appear on modern maps. However, we know from Egyptian sources that the "House of Ramesses II," sometimes called Pi-Ramesses, was a major site. Archeologists have found, in the modern city of Qantir, the remnants of a foundation of a large palace with inscriptions reading "Pi-Ramesses." Thus, modern Qantir has been identified as the first stop of the Israelites on their journey from Egypt.[29]

The second stop on the route of the Exodus was Succoth, and archeologists are satisfied that they have found this site. However, the third stop, Etham, was considered a mystery. One researcher commented, "Unfortunately, with the knowledge presently available, the location and nature of this encampment, as well as the meaning of Etham, will have to remain uncertain."[30] Humphreys took up the challenge, saying, "Etham is important because it is the first named stage of the Exodus journey after the Israelites left Succoth, on the Egypt-Sinai border.... If we do not know where Etham is, then we cannot be sure what route the Israelites took when they left Egypt."[31]

At the head of the Gulf of Aqaba is a place called "El Yitm Peak," and in brackets just below the name, on one map that Humphreys found, is written "Lithm, Etham."[32] Again we see the consonants carrying the root of the name. Etham is found at the head of the Gulf of Aqaba. Was the Gulf of Aqaba the "Red Sea," where the Israelites walked through split waters? There is a great deal of scholarly controversy about the site of "the crossing." The Hebrew term for the body of water is "*yahm sooph*," which means "Sea of Reeds"; thus, many have believed that the crossing was at some smaller, inland body of water and not a major "sea" such as the Gulf of Suez or the Gulf of Aqaba. The name for the Greek translation of the Bible is the Septuagint. Greek Jews who translated the Bible into Greek more than a century before the Common Era rendered the Hebrew "*yahm sooph*" as the Greek "*eruthra thalassa*," meaning "red sea." Some scholars believe that both "*yahm sooph*" and "*eruthra thalassa*" are catch-all terms that have at times referred to different bodies of water in the Middle East.

On a visit to Taba on the coast of the Gulf of Aqaba, Humphreys glanced out the window of his sixth-floor hotel room. He describes what he saw: "The normally deep blue Red Sea was covered with large red patches of color, as if someone had sprayed red paint on it. The effect was very clear and striking and could be seen from some distance away. I was amazed by this spectacular sight. I blinked several times because I thought there must be something wrong with my eyes! But there were no red patches on the white walls of our hotel room.... I rushed excitedly from the room, ran down six flights of stairs, not waiting for the elevator, and strode rapidly out of the hotel, past the swimming pool, and on to the pebbly shore.... I took off my sandals and ran into the warm waters to investigate what was causing the red regions of color. The mystery was revealed. It was low tide, and red coral lay only a few inches below the surface."[33]

To complete the solution of the salt sea-fresh water-reed sea conundrum that he had been unraveling, Humphreys saw reeds near the water where he stood. The guide explained, "These are genuine papyrus reeds.... Syracuse is the only place in the whole of Europe where papyrus reeds grow. The ancient Greeks were so amazed to find a freshwater spring beside the saltwater sea that they wanted to make it really obvious to everyone that it was a freshwater spring."[34]

The site names mentioned in the Torah are also referred to in the literature describing ancient trade routes. Not surprisingly, these trade routes followed water supplies, and abundant water was found in the places where the children of Israel stopped after the Exodus.

Researcher and documentary filmmaker Simcha Jacobovici confirmed Humphreys's route for the Exodus. Both scholars agree that the traditional placing of Mount Sinai in the Sinai desert is not tenable. Following the biblical description and scientific evidence, they come to a site just above the Gulf of Suez, though they differ on precisely which mountain was Mount Khorev, also known as Mount Sinai. They also differ on the reasons the sea turned "red," but both provide scientific understanding of what the children of Israel experienced.

Jacobovici cites the Akhmoshet Stella, an ancient Egyptian stone inscription, that describes "rain, thunder and lightning" of a kind and magnitude that rarely occur in Egypt. The Akhmoshet Stella reports Egypt being "enveloped in darkness" and ascribes the process as occurring when "God [the singular is used] manifested His power."[35] Jacobovici's award-winning documentary is the most convincing evidence yet for skeptical minds that question the reality of the Exodus.

So, Nietzsche, although a Jew of the culture of the Bayt Meedrahsh has no need for such evidence, we can see that those who are accustomed to think of

Biblical stories in terms of "myths" may become more open to a different point of view in the light of such research. We will speak of even more amazing scientific findings later.

Yours,

Ben Moshe

# Letter Nine

February 3, 2006        ה' בשבט תשס"ו

Dear Nietzsche,

As you know, historians and thinkers of other disciplines organize life on the planet Earth into epochs. In each epoch, civilizations rise and fall, many disappearing altogether. The Roman, Babylonian, Mayan, Sinic, Indic, and Syriac civilizations each loomed large in their time, their peoples no doubt believing that the civilizations would exist forever. Yet each has fallen or been absorbed by its successors.

Authors write about Roman, Greek, Byzantine, Arabic, and Persian periods. There were Amalakites, Jebusites, Hittites, Vikings, and many other cultures that no longer exist. We speak of ancient times, the Middle Ages, the Renaissance, and the industrial revolution and document the remarkable changes that took place in these various eras. Historical "eras," though, are merely useful fictions that help us organize history, whereas the culture of the Bayt Meedrash survives them all. Goethe called the Jewish people "the most perpetual people of the earth,"[1] and Tolstoy, whose life overlapped your own, Nietzsche, said of the Jews, "The Jew is the pioneer of civilization. Ignorance was condemned in olden Palestine more even that it is today in civilized Europe."[2]

We have documented at great length the survival of the culture of the Bayt Meedrahsh through thousands of years of history. There is no timeline for this culture. We will examine closely the Jews of the culture of the Bayt Meedrahsh of the twenty-first century and better understand what we have seen already: that "modern" eras come and go, later tagged with some label by

119

an even newer "modern" era. Because the culture of the Bayt Meedrahsh is perpetually the same, it is tagged by each modern era with such descriptions as "behind the times," "out of date," "backward," and so on. And yet, as each "modern" era morphs into the next, the Jew of the culture of the Bayt Meedrahsh remains perpetually modern.

Jews have lived scattered throughout almost all the lands of the earth. The people in each land had their own holidays and festivals to mark different times and seasons. Jews of the culture of the Bayt Meedrahsh, in their dispersion, live spiritually in the land of Israel. They live "outside" their particular geographical space, and their cycles of time are not those of their varied surroundings; rather, their "times" are the cycles of time tied to "the land" in general and to the holy city of Jerusalem in particular. Their language of prayer and study is the holy tongue, Hebrew.

This centrality of a land to a people, Nietzsche, is unprecedented in the history of mankind. We will stress it over and over, because we cannot comprehend the secret of the Jews without understanding their bond to the land of Israel. The sole authority establishing cycles of months, years, leap years, Sabbatical years, and the Jubilee year was the ruling Jewish authority in Jerusalem. "The people remember what has been and anticipate a longed-for future, thereby stretching the present as a midway station on the ongoing journey. The expression of such a world outlook and set of values is particular to Jewish culture."[3]

Explicit in the Torah and *Tahlmood* are mandates for observing and sanctifying cycles of time, the longest cycle being the Jubilee year. Alluded to in the Torah and *Tahlmood* and made more explicit in the hidden wisdom of the Kahbahlistic literature are much larger cycles of thousands of years. These longer cycles, Nietzsche, bring your doctrine of the eternal recurrence closer to Jewish literature. Let us begin with those cycles experienced during the lifetime of a Jew of the culture of the Bayt Meedrahsh. We will begin with the Jubilee and Sabbatical years.

Many people have the misconception that there are 613 commandments incumbent on every Jew. In fact, many commandments can be carried out only in the land of Israel, thus exempting Jews who live outside Israel. The Sabbatical (*Sh'meetah*) and Jubilee (*Yovehl*) years are two commandments applicable only to Jews living in the land of Israel. The Sabbatical year is the last year of a cycle of seven years, and the Jubilee year occurs after seven cycles of Sabbatical years — every fifty years.

The pertinent passages from the book of Leviticus (Vahyeekrah) are a curiosity for most readers of the Bible, but for Jews of the culture of the Bayt Meedrahsh, they are commandments from Hahshehm; the Jubilee years were not extended beyond the destruction of the Temple, but the Sabbatical year continues to be punctiliously carried out in the land of Israel in the twenty-first century. These observances have been "modern" for thousands of years. The details of the observances are found in the *Tahlmood*, the "core curriculum" in every Bayt Meedrahsh.

These seven-year and fifty-year cycles, as well as the cycle of each individual year, are tied to the agricultural rhythms of the Land. This is why the Jewish calendar brings the lunar and solar years together into one unity.

The Jewish calendar served two important purposes for the Jewish people during centuries of dispersion throughout the world: (1) though living in many disparate lands, Jews everywhere were tied to the land of Israel and yearned to return; (2) whether living in Muslim lands using the lunar calendar or in Christian lands using the solar calendar, Jews sanctified the festivals tied to the land of Israel on exactly the same day of the Hebrew calendar. Relative to their surroundings, Jews of the culture of the Bayt Meedrahsh lived outside time and space.

In bringing together cosmic time and historical time, the Jewish calendar ensures that the three pilgrim festivals, *Pehsakh, Shahvoo'oht,* and *Sookoht,* fall at the appropriate season of the year and that all Jews, no matter how scattered and far-flung, observe the holiday on the same day. These three joyous harvest festivals are central to the year for all Jews of the culture of the Bayt Meedrahsh. A large percentage of assimilating Jews celebrate some type of *Pehsakh* (Passover) *seder* (the meal beginning Passover); fewer build a booth, or *sookah,* to honor the Festival of Booths (Sookoht). For many, however, *Shahvoo'oht,* the holiday celebrating the giving of the Torah, goes by unnoticed.

The modal Jewish year has only 354 days, so in order to keep the pilgrim festivals at the proper season, seven times in every nineteen-year cycle, a thirteenth month is added — a sort of "Jewish leap year." The spring month when Passover occurs is Neesahn; the previous month is Ahdahr. Seven times each nineteen years, a second Ahdahr (Ahdahr Shaynee) month is added; this

occurs every third, sixth, eighth, eleventh, fourteenth, seventeenth, and nineteenth year of each nineteen-year cycle.

The beginning of this letter, Nietzsche, is dated ח בשבט תשס"ו. Reading
from right to left, the ח is the Hebrew letter *khet*, which, being the eighth
letter of the Hebrew alphabet, denotes the eighth day of שבט (*Sh'vaht*), the
Hebrew month that falls in February or March of the Gregorian calendar.
The year is תשס"ו—5766, that is, five thousand, seven hundred, sixty-six
years from the creation of the world. The numerical value of the Hebrew
letters is 766; the 5,000 is "understood," assumed.

In the culture of the Bayt Meedrahsh, all schoolchildren, wherever in the
world they live, know this calendar. They know that the Festival of *Sookoht*
begins on the evening of the fifteenth day of the month of Teeshray; they
know that the Festival of Passover begins on the evening of the fifteenth day
of the month of Neesahn; they know that *Shahvoo'oht* begins on the evening
of the sixth day of the month of Sivan. Every day of the calendar begins at
sundown; thus, every Shahbaht (Sabbath) begins at sundown on Friday.
Children know in which Hebrew year and month they were born. Of necessity, adults working in contact with people who use the Gregorian calendar
learn the January-to-December year and its designations, but it is *lo'ahzee* —
foreign; it is not the calendar that governs the rhythms of their universe.

The *Tahlmood* prescribes more than one "New Year." The first day of the
month of *Neesahn* is the New Year for kings. This is more of a legal designation for "dealing with documents" and designating in what year of the rule of
a certain king some event of note took place. "On the first of *Teeshray* is the
New Year for years." This is what is widely known as the "Jewish New Year" —
*Rohsh Hahshahnah*, literally, the "head," or beginning of the year.[4] In the
Tahlmood, *Neesahn* marks the beginning of Jewish history in that it is based
on the redemption from Egypt, and *Teeshray* marks the creation of the
universe. *Rohsh Hahshahnah* ushers in the *Yahmeem Norah'eem* — the Days
of Awe. This term refers to the ten days from *Rohsh Hahshahnah* through
*Yohm Keepoor* — the Day of Atonement, a major day of fasting for Jews.
*Yohm Keepoor*, on the tenth day of the month of *Teeshray*, ends the ten-day
period of the High Holy Days.

As I write this to you, Nietzsche, it is another "New Year." The date is the
fifteenth day of *Sh'vaht*. Tet is the ninth letter of the alphabet, *vav* is the sixth.
They combine to make fifteen, which is pronounced "*too*"; thus, this date is

*Too B'Sh'vaht* — fifteen in the month of *Sh'vaht*. This is the New Year for trees, mandated in the *Tahlmood* for the year tithes were given. In any given year, if a particular fruit has matured to one-third of its full growth, that fruit is part of the previous year; any fruit achieving one-third of its ripening after this day is a result of the blessings of the New Year.

*Too B'Sh'vaht* is not a holiday involving fasting, although seven days in the Jewish calendar do involve abstention from eating and drinking. In addition to *Yohm Keepoor*, the other "major fast" is *Teeshah B'Ahv*, literally, "the ninth day in the month of *Av*." This is the day on which both the First and Second Temples fell. These two days of fasting begin at sunset on the "eve" of the fast day and remain in force until the following evening, when the Jewish day ends.

The five "minor" fast days begin at sunrise and last until sunset. On the third day of the month of *Teeshray*, during the ten Days of Awe, falls the Fast of Gehdalee'ah, or *Tzohm Gehdalee'ah*. This day commemorates the killing of the Jewish governor of Judah, a critical event in the period leading to the destruction of the First Temple and the subsequent Babylonian exile in the sixth century before the Common Era. The Fast of *Tehveht*, on the tenth day of the month of *Tehveht*, marks the beginning of the siege of Jerusalem, leading to the fall of the Second Temple in the first century of the Common Era.

From January 11, 1949, until *Yohm Hahshoh'ah* (Holocaust Remembrance Day) was established on the twenty-seventh day of the Hebrew month of *Neessahn* in 1951, the tenth of *Tehveht* was also observed by some as a memorial day for the six million Jews who died in the Holocaust; it is still used by some as a day to say memorial prayers for those whose date of death is unknown.

The Fast of Esther, on the thirteenth day of the month of *Ahdahr*, commemorates the three days that the Jewish queen Esther fasted before approaching King Ahasuerus to expose his minister Haman's plan to destroy the Jewish people. The fast is connected with the holiday of *Pooreem*, which falls on the fifteenth day of *Ahdahr*. These events occurred at a time coinciding with the end of the Babylonian exile, in the fourth century before the Common Era.

The Fast of the Firstborn, the fourteenth of *Neesahn*, limited to firstborn males, commemorates their being saved from the plague of the firstborn in Egypt. Passover begins on the day after the fast. The final minor day of fasting on the Jewish calendar is the fast of the seventeenth day of the month of *Tahmooz*. This fast recalls the day that the walls of Jerusalem were breached — another major event leading up to the destruction of the First Temple.

Except for *Yohm Keepoor*, Nietzsche, the fast days are virtually unknown to the non-Jewish world — and, indeed, to most Jews outside the culture of the Bayt Meedrash. Terms such as "people of the book" or "the people with a memory" apply specifically to the Jews of the culture of the Bayt Meedrahsh. These days are not simply marked on a calendar; all Jews of the culture of the Bayt Meedrahsh are in synagogues on those days and are saying special prayers to mark those days. On *Teeshah B'Ahv*, the major fast day commemorating the destruction of the Temples, it is the custom to sit on the floor and mourn the destruction of each Temple as if it had only just happened. On Passover, Jews are commanded to tell the story of the Exodus from Egypt as if all Jews had been present.

In the *Hahgahdah*, the "text" for the Passover meal, or *seder*, there is no mention of Moses. Here, as in almost all aspects of the culture of the Bayt Meedrahsh, the emphasis is on the community, the nation. In the culture of the Bayt Meedrahsh, the seder goes on well past midnight as in-depth discussions of the Torah and Tahlmoodic accounts of the Exodus unfold in every home, and song fills the air with the emotions of a people long enslaved whom Hahshehm has finally set free.

Nietzsche, you wrote this of the Jews of your time: "The Jews…are beyond any doubt the strongest, toughest, and purest race now living in Europe; they know how to prevail even under the worst conditions…. The Jews, if they wanted it — or if they were forced into it, which seems to be what the anti-Semites want — could even now have preponderance, indeed quite literally mastery, over Europe, that is certain; that they are not working and planning for that is equally certain."[5] Then you go on to describe the aspirations of the Jews that you knew: "Meanwhile they want and wish rather, even with some importunity, to be absorbed and assimilated by Europe; they long to be fixed, permitted, respected somewhere at long last; putting an end to the nomads' life, to the 'Wandering Jew.'"[6]

Indeed, Nietzsche, the Jews you knew *did* assimilate, at least to the degree that they were allowed; in their family tree, stretching into the twenty-first century, there are no Jewish branches. However, the Jews you did *not* know — those of the culture of the Bayt Meedrahsh — have lustrous, leafy branches spreading into the consciousness of the world of the twenty-first century. They all left Egypt; they all stood at Sinai; they all participate in the continuing acts of creation that are part of every day to come — they all live outside time and space.

In each year there are many other days of note observed by all Jews of the culture of the Bayt Meedrahsh, but I need not overwhelm you with them all. But let us consider one particular day that is observed each month; this is *Rohsh Khohdesh*, the "head," or beginning, of each Jewish month. The commandment to consecrate the first day of the month is the first commandment of the Torah, given to all the Jewish people.[7] Being a day of the Jewish calendar, it is a day outside the "time" of the rest of the world; it is a spiritual "space" outside the space of the rest of the world. In the synagogue, special prayers are said celebrating the renewal of the moon — a physical renewal for the cosmos, and a time of internal renewal for the Jew.

Nietzsche, your contemporary Rabbi Samson Raphael Hirsch, one of the great leaders of the culture of the Bayt Meedrahsh in Germany — and, indeed, in all the world — stressed the spiritual importance of the new moon: "Every time that the moon reunites with the sun and receives new light from it, God wants His people to find their way back to Him and receive new irradiation from His light, no matter where they may be or through what periods of darkness they may have to pass in their path through history."[8]

On the Shahbaht (Sabbath) before the new moon, the community is told, in the synagogue, when the new moon will be born in the following week, and a special prayer is said asking Hahshehm's blessings on the community. At the beginning of each month, one can walk down the street of a community of Jews of the culture of the Bayt Meedrahsh and hear them wish one another, "*Khohdesh tov! Khohdesh tov!* — A good month! A good month!" One can hear it today, you could have heard it in your time, and one could have heard it thousands of years ago.

At least seventy-two hours after the *Mohlahd* — birth of the new moon — the congregation gathers outside the synagogue, at the end of Shahbaht, and says the prayers for sanctification of the new moon. Again, this is *not* a nature-oriented ceremony but a ceremony of renewal for the Jewish people, whose history waxes and wanes like the cycles of the moon. This is a joyous ceremony, to be performed not alone but in the presence of others, to whom each person turns and wishes, "*Shahlohm Ahlaykhem* — Peace be upon you," and receives the same blessing in return.

On *Rohsh Khohdesh* and on the three pilgrim festivals of *Pehsakh* (Passover), *Shahvoo'oht* (Feast of Weeks), and *Sookoht* (Feast of Tabernacles), as well as on the Festival of Lights, *Khahnookah*, a special prayer is chanted in the synagogue. The prayer is called *Hahlehl*, which means "praise." "Hallelujah" is a Hebrew word meaning "Praise to God," with *Ya* being one of the esoteric names of Hahshehm. The *Hahlehl* consists of six psalms, 113–118, chosen for this service because they include the major themes of the Exodus, the giving of the Torah by Hahshehm at Sinai, the future resurrection of the dead, and the coming of the *Mahshee'ahkh* — Messiah. These psalms have a special, joyous melody.

Each month, of course, contains four weeks. Here, too, Nietzsche, this shorter cycle of time is celebrated uniquely by Jews of the culture of the Bayt Meedrahsh. Sunday, the first day of the week, is called simply *Yohm Reeshon* — the first day. Each day is called by its numerical position in the week, except the seventh day, which is *Shahbaht*! It is almost impossible to write this word without exclamation and awe. In fact, formally, each day of the week is regarded as a precursor of the coming Shahbaht, for example, *Yohm Reeshon ba-Shahbaht* — the first day of the week before the coming Sabbath, and so on through the sixth day.

Mondays and Thursdays are "Torah days." This means that inserted in the regular morning service is a Torah service, during which three small sections of the weekly Torah portion are chanted. This custom was instituted by Ezra and the Men of the Great Assembly, hundreds of years before the Common Era.

As *Yohm Sheeshee*, the sixth day, passes the halfway mark and the sun begins to recede in the western sky, a remarkable, palpable change takes place among Jews of the culture of the Bayt Meedrahsh. The women have been feverishly preparing since early morning, and now everything must come into place. The men rush home from work or from the Bayt Meedrahsh, and everyone bathes and changes into their finest clothes. The day winds down as secular time and space recede from consciousness. The most important day of the Jewish calendar, Nietzsche, occurs not once every fifty years, as the beginning of the Jubilee year once did, not once every seven years, as the first day of the *Sh'meetah* (Sabbatical) year still does; not once a year, like *Rohsh*

*Hahshahnah* and *Yohm Keepoor*; not once a month, like *Rohsh Chodesh*, but once *every week*. It is the most central, defining characteristic of life in the culture of the Bayt Meedrahsh. It is *Shahbaht*, and one says the word with a special reverence and awe. The woman of the house, ushers in the *Shahbaht* with the lighting of candles. It is at once a solemn and a joyous moment. Now the family has entered the sacred time and space of *Shahbaht*, and a sense of peace and release is in the air.

Here is a wonderful story about Rabbi Israel Meir HaKohen Kagan, well known as the *Khahfetz Khahyeem* — the name of his famous work on guarding one's tongue from speaking guile and evil. He was your contemporary, Nietzsche. Ah, if only you had met him! He was one of the greatest of his generation, and his *y'sheevah* in Radin, Lithuania, attracted the best students. Once a student of his was found smoking a cigarette on *Shahbaht* — a very serious desecration of the *Shahbaht*. The learned teachers of the *y'sheevah* did everything they knew to turn the young man around. Failing, they told the *Khahfetz Khahyeem* that he must be expelled. The *Khahfetz Khahyeem* asked to see the student. After the rabbi's short visit, the student returned to the *y'sheevah* and told his astonished teachers that he would mend his ways. This is the student's story, as told many years later:

> It was in the late 1920s. I was very young, and the Chafetz Chaim was already in his eighties. He was also much shorter than I, hardly coming up to my shoulder. I never really spoke to him. He stayed in his grocery store for the first hour of the day, and then he would go home and study, but when he was in the street, he would never let anyone say hello to him first; he always greeted the individual first. So, I got greetings *from* him, but I never spoke *to* him. When I was told he wanted to see me, I didn't know what to expect. When I walked into his house after being summoned, although I was dazed by the prospect of being addressed by the Chafetz Chaim himself, I couldn't help noticing how poor everything seemed. In the room where I was standing, there wasn't one piece of furniture that was not broken. But before I could get my bearings, there was the Chafetz Chaim right in front of me. I am sure he must have looked at me, but all I remember is a face larger than life. Suddenly he grabbed hold of my hand, clutching it tightly, and out of his mouth I heard the word

"*Shabbos*" [Yiddish for Sabbath] said with such feeling, as if he were uttering the name of the most beloved object in the world. Then there was a silence, and then he began to cry — not sniffles, but streams of tears, and the tears from his eyes fell on the palm of my hand. Even if I live until one hundred and twenty, I will never forget the feeling of how hot those tears were; they actually burned my hand! And then I heard one more word, "*Shabbos*," [Shahbaht] with the same awesome sense of love and anguish and still holding my hand, he took me to the door.[9]

In the *Tahlmood* is a description of the coming of *Shahbaht* entering on Friday night: "Rabbi Chanina robed himself and stood at sunset of Sabbath eve and exclaimed, 'Come and let us go forth to welcome the queen Sabbath.' Rabbi Jannai donned his robes on Sabbath eve and exclaimed, 'Come, O bride, Come, O bride!'"[10]

Here is a beautiful description of the place of *Shahbaht* in time; it mentions a well-known song about greeting the *Shahbaht* "bride": "The Sabbath is a primary junction between the cosmic cycle and the course of history as they are both marked in the calendar. By its very repetition, the Sabbath accords cyclical cosmic time a purposeful direction from Creation to Redemption, setting sabbatical and jubilee years.... It is likened to a bride in the ritual poem *Lecha Dodi* and welcomed in song by Jewish communities throughout the world."[11]

There is not a single scholarly commentator who does not come under the magic spell of *Shahbaht*. Rabbi Emanuel Rackman, a current rabbinic authority, explains that through *Shahbat*:

Man can demonstrate that he is not the slave of greed and envy. When, by self-discipline, man shows that it is in his power to call a halt to the acquisition of things and the exploitation of natural resources, it can be said that his craving for economic power is not altogether his master.... Thus the Law made the Sabbath a means for the cultivation of personal ethics.... The Sabbath was actually a day of transformation. The most bitter existence of peasant or laborer was transformed into something heavenly. From painful preoccupation with means all week, the higher man finally came into his own on the Sabbath. Is it any wonder then that slaves too were to rest?

How could a day dedicated to ends permit the exploitation of human beings as means?[12]

Rabbi Rackman goes on to make reference to "higher man." Nietzsche, you made frequent use of this term. In one section of *Human, All Too Human*, though you were not commenting about the *Shahbaht*, you could very well have been describing this holy day: "Everyone has his good days when he discovers his higher self; and true humanity demands that everyone be evaluated only in the light of this condition and not in that of his working-day unfreedom and servitude.... Many live in awe of an abasement before their ideal and would like to deny it: they are afraid of their higher self because when it speaks it speaks imperiously."[13]

Emphasizing the evolution of Jewish law designed to safeguard what the Torah calls holy, Rabbi Rackman explains why, for Jews of the culture of the Bayt Meedrahsh, additional "rules" do not interfere with the sanctity of the day, though they find disfavor among "moderns."

> The Rabbis of course found it necessary to make additional rules, to safeguard the Sabbath. In the main, these are the rules against which moderns are most rebellious. As a matter of fact, moderns frequently visualize the Rabbis as misanthropes whose sole purpose is to make our lives as miserable as possible. There have been others in the past who could not understand the Sabbath. Sadducees and Karaites regarded the prohibition against fire as a prohibition against its use, instead of a prohibition against its creation and the use of its potential for still further creation. In darkness they sanctified the Sabbath. Many even outlawed food and sexual intercourse for the day. For them, misery was the keynote of the Sabbath.
>
> The point of view of the Rabbis, however, stands in bold contrast — in fact, as a protest against these tendencies. The Rabbis prescribed the lighting of candles and made the Sabbath lights in the home one of the most significant features of the day. And they made eating and cohabitation on Sabbath not only permitted functions but virtually mandatory ones. The Sabbath was not to frustrate man, but to help him fulfill himself.
>
> Further, to prevent the many Sabbath prohibitions from becoming a barrier to the fulfillment of the Law's ideal, the Law emphasized

two positive conceptions — *Kibud* and *Oneg* — the honor and joy of
the Sabbath. The Sabbath was honored by festive dress and enjoyed
with festive meals; it was welcomed with songs and candlelight; its
departure was toasted with wine and incense.[14]

Aryeh Kaplan, a brilliant twentieth-century physicist and rabbinic authority
on Jewish law and the Kahbahlah, writes about the legal reaction to those
who desecrate the Sabbath, and the struggle among the rabbis to find a more
lenient interpretation: "Many people claim that, to be a 'good Jew,' one need
only observe the Ten Commandments. But if you do not keep the Sabbath,
then you are only keeping nine of them.... The Torah openly states (Exodus
31:14), 'You shall keep the Sabbath, for it is holy to you; any one who profanes
it shall be put to death. For whoever does any work on that day shall be cut off
from his people.' Put to death... Cut off from his people... Very strong terms
indeed.[15]

How can one understand this seemingly harsh decree? Some authorities
adopt a more lenient view, writing that "in modern times, one may extend to
a Sabbath violator the privileges of being a Jew, for a very interesting reason.
They state that no one would violate the Sabbath if he truly understood its
meaning. Therefore, unless we have contrary evidence, we assume that a
person violating the Sabbath is doing so out of ignorance, and therefore we
treat him with sympathy and understanding rather than harshness."[16]

The gulf between "Jews on the way out" and Jews of the culture of the Bayt
Meedrahsh is nowhere as great as on the subject of honoring *Shahbaht*. One
feels the strain among the authorities of the culture of the Bayt Meedrahsh
searching for some way *not* to write off those Jews who desecrate *Shahbaht*;
indeed, there is a sense of disbelief that any Jew would willingly give up the
gift of *Shahbaht*.

One who violates the sanctity of *Shahbaht* is subject to *kahreht* — to being
cut off from the Jewish people. However, in Jewish law, this is not an act of
excommunication carried out by rabbinic authorities; rather, it is an act of
Hahshehm. This is fascinating, Nietzsche, because we see that those who
consciously leave the culture of the Bayt Meedrash very soon stop honoring
*Shahbaht* and stop having large families. Within three to five generations,
typically there are no more descendants who identify themselves as Jews.

Whether one considers this as an act of Hahshehm or a self-inflicted *kahreht*, it surely is a cutting-off from the Jewish people.

Since all Jewish days begin at sundown and continue until the following sundown, Friday night is *ehrehv Shahbaht* — the evening beginning *Shahbaht*. After the evening prayers at the synagogue, where there is a special *Kahbahlaht Shahbaht* (Receiving the Sabbath) service just before the regular evening service, the family returns home.

Around the *Shahbaht* table, all families of the culture of the Bayt Meedrahsh sing *Shahlohm Ahlaykhem* — "Peace be with you," a song involving Hahshehm's ministering angels that speaks of peace and prays for peace. The Friday night meal is a festive meal, a meal that creates communion and community.

At this point, the husband, often with the children participating, sings *Ehshet Khayeel* — "A Woman of Valor." This, Nietzsche, is the last of King Solomon's Proverbs, giving praise to the woman of the home. At some point between the return from synagogue and the beginning of the Sabbath meal, it is the custom in most families for a parent (usually the father) to put his hands on each child's head and bless them quietly; the boys are likened to Ephrahyeem and Menahsheh, the sons of Joseph, and the girls to the matriarchs: Sarah, Rebecca, Leah, and Rachel.

You may ask, why Ephrahyeem and Menahsheh? When the patriarch Jacob was dying, he called his children to him and gave each a blessing. He allotted to Joseph, by blessing each of his sons, two portions in the house of Israel — two tribes: "On that day he [Jacob] blessed them, saying, 'In time to come, Israel (the Jewish people) will use you as a blessing.' They will say, 'May God make you like Ephrahyeem and Menahsheh.'"[17] Whereas there was much strife between Isaac and Ishmael, between Esau and Jacob, and between Joseph and his brothers, Ephrahyeem and Menahsheh had a more peaceful relationship, and despite being raised surrounded by Egyptian culture, they were raised by Joseph with the learning and customs of the culture of the Bayt Meedrahsh.

*Shahbaht* is officially consecrated by the *Keedoosh* — the blessing of this holy day over a cup of wine. The first paragraph of the *Keedoosh* recalls Hahshehm's act of creation: "The sixth day. The heavens and the earth were finished and all their array. On the seventh day, the Lord completed His work which He had done, and He rested on the seventh day from all His work which He had done. The Lord blessed the seventh day and hallowed it, because on it, He abstained from all His work which the Lord did to create it."

Then comes "Blessed are You, Hahshehm our Lord, King of the universe, Who creates the fruit of the wine." The third part is the official sanctification of the *Shahbaht*: "Blessed are You, Hahshehm our Lord, King of the universe, Who has sanctified us with His commandments, took pleasure in us, and with love and favor gave us His holy Sabbath as a heritage, a remembrance of creation. For that day is a beginning of holy acts, a remembrance of the Exodus from Egypt. For us did You choose and us did You sanctify from all the nations. And Your holy Sabbath, with love and favor, did You give us as a heritage. Blessed are You, Hahshehm, Who sanctifies the Sabbath."

Here is the creation of the universe, the remembrance of deliverance from slavery, and the gratefulness for being chosen to receive the Torah. "Jews are a people with a memory," it is often said, but the emphasis on the past misses the point, Nietzsche. The act of creation goes on every day, and since one learns more and more each day about the Torah, one receives it every day.

That the term "chosen people" has often been cited as an accusation of a belief in "superiority," ethnic, racial, or otherwise, is really a problem for the accusers. Abraham lived in a world awash with idol worship, violence, and greed. Has the world changed so much? Abraham was told that his seed would become a great nation. Clearly, there were conditions, and clearly, anyone could join, then and now. That many find the requirements too stringent and throw them off is also clear — after all, one has free choice.

Rabbi Rackman avers, "The chosenness of the Jews flows from the fact that God redeemed them from bondage and gave them the Torah that they might become a holy people and a kingdom of priests. Whether or not they had a mission as such to the non-Jewish world is debatable. Perhaps their achievement for humanity was to be only an incident of their service to God. What is not debatable is that there exists a special relationship between them and God pursuant to the covenant."[18]

Is there a question of superiority here? Again we look to Rabbi Rackman:

> My belief that God chose Abraham and his seed for the covenant is no warrant for any feeling of superiority over my fellow man. Abraham, according to the record, was selected because God recognized him to be one who would transmit to his posterity a sense of mission

with regard to justice and righteousness. His seed had only the merit of the fathers — especially Abraham's. In Abraham's case, the merit was not that of Terah [Abraham's father]. Certainly neither Moses in Deuteronomy nor the prophets anywhere were enamored of Israel's virtue. Yet my existence has been ennobled because of the mission. I have inherited that which I seek to fulfill. I cannot impose it on anyone other than my children — but anyone who wants to share it is free to do so.[19]

On the other hand, Rabbi Abraham Isaac HaKohen Kook, a revered rabbinic authority of the first half of the twentieth century and a lyrical writer of poems, aphorisms, and other commentaries, had no compunctions about identifying with the term "chosen people." He wrote in one of his most important works, *Orot* (*Lights*): "A great mistake is turning back from all of our advantage, the cessation of the recognition that, 'You have chosen us.' Not only are we different from all the peoples and tongues, but we are also exalted and much greater than any people. If we know our greatness, then we know ourselves, and if we forget our greatness, then we forget ourselves, and a people that forgets itself certainly is small and lowly."[20]

Returning to the *Shahbaht* table, after the *Keedoosh* over the wine, all family members go to a sink for ritual hand washing — *n'teelaht yahdahyim*. Even a child who does not yet speak is lifted up and water spilled over his hands, and the *b'rahkhah* — blessing — is recited for him. It is a source of great pride, for the child and the family, when the child is first able to recite the *b'rahkhah* without help.

The family returns to the table for the *mohtzee* — the blessing over the special bread, the *khahlah*. Two loaves of (usually braided) bread are lifted, the appropriate blessing is sung, and a piece of bread is distributed to everyone present at the table. The reason for two loaves of *khahlah* is that on the day before *Shahbaht* in the desert, after the children of Israel's exodus from Egypt, manna fell from heaven in double portions, so the Jews would not have to gather the manna on *Shahbaht*.

Jews sing around the *Shahbaht* table, Nietzsche, and they sing loud and long, thumping on the table, swaying back and forth. It is time to rejoice, to celebrate the most important gift of Hahshehm: the gift of *Shahbaht*. Interspersed with the singing are *deevray Torah* — words of Torah. The *Tahlmood* informs us, "Rabbi Shimon said, If three have eaten at one table and have not spoken over it words of Torah, it is as though they had eaten of the sacrifices of the dead.... But if three have eaten at one table and have spoken over it words of Torah, it is as if they had eaten from the table of Hahshehm."[21] From the most learned adult at the table, to the smallest child, teachings from the Torah may be shared. Issues of *khol* — secular time — are put aside and words of Torah are exchanged as precious gifts.

In the synagogue on *Shahbaht* day, the *Pahrahshaht Hahshahvoo'ah* — the Torah portion for the week — is chanted. This is followed by an additional chanting — the *Hahftahrah* — a selection from the Prophets. Then the families return home for the *Shahbaht* midday meal. Again the *Keedoosh* is sung over a cup of wine, the blessing over the *khahlah* is recited as it is on Friday night, and the festive meal begins anew, with more words of Torah, more singing, more rejoicing. Between the afternoon *Meenkhah* service and the evening *Mah'ahreev* service, there is a third meal, *s'oodah sh'eesheet*, which is generally light and accompanied by words of Torah and singing.

When three stars appear in the sky signifying the end of *Shahbaht*, the evening *Mah'ahreev* service begins. After the service, family members gather for *Hahvdahlah* — separation. This short service ushers out the *Shahbaht*. There is sadness in letting go of this holy time and space and returning to *khol* — the secular, or mundane, time and space. The final blessing of the service thanks Hahshehm, "...who distinguishes between the holy and the mundane, between light and darkness, between the Seventh Day and the Six Days of the week..." Yet the *Shahbaht*, the most important day of the Jewish calendar, will not return in a year or in a month, but in another week.

Between two *Shahbahts* are the days of the workweek. What occurs in the culture of the Bayt Meedrahsh during this time will perhaps astonish you, Nietzsche. Since other cultures have some semblance of a *Shahbaht*, perhaps the "average" day of Jews of the culture of the Bayt Meedrahsh will serve to illustrate the unique qualities of this culture. It will show that for the Jews of this culture, there is no such thing as "religion," which one "practices" apart from what one does the rest of the time. I will write about this soon.

Yours,

Ben Moshe

# Letter Ten

February 19, 2006                                  כ"א בשבט תשס"ו

Dear Nietzsche,

By looking at *khol* — the "mundane" workweek of the Jew of the culture of the Bayt Meedrahsh — we can understand how, if the *Shahbaht* of any other culture were as spiritual and dedicated to values and virtue, there would be little reason for the Jews of the culture of the Bayt Meedrahsh to seek to live in seclusion, apart from that world.

Some might wonder, "Why in the world would one write to Nietzsche about virtue?" Many who think they know you would swear that you never bothered yourself with such things, let alone wrote anything like this: "We do not hesitate to take the path to a virtue even when we are clearly aware that the motives which impel us — utility, personal comfort, fear, considerations of health, of fame or reputation — are nothing but egoism. These motives are called selfish and ignoble; very well, but when they incite us to a virtue… That is why education ought to compel to virtue as well as it can and according to the nature of the pupil: virtue itself, as the sunshine and summer air of the soul, may then perform its own work on the soul and bestow maturity and sweetness upon it."[1]

Dear Nietzsche, you are in sweet accord with the *Tahlmood*: "A man should always occupy himself with the Torah and [its] precepts, even though it be for some ulterior motive, for the result will be that he will eventually do them without ulterior motive."[2]

You suggest that education should "compel to virtue." Is this possible? Rabbi Eliezer Berkovits agrees with you: "The only way of educating the bio-

135

physical instrument of action is by making it perform and do."[3] The "making it perform" first includes the choice, the desire to perform, and then — as no one recognized more than you, Nietzsche — the need to "overcome." In *Human, All Too Human*, you wrote, "The man who has overcome his passions has entered into possession of the most fertile ground."[4]

In the culture of the Bayt Meedrahsh, "overcoming" is mediated by the *pro*scriptions of the negative commandments, the "thou shalt nots," and the *pre*scriptions of the "thou shalts." These commandments were given with the Torah, and the methods of implementing this moral education are found in the Oral Law. At times of crisis, "great men of the spirit," such as Ezra and the Men of the Great Assembly, arose to give direction to the culture of the Bayt Meedrahsh, as I have written to you before.

I put "great men of the spirit" in quotation marks because I borrowed the phrase from you: "Greatness means giving direction. No river is great and abundant of itself: it is the fact that it receives and bears so many tributaries that makes it so. Thus it is, too, with all great men of the spirit. All that matters is that one supplies the direction which many inflowing tributaries then have to follow, not whether one is poorly or richly gifted from the beginning."[5]

You clearly understood the reason for living with like-minded people and for a hallowed tradition: "Sometimes this clinging to one's own environment and companions, one's own toilsome customs, one's own bare mountainside, looks like obstinacy and ignorance — yet it is a very salutary ignorance and one most calculated to further the interests of the community.... The contentment of the tree in its roots, the happiness of knowing that one is not wholly accidental and arbitrary but grown out of a past as its heir, flower and fruit, and that one's existence is thus excused and, indeed justified — it is this which is today usually designated as the real sense of history."[6]

In fact, Nietzsche, without having any contact with Jews of the culture of the Bayt Meedrahsh, you wrote of them, of those who, you thought, no longer existed: "I have been on the lookout for learned, bold and industrious comrades in arms — I am still looking. The object is to explore the huge, distant and thoroughly hidden country of morality, morality as it has actually existed and actually been lived, with new questions in mind and with fresh eyes."[7] To those bold and industrious comrades in arms...history thus belongs...to him who preserves and reveres — to him who looks back to whence he came into being, with love and loyalty; with this piety he, as it were, gives thanks for his existence. By tending with care that which has existed from old, he wants to preserve for those who shall come into existence after him the conditions under which he himself came into existence — and thus he serves life."[8]

Whether the terms we use are yours, Nietzsche, or those of the culture of the Bayt Meedrahsh, you knew and praised the values. As we go through the daily cycle of the Jews in this culture, you will see the ongoing education to virtue and values; you will see "him who looks back to whence he came into being, with love and loyalty; with this piety he, as it were, gives thanks for his existence."

When Jews of the culture of the Bayt Meedrahsh awake in the morning, they immediately say the prayer *Modeh Ahnee:* "I gratefully thank You, O living and eternal King, who has returned my soul within me with compassion — abundant is Your faithfulness." They then arise and go to a sink (or, in some homes, a pail and basin kept at the bedside), do a ritual washing of the hands and say the accompanying *b'rahkhah* — blessing: "Blessed are You, Hahshehm our Lord, King of the universe, Who has sanctified us with His commandments and has commanded us regarding the washing of our hands." All these blessings are said in Hebrew, *lahshohn hahkodesh* — the holy language.

When getting dressed, a Jewish man puts on *tzeetzeet.* This word, meaning "fringes," refers to a four-cornered undergarment with knotted fringes hanging down from each of the four corners. This is the accompanying *b'rahkhah* (blessing): "Blessed are You, Hahshehm, our Lord, King of the world, Who has sanctified us with His commandments and has commanded us regarding the wearing of *tzeetzeet.*" A male child begins wearing *tzeetzeet* at the age of three. In addition to the *keepah* (skull cap), the *tzeetzeet* is an immediate identifying marker of a Jewish male of the culture of the Bayt Meedrahsh. Although *tzeetzeet* is an undergarment, the strings are sometimes worn hanging outside, over the pants.

We are just beginning with the many blessings the Jew of the culture of the Bayt Meedrahsh pronounces each day, but the pattern of many of the *b'rahkhot* (plural of *b'rahkhah* — blessing) can already be discerned. The Jew is one who is "commanded." Many of the commandments have a specific reason, but some have no other reason than that it is "the will of Hahshehm."

Many believe that even when there is no stated reason for a commandment, it is because Hahshehm wills only that which is good and correct. One accepts with obedience whatever is His will.[9]

Each of these commandments, Nietzsche, is discussed in depth in the *Tahlmood*. The importance here is to see the pattern of piety and devotion in the everyday life of Jews of the culture of the Bayt Meedrahsh.

When the need arises to relieve oneself in the washroom, the Jew leaves the washroom, stops, and says: "Blessed are You, Hahshehm our Lord, King of the universe, Who fashioned man with wisdom and created within him many openings and many cavities. It is clear and known before Your throne of glory that if but one of them were to be ruptured or but one of them to be blocked, it would be impossible to survive and to stand before you. Blessed are You, Hahshehm, Who heals all flesh and acts wondrously." Whether one relieves oneself once or ten times a day, each time, this *b'rahkhah* is recited.

If one studies Torah before going to the synagogue, he first says the appropriate *b'rahkhah*; if the morning service is the first Torah study, the *b'rahkhah* may be recited in the synagogue: "Blessed are You, Hahshehm, our Lord, King of the universe, Who has sanctified us with His commandments and has commanded us to be involved with words of Torah. Please, Hahshehm, our Lord, sweeten the words of Your Torah in our mouth and in the mouth of Your people, the family of Israel. May we and our offspring and the offspring of Your people, the house of Israel — all of us — know Your Name and study Your Torah for its own sake. Blessed are You, Hahshehm, giver of the Torah."

Your words, Nietzsche, quoted above, put it similarly: that history belongs to him who "preserves and reveres.... By tending with care that which has existed from old, he wants to preserve for those who shall come into existence after him the conditions under which he himself came into existence — and thus he serves life."

In addition to the ritual washing of the hands, many Khahseedic Jews immerse themselves every morning in a *meekvah*, a ritual bath. This cannot be a bathtub or swimming pool. This is a pool whose size and natural waters are specified in detail. We will discuss this at greater length when we talk about women of the culture of the Bayt Meedrahsh.

Now it is time for *Shahkhahreet* — the morning prayers. One can in a case of great necessity *dahven* (pray) alone at home or at the workplace, but it is highly encouraged to *dahven* with a *meenyahn* — a group of at least ten males at least thirteen years of age. While it may be difficult for some men to make it to a synagogue for the afternoon and evening prayers, the morning *Shahkhahreet* is attended by a very high percentage of men in any given community. "Difficult" is a relative term, and there are elderly men who have never in their lives missed praying all three times each day with a *meenyahn*.

Before the service begins, the men don *tahleet* and *t'feeleen*. The *tahleet* is a prayer shawl. *T'feeleen* are two small black boxes known in English as phylacteries; one is attached just above the forehead with the straps going to the back of the head, then over the shoulders to the front; the other is attached with the straps to the underside of the upper arm, positioned opposite the heart. The straps are wrapped around the lower arm, then onto the hand and fingers, in a prescribed way. The contents of each box are the same four passages from scripture. In the arm *t'feeleen* the passages are written on one piece of parchment, prepared from the skin of a kosher animal, whereas the head *t'feeleen* has four separate compartments, with each passage written on a separate piece of parchment.

The first verse, from *Exodus* 13:1–10, speaks of the remembrance of the Exodus from Egypt through the Passover service. It also commands that the story be told to children. "And it shall be for you a sign on your arm and a reminder between your eyes...." From this verse, the rabbis of the period of the *Tahlmood* redaction derived the commandment for wearing *t'feeleen* on the head and the arm. The second passage continues with *Exodus* 13:11–16 and again commands passing on the story of the Exodus: "With a strong hand Hahshehm removed us from Egypt, from the house of bondage." The last two passages in the *t'feeleen* are the first two paragraphs of the three-paragraph *Sh'mah*. This prayer you read about, Nietzsche, in a previous letter. It is the central, most universally known prayer among Jews. Almost all Jews in all streams of Judaism know the opening statement of unity proclaiming that Hahshehm is our sovereign and that he is a single, indivisible unity: "Hear, O Israel, Hahshehm is our Lord, Hahshehm is One." Every schoolchild in the culture of the Bayt Meedrahsh can recite all three paragraphs of the *Sh'mah* in Hebrew, by heart.

The first paragraph of the *Sh'mah*, from Deuteronomy 6:5–9, recognizes Hahshehm as sovereign and also stresses passing the tradition to the children: "You shall love Hahshehm, your Lord, with all your heart, with all your soul and with all your resources. Let these matters that I command you this day be upon your heart. Teach them diligently to your children and speak of them while you sit in your home, while you walk on the way, when you retire and when you arise. Bind them as a sign upon your arm and let them be as frontlets between your eyes; and write them on the doorposts of your house and on your gates."

The second paragraph of the *Sh'mah* is from Deuteronomy 11:13-21. It promises rewards for following Hahshehm's commandments, and consequences if "your heart be seduced and you turn astray and serve gods of others..." and returns to a theme that is an important part of the secret of the Jews: "You shall teach them to your children, to discuss them, while you sit in your home, while you walk on the way, when you retire and when you rise up." Then follows the commandment of *m'zoozah*, the small elongated box fixed at the door of Jewish homes: "And you shall write them on the doorposts of your house and upon your gates." The *m'zoozah* contains the first two passages of the *Sh'mah* but not the other two paragraphs that are written on parchment inside the *t'feeleen*.

One often sees Jews of the culture of the Bayt Meedrahsh put their hand to the *m'zoozah*, then kiss their fingers. The *m'zoozah* is not only on the outer doorposts but also on most doorposts within the house.

At the beginning of *Shahkhahreet*, or morning service, fifteen blessings are recited, in which one thanks Hahshehm for many aspects of life. The prayer leader recites the blessings, and the congregation responds, "Amen." Many *T'heeleem* — Psalms — are recited. Each individual recites the three paragraphs of the *Sh'mah* silently. Then follows the *Ahmeedah* — literally, "standing" — prayer. It is first said silently by the congregants, then repeated aloud by the *shahlee'ahkh tzeeboor* — the "representative of the congregation" who is leading the prayers. After the *Sh'mah*, the *Ahmeedah* is the most important prayer of the Jewish people. It contains recognition of Hahshehm's sovereignty, gratefulness for his blessings, and entreaties for insight, health, prosperity, and other divine gifts. One can include other personal, pertinent prayers, but the prayers of the *Ahmeedah* are largely for the good of the community.

In the morning service on Mondays and Thursdays, the Torah is removed from the Ark, and three brief sections from the specific Torah portion of the week are chanted aloud. Of the three daily services, *t'feeleen* are worn only during the morning service, and the Torah is read only at the Monday and

Thursday morning services. The only exception is *Shahbaht*, when the entire Torah portion of the week is chanted at the morning service; at the *Shahbaht* afternoon service, three short portions of the coming week's Torah portion are read out. *T'feeleen* are not worn on *Shahbaht*, for the day is so holy that there is no need for the *k'dooshah* (holiness) that *t'feeleen* bring to a weekday.

The afternoon service, called *Meenkhah*, is briefer than the morning service. The *tahleet* (prayer shawl) and *t'feeleen* are not worn. The *Sh'mah* is not recited, but the central prayer, the *Ahmeedah*, is recited, first quietly by all the congregants and then by the leader, just as in the morning. Ad hoc *meenyahneem* are sometimes formed by men at work who have no synagogue nearby; by gathering ten Jewish men to constitute the quorum required for a *meenyahn*, together they may conduct the afternoon service wherever they are. If a *meenyahn* is not available, a man may close his office door and pray alone. When praying alone, some parts of the service must be omitted. The preference is to pray in the synagogue with a *meenyahn*.

The evening service, like the morning service, includes all three paragraphs of the *Sh'mah*, as well as the *Ahmeedah*. *Tahleet* and *t'feeleen* are not worn. However, morning, afternoon, and evening prayers are invariably recited by Jews of the culture of the Bayt Meedrahsh, either as part of a *meenyahn* or alone. As you can see, Nietzsche, "religion" is not something that the Jew of the culture of the Bayt Meedrahsh "practices" when not doing something else. Being aware of Hahshehm and his commandments, executing those commandments, and being thankful for Hahshehm's blessings constitute an attitude integral to every day, every hour, every act. On awakening, on emerging from the washroom after relieving oneself, passing through a doorway and kissing the *m'zoozah*, while attending three services a day, the Jew is constantly aware of his presence before his Creator, of his good fortune to be a Jew who receives Hahshehm's blessings, and of Hahshem's expectation that he behave in accordance with the ethics and values prescribed in the Torah.

These daily, weekly, monthly, and yearly cycles, as well as the seven-year *Sh'meetah* cycle, speak to why the designation "culture of the Bayt Meedrahsh" is preferable to "religion." The term "religion" lends itself to comparison with other "religions," whereas there is no culture comparable to that of the Bayt Meedrahsh. Nor does the lifestyle of assimilating Jews compare to that of Jews of the culture of the Bayt Meedrahsh.

Ah, Nietzsche, we are just getting started! We have not yet even mentioned food and drink. These are a gift bestowed on mankind, and the Jew pronounces blessings before and after partaking of this bounty. *All* foods? Yes. One goes to the faucet for a glass of water, fills the glass, pauses to recite a blessing, drinks the water, puts the glass down, and then pauses again to recite the after-blessing. These blessings are recited before and after each drink, be it once, twice, or ten times a day. A variety of blessings are said before and after eating or drinking, depending on what is included in the snack or meal. How does one know what to say and when? All the procedures for arising in the morning, eating food, passing by a *m'zoozah*, praying three times a day, and for many other occasions are contained in the core curriculum of the Bayt Meedrahsh — the Torah and *Tahlmood*.

Could I pass off the following as coming from Jewish scriptures? "The young person should be taught to regard himself as a failed work of nature, but at the same time, as a witness to the grandiose and marvelous intentions of this artist: nature has done badly, he should say to himself, but I will honor its great intentions by serving it so that, one day, it may do better. Anyone who believes in culture is thereby saying: 'I see above me something higher and more human than I am; let everyone help me to attain it, as I will help everyone who knows and suffers as I do: so that at last the man may appear who feels himself perfect and boundless in knowledge and love, perception and power, and who in his completeness is at one with nature, the judge, the evaluator of things.' It is hard to create in anyone this condition of intrepid self-knowledge because it is impossible to teach love; for it is love alone that can bestow on the soul, not only a clear, discriminating and self-contemptuous view of itself, but also a desire to look beyond itself and to seek with all its might for a higher self as yet still concealed from it."[10]

This quote is, of course, from your *Untimely Meditations*. You knew, Nietzsche, what you desired to find in the *Übermensch* and in the ideal culture. You just did not know the Jews of the culture of the Bayt Meedrahsh; you did not know that they existed in your time, thousands of years before your time, and that they would continue to exist thousands of years after your time. There is no "time" for them. As Goethe said, "It is the most perpetual people of the earth; it was, it is, it will be to glorify the name of Jehovah through all times."[11]

A child sees and lives devotion to Hahshehm's will every day — the observance of the values of the culture of the Bayt Meedrahsh. Boys and girls see the daily behavior of the parents and older children in the home and are taught, by word and example, what to do and what not to do. Before he can speak, a young child is held up to the sink to "wash" before a meal that includes bread. The *b'rahkhah* (blessing) is said for the child, and almost by the time he can speak, the child has the blessing memorized. These are practices the child sees observed with joy and thankfulness, not with stern prohibitions and dire warnings of punishment. The child is not taught "religion"; rather, the child is taught how to live in the culture of the Bayt Meedrahsh, grateful for the gifts of Hahshehm.

Every prayer, every benediction, every act is more than simply the act itself; it is an attempt to draw closer to Hahshehm. If one is aware of being created in the image of Hahshehm, that is, the moral and ethical image of Hahshehm, which is perfection, then each act during the day is a seeking of that elevation of deed and spirit, a reaching "higher" — a concept, Nietzsche, that you used often.

Thus, when a Jew sets aside a certain time each day to study Torah, to study *Tahlmood*, he is not only involved in an intellectual undertaking of the highest order, he is also involved in a spiritual undertaking of the highest order.

In the blessings at the beginning of the morning service — *Shahkhahreet* — one of the passages read is from the *Tahlmood*: "These are the precepts whose fruits a person enjoys in This World, but whose principal remains intact for him in the World to Come. They are: the honor due to father and mother, acts of kindness, early attendance at the house of study [Bayt Meedrahsh] morning and evening, hospitality to guests, visiting the sick, providing for a bride, escorting the dead, absorption in prayer, bringing peace between a man and his fellow — and the study of Torah is equivalent to all of them."[12]

There is an important concept of studying Torah *leeshmah* — for its own sake and not for some specified purpose. Is not observing the commandments more important than studying them? Is that not why one studies them? Many sages of the *Tahlmood* bring this argument. Also presented are opinions of others who say that the study of Torah itself is the highest virtue because it brings one closer to Hahshehm in his perfection, and that the fulfillment of all the commandments flows from studying Torah. This is one of the many examples of antinomies that fill the Torah and *Tahlmood*, an illustration of the Jew of the Bayt Meedrahsh's comfort with abstract thinking. The discussion that I have just very briefly summarized is examined in great detail in Jewish texts.

It is worth reiterating here, Nietzsche, what I mentioned in an earlier letter: In its specific use, the word "Torah" refers to the scroll of the Five Books of Moses, the basis of all study in the culture of the Bayt Meedrahsh. In its broader sense, "Torah" means "teaching," and studying Torah means immersing oneself in the Written and Oral Law and all the elucidating texts expounding on them.

The roles of men and women are very different in the culture of the Bayt Meedrahsh. Here we identify a crucial element in the secret of the Jews of this culture. No culture can perpetuate itself against great odds without exceptionally strong men *and* women. While the family has traditionally been the center of life in many cultures, there have been clear shifts within "modern" times. Today, in the early twenty-first century, with fewer children in the home and more women working outside the home, churches and synagogues have become centers not only of worship but of family, social, and leisure activity. In the culture of the Bayt Meedrahsh, the home remains the cultural center, and there is great pride in the woman's role as the mother, the primary influence on the moral and ethical education of the young children, and a helpmate to her husband.

*Hahshehm* has no gender. "He" is a convenient pronoun, but as we have seen, *Hahshehm* has neither form nor attributes. Many words pertaining to Hahshehm are, in Hebrew, of the feminine gender, most importantly Hahshehm's *Sh'kheenah*. The *Sh'kheenah* is the expression of Hahshehm's presence in the world. Hahshehm fills the universe, but when there is a high level of holiness at any given place, it is said that the *Sh'kheenah* rests there.

In an earlier letter, we spoke of *khokhmah* and *beenah* as the highest levels of mental activity. *Khokhmah* is undifferentiated nonverbal thought, whereas *beenah* represents understanding, conceptual knowledge, and reason. Women are endowed with a higher level of *beenah* than men.

This trait is seen at a high level in the Jewish matriarchs: Sarah, Rebecca, Leah, and Rachel. It is Sarah who discerns that Isaac, not Ishmael, is the proper successor to Abraham; Abraham has to be convinced to send away Hagar and Ishmael. Isaac cannot foresee that Jacob is the one destined to become "Israel" and lead the development of the Jewish people; it is Rebecca who has to overcome his "blindness" and make him see, understand, differentiate between Jacob and Esau. Laban refuses to let Rachel be the first to marry Jacob, as Leah is his elder daughter, and so the two sisters, with great compassion and discernment, work together to ensure Jacob's spiritual development.

Women's roles in general society have changed significantly over time. The concept of "modern," where women are concerned, changes more quickly than most societal phenomena. Women's roles in the workplace and in the home have been modified dramatically. They tend to marry later and have fewer children. Women have become a heavily targeted element in commercial markets; the women's fashion industry reaps billions of dollars in profits each year. Fashions in apparel, makeup, and hairstyles are constantly shifting.

While styles fluctuate, the movement toward ever more revealing clothing has been steady. "Sexy" sells. Low-cut blouses and dresses are commonplace, as are short skirts. In men's magazines, it was "modern" in the twentieth century to show bare-breasted women in sensual poses; today it is "modern" to show completely nude women, and men as well, and explicit scenes of sexual intercourse are common fare in movies.

"Freedom" granted to teenage girls and boys has seen teenage pregnancy rates rise throughout the years since you left us, Nietzsche, and divorce rates have risen apace. Divorce rates have risen in the culture of the Bayt Meedrahsh, too, but they remain significantly less than that of "modern" society. Premarital pregnancies are virtually unheard of in the culture of the Bayt Meedrahsh.

In the education of boys and girls, *tz'neeyoot* — modesty — is held in very high esteem. One is modest before his Creator and before his fellow Jew. High standards in knowledge and behavior are constantly reinforced; there is no need for competition for these traits to come to the fore. Knowledge is knowledge of Hahshehm and His will, which leads to behaviors that flow naturally from adhering to the positive and negative commandments.

When dealing with relationships between men and women as well as between boys and girls, *tz'neeyoot* is of the highest value. The Torah recognizes sexual behavior as natural. In the context of a loving marital relationship, it is imbued with *k'dooshah* — holiness. The Torah and *Tahlmood* discuss in depth sexual behavior that is exploitative and extramarital. Rape and how to deal with it are important topics. All people have a *yehtzehr hahrah*, the evil impulse, and a *yehtzehr hahtov,* the impulse to ethical, "higher" behavior. Observance of the commandments reinforces the *yehtzehr hahtov*, which helps one to overcome the *yehtzehr hahrah*.

Freud gives sexual and aggressive drives center stage in his view of man. Nietzsche, you recognized the power of the sexual drive, though you subordinated it to the will to power. The healthy will to power is to overcome the unchecked will to power. "To *sow* the seeds of good spiritual works in the soil of the subdued passions is then the immediate urgent task."[13]

Young children in the culture of the Bayt Meedrahsh, and especially young girls, imbibe from their mothers' behavior and from explicit teaching that their body has *k'dooshah* — holiness; it belongs to them, and it is their responsibility to guard this *k'dooshah*. This is accomplished through *tz'neeyoot* — modesty. Above all, *tz'neeyoot* means respect, for others and for one's own body. *Tz'neeyoot* calls for clothing that covers the body, yet it need not be monastic, austere clothing. Many non-Jewish women choose modest clothing as a preference of style. Many women of the culture of the Bayt Meedrahsh wear stylish clothing, but always *modest* stylish clothing. This ethic is absorbed by a girl beginning in her earliest years. *Tz'neeyoot* means that low-cut blouses and dresses are out, as are short skirts.

*Tz'neeyoot* also means limitation of physical contact between men and women, girls and boys. One who visits a home imbued in the culture of the Bayt Meedrahsh may well find a friendly two-year-old girl approaching with a smile and asking to be picked up and hugged by the visiting man or woman. Return a year or so later, however, and the same little girl, while still outgoing and friendly, may well shy away from physical contact with a man, while a boy refrains from physical contact with a woman once he has turned nine. The exact stage at which this change takes place varies from family to family and child to child, but it generally begins before school age. Being outgoing and friendly is a way of showing affection; refraining from physical contact is a way of showing respect.

Physical affection between men and their male friends, as well as between women and their female friends, is common in the culture of the Bayt Meedrahsh. There is no self-consciousness about being considered homosexual. Within these parameters, there are, of course, the differences one sees in the general population regarding issues of personal space and displays of physical affection. While public displays of physical affection among married couples are not normally seen in the culture of the Bayt Meedrahsh, this is not an issue of prudishness but an expression of the *k'dooshah*, or holiness, of the marital relationship.

Because the separate roles of men and women are valued in the culture of the Bayt Meedrahsh, women do not have the same requirements as men in *hahlahkhah* — Jewish law. As a general rule, women are not obligated to observe the positive commandments that are time-specific, though they are not *prohibited* from observing these commandments. This topic, Nietzsche, like many in the *Tahlmood*, has shades of gray. For example, if the woman performs a positive act that is a commandment but from which she is exempt, does she say before the act the blessing that includes the words "Blessed are You, Hahshehm, our Lord, King of the universe, Who has commanded us..."? These issues are discussed in depth in different sections of the *Tahlmood*, but often no definitive *hahlahkhah* — law — is proclaimed. This opens the way for different commentators and codifiers of Jewish law to make their own rulings. There may be differences, and in the end, a *pohsehk* — an accepted authority on *hahlahkhah* — can render a decision for his particular community. Thus, there may be different decisions about the same issue.

This process leads many uninitiated in the ways of *Tahlmood* to believe that rules are made arbitrarily. However, the rulings are always grounded in much scholarly research. This process is rather like the issuing of majority and minority opinions in a Supreme Court case, or more precisely, like those occasions when a higher court refuses to hear an issue and leaves it to various local jurisdictions to decide for their communities.

The clear majority of opinions rules that women indeed may carry out the positive commandments to which they are not obligated; moreover, it is generally held that they may say the blessing before the act, the opinion broadly based on the belief that the Torah was given to the entire community of Israel. Today Ashkenazic communities allow women to say the blessings even if they are not bound by the commandment, whereas Sephardic communities prohibit this practice. Rabbi Moses Maimonides, the Rahmbahm, ruled that women can fulfill the commandment of wearing *tzeetzeet*,[14] the four-fringed undergarment mentioned above, and went on to apply this ruling to all positive commandments from which women are exempt, such as wearing *t'feeleen*.

However, women in the culture of the Bayt Meedrahsh have no desire to blur distinctions between the roles of women and men; one does not see women wearing *tzeetzeet* or *t'feeleen*. This is another example of the continuous modernity of the culture of the Bayt Meedrahsh, in contrast to the ever-changing aspirations and customs of women in most cultures, which have changed so frequently that what is "modern" in one decade becomes old-fashioned in the next, with a new "modern woman" succeeding the last.

One significant trend for women in the culture of the Bayt Meedrahsh is toward more and more study of *Tahlmood* and serious scholarship. In the past, women's studies have been confined to general principles and to specifics in the laws that apply to women. One can point to many commentators in the past who have discouraged the practice of women studying *Tahlmood*; some present-day *pohskeem* (plural of "*pohsehk*" — "legal authority") look favorably on this trend.

Despite the fact that you never married, Nietzsche, you addressed both the negative and positive possibilities: "Sexual love betrays itself most clearly as a lust for possession: the lover desires unconditional and sole possession of the person for whom he longs; he desires equally unconditional power over the soul and over the body of the beloved; he alone wants to be loved and desires to live and rule in the other soul as supreme and supremely desirable...a *shared* higher thirst for an ideal above them. But who knows such love? Who has experienced it? Its right name is *friendship*."[15]

I will write more about marriage and family relationships in the next letter, Nietzsche. Until then I remain

Very truly yours,

Ben Moshe

# Letter Eleven

March 2, 2006                                              ב' באדר א' תשס"ו

Dear Nietzsche,

Let us continue with your writings about love and marriage, for some are quite consistent with the values of the culture of the Bayt Meedrahsh: "The best friend will probably acquire the best wife, because a good marriage is founded on the talent for friendship."[1] You encouraged those considering marriage to look at the value it can bring: "Thus I counsel all who are honest; and what would my love for the *Übermensch* and for all who shall yet come amount to if I counseled and spoke differently? Not merely to reproduce, but to produce something higher — toward that, my brothers, the garden of marriage should help you."[2]

The reason, dear Nietzsche, that marriages in the culture of the Bayt Meedrahsh are more enduring than those outside the culture is that they are "not merely to reproduce" but, in fact, "to produce something higher." And the "something higher" is a family committed to ethical and moral values and closely bound to a culture subscribing to the same values — values it has upheld for millennia.

This sanctification of love is beautifully illustrated by the *Song of Songs*, from which I quoted in another letter. It is part of the *Tahnahkh* — the Bible. King Solomon wrote this poem of love as an allegory to the love between Hahshehm and the people of Israel. Marriage is as much a part of the life cycle of Jews of the culture of the Bayt Meedrahsh as is birth and death. In order for mankind to join Hahshehm in the perfecting of the world — *teekoon ohlahm* — marriage is a necessity.

149

Many references in the *Tahlmood* make it clear that marriage is an obligation, and the sooner it takes place, the better. When a brilliant scholar, Rabbi Hahmnoonah, was praised to Rabbi Hoonah, the latter asked that the scholar be brought to him. When he discovered that Rabbi Hahmoonah was not married, he said, "See to it that you do not appear before me before you are married."[3] The discussion goes on to consider the best age for marriage, and the range decided on was sixteen to twenty-two.

Given the strictly observed laws of *tz'neeyoot* — modesty — it is easy to see why premarital pregnancies do not occur in the culture of the Bayt Meedrash. There is no such thing as "dating" for young men and women except in the context of choosing a life mate. Stories of matchmaking where the parents make all the decisions and the young people have no say in the matter are a myth. A potential match may well be thought of first by parents, but it might also be suggested by friends or even by one of the young people, who hears about someone he or she would like to meet. The meetings between the potential couple are in public settings, such as a hotel lobby that is open to all. If it is clear from the beginning, to either participant, that they are not compatible, the matter ends there. This possibility is understood from the outset; thus, feelings of rejection are minimized. No further "casual" get-togethers are planned, since their sole purpose is to determine whether there is the possibility for building a married life together.

The discussions center on background, work, and family interests. It will not surprise you, Nietzsche, that even without any physical contact at all, there still is an awareness of physical attraction or the lack of it. By the third or fourth meeting, the couple generally know whether they are suited to each other, though a more lengthy process is possible. It is rare for such a process to go on for even several months. The custom is for the young man to propose marriage; if the woman accepts, they consider themselves engaged.

The next step involves meeting the parents; then the two sets of parents meet, generally in the presence of the couple. While all involved hope for the blessings of the parents, it is not a requirement, for the couple has the right, under Jewish law, to marry without parental consent. An engagement party, involving family and friends, is often held. There are words of Torah and introductions. There may be dancing, but not mixed dancing. We will discuss this in greater detail when we get to the wedding. Nietzsche, there is no joy like the joy that accompanies a wedding in the culture of the Bayt Meedrahsh.

In Ashkenazic communities, it is customary for the couple not to see each other the week before the wedding. On the *Shahbaht* before the wedding, the groom, or *khahtahn*, is called to the Torah in his synagogue, and a special blessing is read for the upcoming wedding. The *khahtahn* and his friends often have a *Shahbaht* meal at the home of his parents. The bride, or *kahlah*, and her friends celebrate the *Shahbaht* meal at her home. As at other *Shahbaht* meals, there is singing as well as *deevray Torah* — words of Torah. The passages of Torah are tied to the upcoming *seemkhah* (happiness or happy celebration). The couple enhance the anticipation and *k'dooshah* — holiness — of the wedding day by fasting. The woman — and often, sepa-rately, the man — immerses herself in a *meekvah*, a ritual bath, the week before the wedding, sometimes on the wedding day itself. The wedding date is timed according to the woman's menstrual cycle, for reasons we will discuss more fully when we speak of relationships after the wedding.

At the reception before the wedding, a *m'kheetzah*, or partition, is set up between the men's side and the women's side. On the women's side, the bride, sitting on a platform on a quasi throne befitting a queen, receives good wishes and is asked by many for a blessing, because her elevated status as a bride enables her to entreat Hahshehm for health, enhanced learning of Torah, or a good marital match for her yet unmarried friends. On the men's side, the groom may say words of Torah appropriate to the occasion. The wedding contract — *k'toobah* — is reviewed and signed by two witnesses. This contract defines the personal and monetary obligations in the marriage, most of which concern the husband. The men gather around for fellowship with the groom, often chanting *neegooneem* — tunes without words. The mood at this point is reserved, quiet, in recognition of the *k'dooshah* of the upcoming ceremony under the *khoopah*, or wedding canopy.

Then, Nietzsche, comes a beautiful moment: the *b'dehken*, literally, "covering-up." The groom, accompanied by his father, the father of the bride, and other male family members and friends, crosses over to the women's side of the partition. At many weddings, the friends of the groom dance backward — facing him, arms around one another's shoulders, as he begins the proces-sion to the bride. The bride and groom now see each other for the first time in a week. The bride, her veil lifted, is identified by her intended as the woman he wants to marry. This is in reminiscence of the story of Jacob, who thought he was marrying his beloved Rachel, but under the veil was Leah, her older sister. The groom lowers the veil back over the bride's face and then, accompanied by the male entourage, proceeds to the *khoopah*, the wedding canopy.

There are many customs not directly related to *hahlahkhah*, and often differing reasons are cited for a given custom. The reason for the bride wearing a veil at all is connected by some to a passage in the Torah concerning Rebecca as she was about to meet Isaac: "She took a veil and covered herself."[4] There is a variation in customs between Ashkenazic and Sephardic Jews, though the basic structure of the wedding is the same.

The *khoopah* is a length of fine cloth (sometimes a *tahleet* — a prayer shawl), held aloft by poles at each of its four corners. Four people are selected to hold the poles and thus are close to the ceremony. The canopy symbolizes the home that the bride and groom will build. It is open on all four sides, symbolizing the "open house" of Abraham. Abraham had many outstanding attributes, and one of the most noted was his welcoming of guests; his house was open to wayfarers coming from all directions. According to many Jewish sources, Hahshehm erected a canopy for Adam and Eve and performed their marriage ceremony in the Garden of Eden. Under the canopy he commanded them, "Be fruitful and multiply."[5]

The bride approaches with her entourage. She is accompanied by her mother and the mother of the groom, carrying candles to symbolize the light and joy that should always accompany the couple. The groom wears a white robe-like garment, known as a *keetle*, over his clothing. Again, there are many suggestions about the reason for this custom: white symbolizes purity and elevates the groom spiritually; he is like a king; the high priest wore white on the holy day of *Yohm Keepoor*.

The bride arrives under the canopy and circles the groom — three times according to one custom, seven times according to another. The custom is generally observed only at weddings of Ashkenazic Jews. The *Tahlmood* teaches, "Whoever lives without a wife lives without a wall." The bride circles the groom, indicating that she will be like a wall protecting her husband from temptation.[6] The number three can symbolize the three obligations the groom has to his bride: to provide her with food, clothing, and satisfaction of her desires. In Jewish law, the man has an obligation to fulfill his wife's sexual desires; the woman has no such obligation toward the man. In the tradition of the Kahbahlah, seven circles around the groom represent the seven revolutions of the earth during the seven days of creation. Also, the number seven has a spiritual meaning of closeness to Hahshehm. There are seven days in the week, seven years in the *Sh'meetah* cycle, and seven *Sh'meetah* cycles culminating in a Jubilee year. There are many other times when the number seven appears in the tradition of the Jews.

In earlier times, the engagement of the couple often preceded the wedding by some months. The bride remained in her parents' home and was "as if" married in terms of prohibition of contact with other men, but the engaged couple could not have relations together. In our day this official engagement (*Keedoosheen*) takes place as part of the ceremony, with the giving of the ring.

The rabbi conducting the ceremony welcomes the couple and chants the sanctification over a cup of wine. On behalf of the man, this blessing is recited: "Blessed are You, Hahshehm our Lord, King of the universe, Who has sanctified us with his commandments and commanded us regarding sexual prohibitions, forbidding to us [women] who are merely betrothed, but permitting to us [women] who are married to us through the wedding ceremony (*khoopah*) and sanctification (*keedoosheen*). Blessed are You, Hahshehm, Who sanctifies Israel through *khoopah* and *keedoosheen*."[7]

The two witnesses come forward. The groom produces the ring for the bride. The rabbi asks if the ring belongs to him; then the rabbi asks the witnesses to examine the ring and verify that it is worth at least a *p'rootah* — the smallest coin in earliest Jewish tradition. The groom places the ring on the forefinger of his bride's right hand and repeats after the rabbi, in Hebrew, the traditional words that mean "Behold, you are consecrated to me with this ring according to the law of Moses and Israel." The thirty-two letters in this recitation parallel the number of times Hahshehm's name, as *Ehloheem*, is mentioned in the first chapter of Genesis — the creation of the world. Also, the Hebrew letter representation of thirty-two is *lamed beht*, which spells the Hebrew word for "heart."[8]

While it is "modern," Nietzsche, for weddings to be "double-ring" ceremonies — a ring for the bride and a ring for the groom — this is not found in weddings of the culture of the Bayt Meedrahsh. The ring is a gift from the groom to the bride; the bride must accept it freely. Indeed, such an exchange can raise questions about the legality of the marriage in Jewish law.[9] Also, the bride is the center of the wedding ceremony — it is *she* who is sought after.

Moreover, there is a question of *tz'neeyoot* (modesty); men generally eschew wearing jewelry.

The Hebrew for "you are consecrated to me," which begins the recitation of the ring ceremony, is *"Aht m'koodehsheht lee."* At the end of the ring ceremony, many guests say aloud, *"M'koodehsheht"* — "Consecrated!" This marks the end of the *k'doosheen* part of the ceremony, and the couple is considered linked, but not yet permitted to live together. While not originally part of the wedding ceremony, for almost a thousand years it has been the custom to read the *k'toobah*, or "wedding contract," at this point. This divides the two parts of the ceremony.

Just as the first part of the rite began with sanctification over a cup of wine, so, too, does the second part. The essential part of the actual wedding ceremony is the chanting of the *shehvah b'rahkhot* — the seven blessings. Family members and friends receive the honor of being called under the canopy to face the bride and groom and chant the blessings. Again we have the number seven, alluding to the seven days of creation. The first blessing is given over the wine; the second proclaims that Hahshehm created all things for his glory. The third blessing thanks Hahshehm for creating man, and the fourth declares thankfulness for man having been created in Hahshehm's image. As we mentioned before, dear Nietzsche, the "image" is not physical but is a mirror image of the goodness that Hahshehm bestows on man — so, too, should man be good to his fellow man.

The fifth blessing asks that "the barren [land] rejoice and be glad when its children are gathered back to it in joy." The sixth blessing asks Hahshehm to "grant great joy to this beloved couple, just as you granted happiness to the work of your hands long ago in the Garden of Eden."

The seventh blessing joyously involves all the guests at the wedding. It begins with the traditional opening: "Blessed are You, Hahshehm, our Lord, King of the universe...." At this point, all join in chanting the Hebrew words that complete the blessing: "...who created happiness and joy, bridegroom and bride, rejoicing and song, delight and cheer, love and harmony, peace and fellowship. Soon, Hahshehm, our Lord, may there be heard in the cities of Judah and in the streets of Jerusalem a sound of gladness, a sound of joy, the sound of the bridegroom and sound of the bride, the sound of rejoicing from bridegrooms at their weddings, and young people at their feasts of song.

Blessed are You, Hahshehm, Who grant joy to the bridegroom with the bride."

In the teaching of the Kahbahlah, the seven blessings represent the seven voices that the people of Israel "saw" at Mount Sinai. The teaching is taken from the portion in Exodus that says, "All the people saw the voices."[10] The seven blessings complete the wedding ceremony. At this point the traditional breaking of the glass is done, though some do so at the end of the *keedoosheen*. A glass is wrapped in a napkin and placed on the floor; the groom smashes it with his right foot. All present erupt with a joyous "*Mahzahl tov!*" These words literally mean "good luck" but intend "Congratulations!"

Several reasons are given for breaking the glass: joy is often tempered with sadness; it represents the destruction of Jerusalem and the Temple; it is a reminder of the breach of faith that took place after the wedding of Adam and Eve in the Garden of Eden; and there are many more.

In the culture of the Bayt Meedrahsh, the bride and groom do not kiss under the canopy, because physical affection is a private matter. Again, Nietzsche, *tz'neeyoot* — modesty. Singing and dancing punctuate the recessional of male family and friends of the bride and groom. Again facing the bride and groom, they dance backward and lead the couple to a room for their first opportunity to be alone. A light meal awaits the bride and groom, who have been fasting all day. This is not the place where the marriage is consummated; their time alone generally lasts twenty to thirty minutes.

While the couple is alone together, the guests gather at tables. There are areas for *n'teelaht yahdahyeem* — the ritual hand washing before a meal. The guests eat the first course of the meal, and there is much talk about the bride, the groom, and the wedding ceremony. Suddenly there is a stir from one corner of the room. The guests jump to their feet as the band fills the room with lively, pulsating festive music. The backward-dancing friends lead the new couple toward the dance floor, where the bride moves to the women's side of the partition, and the groom to the men's side. All the guests spill onto the dance floor.

For forty minutes to an hour the music is nonstop, with concentric circles swirling around to the beat. The men, on their side of the partition, as well as the women on their side, are holding hands and dancing in a circle, a celebrating mass of humanity honoring the new union with an unrestrained

outpouring of happiness and joy. In the center on the men's side, various cele-
brants join the groom. He dances with his father, his father-in-law, all three
together, his grandfathers, and sometimes even great-grandfathers. Then
come brothers, cousins, and friends, with the rest of the community moving
around them on the outside. The next moment, the groom is dancing with his
teachers. Distinguished rabbis, who in other settings are taciturn and quietly
dignified, join in the festivities. "This is the day Hahshehm has made,
*nahgeelah v'neesm'kha bo*," go the lyrics to an old Jewish song: "...we shall
rejoice and be happy on it."

On the women's side, the scene is, if possible, even more *khageegee* —
celebratory — as the outpouring of love and support for the bride grows.
Suddenly, the bride and groom see each other over the partition. How does
this happen? The bride has been placed on a chair and hoisted into the air by
close friends. The same scene is repeated on the groom's side, as he is raised
on a chair or onto the shoulders of a friend. Then the father and father-in-law
may be raised as well; they all join hands, and the circling and shouts of joy
continue to fill the air.

Back on the ground at last, the dancing continues. The pace is fast and a
little wild, and the clothes of all the participants are soon soaked with perspi-
ration, but no one cares. Dancers back out of the center to catch their breath
and are replaced by others, but the bride and groom have no rest until someone takes pity on them and gives them chairs. The dancing goes on and on, as
if the needed energy were being tapped from an inner reservoir reserved for
just this occasion. Nietzsche, you have never seen anything like this, nor has
most of the rest of the world!

Finally the music winds down, and everyone, still filled with vigor and
excitement, moves to the tables for dinner. The musicians — often a guitarist,
clarinetist, keyboard player, and singer — take a break. The music has been a
continuous stream of Hebrew and Yiddish melodies. At dinner different
communities of the culture of the Bayt Meedrahsh have their own customs.
In some, the men and women dine on different sides of the partition. In other
communities, the seating is mixed for dinner. The eating and socializing go
on for only a short time, and then the dancing begins anew.

In some communities, after another furious round of dancing, the bride
on her side and the groom on his are allowed to be seated and are entertained
like a king and queen. The couple may sit together, first on one side of the

partition, then on the other. Parading before them are various entertainments: a juggler, someone balancing a ladder on his chin or with a cup full of wine on his head, others doing back flips or walking on their hands — displaying talents that few knew they possessed, to the delight of the honored couple. Then everyone goes back to the tables to finish the meal. Singing of the *beerkaht hahmahzohn* — the blessing after the meal — officially brings the festive meal to an end.

The wedding ceremony itself is one of holiness, requiring the presence of at least ten men aged thirteen or more, and it is fitting that the evening end with a ceremony of gratefulness to Hahshehm. Often, most of the guests have left by this time, but family and close friends of the couple, who have also remained, gather around for a repeat of the *shehvah b'rahkhot* — the seven blessings that were chanted under the wedding canopy. A cup of wine is passed from one man to another, usually not the same people who performed the rite during the wedding ceremony. The evening comes to a close, and the bride and groom leave to spend their first night together.

What then — off to a secluded honeymoon? Not yet. The celebration of the new couple is extended another six nights as various friends and relatives host celebratory dinners. The custom is to include also friends who were not present at the wedding. At each dinner, the seven blessings are chanted. The themes of gratefulness to Hahshehm, of joyousness, of the Jewish people, of Jerusalem and the land of Israel, fill the air over and over again. One of the oft-repeated songs includes these lyrics: "There shall once again be heard in the cities of Judah and the streets of Jerusalem a sound of joy, a sound of gladness, a sound of the bridegroom, a sound of the bride." You were aware, Nietzsche, of this longing to return to Zion, to return to the land of Israel. I will write much more about this in future letters.

How do the new bride and groom relate to each other? How do they keep the fires of the excitement and the *k'dooshah* — holiness — of the wedding ceremony burning in their everyday lives? What about the issue of sexual intimacy? Outside the culture of the Bayt Meedrahsh, many young people have lived together and slept together for a year or more before marriage. Young people, as I have mentioned, are not marrying as young as in earlier times, and they are having fewer children.

Whereas outside the culture of the Bayt Meedrahsh, marriage between two virgins has become a rarity, within the culture it is the rule. The Torah and *Tahlmood* have much to say on this point. The groom has already pledged to feed, clothe, and satisfy his bride sexually. The "ancient" rabbis understood individual psychology very well. The groom's anxiety over the first sexual encounter was acknowledged by exempting him from certain prayers and observances.[11] The man has an obligation to satisfy his wife sexually, and she has no such obligation to him. A man is explicitly forbidden from forcing his wife to have sexual intercourse.

So we see, Nietzsche, sexual relations are not only for the purpose of procreation. The nature of men and women was fully recognized and dealt with in much more detail that I can give in this letter. Because there is special holiness associated with *Shahbaht* and certain holidays, sexual relations are encouraged during these times. The process is clearly to give the woman control over her own body and to respect her natural physiological responses. This is very different from most cultures, in which the man is considered the dominant and dictating force in sexual relationships. The ethic of the culture of the Bayt Meedrahsh is that the process should help the man overcome his instinct to dominate and to overindulge in sexual relations.

A common problem among couples is sexual boredom. The culture of the Bayt Meedrahsh greatly reduces the likelihood of this by providing for physical separation between the man and woman for approximately two of the four weeks of the month. This separation occurs during the time a woman is menstruating and the week afterward. The concept of *toomah* — ritual impurity — has nothing to do with physical impurity; it is a spiritual phenomenon. There are extensive laws on ritual impurity that concern men, women, food, and many other things.

It is strictly forbidden to have sexual relations while a woman is menstruating. To distance the couple from any temptation during the woman's period of menstruation and for a week following, the husband and wife should not have physical contact of any kind. Conversation and behavior that could lead to temptation are prohibited. This has nothing to do with the woman's being "untouchable." The man is enjoined to treat his wife with love, kindness, and support. This also reinforces that the expression of love and affection need not be exclusively physical. This period of *needah* — separation — exists from the onset of menses until the woman immerses herself in a *meekvah* — ritual bath.

We discussed in an earlier letter that many men immerse themselves in a *meekvah* each morning. Men and women alike find this a spiritually enriching experience, a reaching higher above the everyday preoccupations of the physical, material world. When the woman emerges from the *meekvah*, the husband and wife celebrate life and the sanctity of their marriage with a physical reunion. What an amazing way to avoid the pitfall of sexual boredom and celebrate the physical and spiritual union of man and wife!

Although, as we discussed, sexual relations are not only for procreation, childbearing is nonetheless a tremendously important part of the culture of the Bayt Meedrahsh. All begins with the Torah; the very first positive commandment is *p'roo oor'voo* — "Be fruitful and multiply."[12] This, like many of the commandments, is appreciated not just as a "thou shalt" but as a blessing as well. While the birthrates in various cultures have changed over time, the culture of the Bayt Meedrahsh has remained forever "modern." Despite centuries of persecution, massacres, and threats, the blessing of having children has been of key importance. From the time Moses was conceived in secret and hidden from the Egyptians, nothing has discouraged Jews from expressing this joyous *meetzvah*, or commandment.

The beloved rabbi Isaac HaKohen Kook taught,

> The fact that *peru urevu* (procreation) is a *mitzvah* from God indicates that this activity is rooted in absolute holiness and goodness. Indeed, this viewpoint is the very basis for human morality. If the continued survival of the human race is not based on goodness, then life itself is merely the lamentable victory of our natural drives and instincts over the will for good. This dark view is the root for all negative character traits and immoral behavior, both in the family unit and in society. The final conclusion of such an outlook is that "might is right" — the strong and the fit deserve to rule over the weak. Nevertheless, we know that life is not easy. Life in this world is full of pain and suffering.... How can we bring children into such a world? Just as this *mitzva* reinforces our natural aspirations for goodness, it also elevates the mind and expands our horizons to recognize the unity of reality over time. The past, present, and future are all bound together.[13]

Dear Nietzsche, what could be a more life-confirming attitude! The birthrates for Jews outside the culture of the Bayt Meedrahsh have fallen below replacement levels. For centuries, Catholics and Protestants held the same theological position as Jews of the culture of the Bayt Meedrahsh, but this value eroded in the twentieth century. In the 1950s, researchers produced the first oral contraceptive. This was a revolutionary moment on a global scale. For reasons of "population control" or "freedom" to have sex without fear of pregnancy, many enthusiastically welcomed this development. While the pope denounced use of contraceptives, many theologians opposed him. The results are found in the homes. Birthrates in largely Catholic Spain and Italy are among the lowest in Europe, below 1.5 children per family.

Before "the pill," the favored method of birth control was referred to as the "rhythm method." Couples easily calculated the likeliest time of conception in the woman's physiological menstrual cycle and avoided sexual relations then. The calculation is not difficult; indeed, it was revealed in the Torah thousands of years ago: two weeks after the onset of menses, when the woman of the culture of the Bayt Meedrahsh emerges from the *meekvah* and renews sexual relations with her husband, she is at the precise time when conception is most likely. This "reverse-rhythm method" works quite well in keeping conception rates high in the culture of the Bayt Meedrahsh.

There is extensive discussion in the *Tahlmood* about the number of children needed to fulfill the blessing of *p'roo oor'voo* — to be fruitful and multiply. The minimum number of children required in the Tahlmoodic trachate *Y'vahmoht* is one boy and one girl; yet another opinion is two boys and one girl. Couples keep conceiving until this minimum is met. While this fulfills the commandment, one does not then cease to affirm life by engaging in contraceptive methods. This affirmation of life acquired new and dedicated emphasis in the wake of the murder of one and a half million Jewish children by the Nazis in World War II. While no precise statistics are available, it is clear that the *average* number of children per family, in the culture of the Bayt Meedrahsh of the twenty-first century, is more than five.

The figure of five children per family is conservative — many families have seven and more. They begin to have children early and, thus, are already grandparents in their forties and great-grandparents in their sixties. This is not theoretical, Nietzsche. Every Jew of the culture of the Bayt Meedrahsh knows many couples in their seventies who have more than sixty

grandchildren, some more than eighty. They do not just "have" these grandchildren; they dance at their weddings and celebrate a myriad of life-affirm-
ing events along the way. They see their children, grandchildren, and great-
grandchildren dedicate their lives to Torah in the broadest sense; this means
studying Torah and *Tahlmood* from an early age and living the life of values
derived from that study.

We have discussed some of these values in our letters, Nietzsche, and now
we will take a deeper look. At the same time, we will also focus on *your* values.
Just as part of the secret of the Jews of the culture of the Bayt Meedrahsh is
that few actually know these Jews up close, we will find that part of the "secret
of Nietzsche" is that few people know your writings up close.

I will write again soon.

Yours always,

Ben Moshe

# Letter Twelve

March 16, 2006                                        ט״ז באדר תשס״ו

Dear Nietzsche,

"Morality" and "values" are powerful words — or are they? Perhaps they are actually *weak* words. Perhaps there is no such thing as values at all. Isn't this why you wrote about the need for a "reevaluation of all values"? Is not power everything? And are not restraints on it an abuse of the human will? Is not "liberty" the freedom from restraints? Is not the God of the Jews a stern God of retribution and vengeance?

There are still many people in the twenty-first century who believe all these things about you, Nietzsche, and about the "stern" God of the Jews. Just as you admonished your readers to read all your words before pretending to understand them, one must also read the entire Torah and *Tahlmood* and the authoritative commentaries on them in order to know and understand them. Indeed, your own misunderstanding of the culture of the Bayt Meedrahsh resulted from your incomplete reading of the necessary texts.

In this letter, we will see that values, ethics, and morality are vitally important for you and for the culture of the Bayt Meedrahsh — and indeed that your values are one and the same with those of the culture of the Bayt Meedrahsh.

Unfortunately, many people are still confused about your works, including a number of academic "authorities," and it is high time to set the record straight. For instance, Geoffrey Clive finds in your writings "numerous passages conveying an almost vindictive contempt for the weak."[1] Calling your attitude toward Germans "ambivalent," he goes on to say, "At times his contempt is a clear case of projected self-hatred."² Moreover, he maintains that misinterpretations of your works have to do with the "failure to see him in his love-hate relationship to himself."³ Clive points to your *Beyond Good and Evil* as ample proof of "antimoralism."⁴

Lest you think these are merely the crotchets of one isolated scholar who has missed your intent altogether, here is a comment from Max Dimont, a historian who has written praiseworthy books about the Jews: "Nietzsche, with all due regard for his nervous, brilliant prose, is the 'father' of Nazism, and his ethic is not the ethic of Torah and Testament, but the limited code of the Nazi."⁵

Neither of these writers cites even a single source to support these assertions — a blatant failure of the obligation to scholarship and truth. They could cite no references, because *nothing* in your writings supports their misconceptions.

Clive, the philosophy professor, is no psychiatrist, yet he makes a major point of what he calls your "self-hatred." Of course, he need not be a psychiatrist to bring examples from your writing to buttress his analysis, but there are no such examples to bring. Thus, he limits himself to baseless pronouncements, which are rendered nonsense by the entire corpus of your works.

The references to your "ambivalence" toward Germans, and Dimont's reference to you as the "father of Nazism," are merely a passing on of misinterpretation, not to be confused with scholarship.

Much of the misunderstanding derives from your writing about powerful people and your central concept of the will to power. In examining this, we begin bringing together your values and those of the culture of the Bayt Meedrahsh.

Your extensive writings on going "beyond good and evil," of course, have nothing to do with "antimoralism," for they neither exalt evil nor shun traditional values. The objection was clearly to a phantom "dichotomy" between the two terms, as if one were either good or evil and as if conceptions of good and evil could be judged in the context of utilitarianism. You wrote in *The Gay Science*, "Nowadays there is a profoundly erroneous moral doctrine that is celebrated especially in England: this holds that judgments of 'good' and 'evil' sum up experiences of what is 'expedient' and 'inexpedient.' One holds that what is called good preserves the species, while what is called evil harms the species. In truth, however, the evil instincts are expedient, species-preserving, and indispensable to as high a degree as the good ones; their function is merely different."[6]

In a footnote to this part of *The Gay Science*, Walter Kaufmann, the authoritative translator and scholar of your works, writes, "Nietzsche's refusal to accept any simplistic contrast of good and evil is one of the central motifs of his philosophy. All interpretations that overlook this anti-Manichaean subtlety and assume that he simply reverses traditional valuations are untenably crude."[7]

In this context, I again refer to your contemporary Rabbi Samson Raphael Hirsch, one of the great leaders of the culture of the Bayt Meedrahsh in Germany and all of Europe. Commenting on what, on the surface, could be seen as a clear dichotomy between good and evil — Cain's murder of Abel — Hirsch writes,

> Its [sin's] power is not to be underestimated. It has the power to master you, but it remains quietly at your door. It does not come in to you by itself, uninvited. If it is at home with you, yea, finally to become master of your house, you must in the first instance have invited it in, set a chair for it at your table. By itself it remains quietly before your door. More, all its desire is that you should master it and direct it. God has given sensuality an appeal to your senses, not that it should master and direct you, but that you should master and direct it, not that you should suppress or kill it, but *timshal*, regulate it, rule over it and direct it.... *For there is not a single natural tendency in Man which is, in itself, either good or bad* [emphasis added].[8]

A commentary on the *Sayfehr Y'tzeerah* — a very early text of the esoteric wisdom of the culture of the Bayt Meedrahsh — tells us, "Man has both an urge for good and an urge for evil, the *Yetzer Tov* and the *Yetzer HaRa*. In a purely spiritual sense, these are poles apart. Without a physical world, they could never be brought together in a single entity.... It is only in a physical being that both good and evil can exist together.... One reason why God created man in a physical world was to allow him to have freedom of choice."[9]

This is Hahshehm, Nietzsche. Physical man — *every* physical man — is made up of both good and evil. You contrasted what you say is a possible "healthy god" (you used a lower case "g") to the Christian godhead; you also provided for the possibility that religion can be a "form of thankfulness":

> A people that still believes in itself retains its own god. In him it
> reveres the conditions which let it prevail, its virtues: it projects plea-
> sure in itself, its feeling of power, into a being to whom one may offer
> thanks. Whoever is rich wants to give of his riches; a proud people
> needs a god: it wants to sacrifice. Under such conditions, religion is a
> form of thankfulness. Being thankful for himself, man needs a god.
> Such a god must be able to help and to harm, to be friend and enemy
> — he is admired whether good or destructive. The anti-natural
> castration of a god, to make him a god of the good alone, would here
> be contrary to everything desirable....[10] How can anyone today still
> submit to the simplicity of Christian theologians to the point of
> insisting with them that the development of the conception of God
> from the "God of Israel," the god of a people, to the Christian God,
> the quintessence of everything good, represents progress.[11]

Many of your readers, Nietzsche, take a simplistic approach, seeing only your
"philosophy" or only your "psychology"; therefore, they miss your subtleties.
For the culture of the Bayt Meedrahsh, man is made up of his *yehtzehr hahtov*
and *yehtzehr hahrah* — good and evil impulses — and must use his inclination for good to overcome his inclination for evil. This was your conviction,
too. You ranted against what you saw as the attempt of Christianity to "emas-
culate" man — to extirpate the impulse toward evil rather than understand
that, through "overcoming," a positive will to power becomes a moral force
for good by rising above the negative will to power.

For you, for the culture of the Bayt Meedrahsh before you, and for Freud
after you, there are unconscious forces at work, and the goal is not to uproot
them but to recognize them and gain mastery over them. You warned that
these thoughts were "dangerous insights" and that "there are in fact a hundred
good reasons why everyone should keep away from it who — *can*."[12] But for
one who is swept into the whirlwind or, in your words, "drifted there with
one's bark, well! Let us clench our teeth! Let us open our eyes and keep our
hand firm on the helm! We sail right over morality, we crush, we destroy
perhaps the remains of our own morality by daring to make our voyage there
— but what matter are we! Never yet did a profounder world of insight reveal
itself to daring travelers and adventurers."[13]

Aha! So there he is! The "dangerous" Nietzsche, who advocates that we

destroy our own morality in favor of being "daring travelers and adventurers."
So it is for those who read you incompletely. While the above-quoted passage
may be too subtle for some, there is nothing subtle about your repeated attack
on preachers of morality who look down with pity on those they deem evil —
who pitilessly flog their flock to extirpate their evil, and, in the process,
castrate them.

Did you care about those in need of help? You said through Zarathustra,
"I wash my hand when it has helped the sufferer; therefore I wipe even my
soul. Having seen the sufferer suffer, I was ashamed for the sake of his shame;
and when I helped him, I transgressed grievously against his pride.... But I
am a giver of gifts: I like to give, as a friend to friends. Strangers, however, and
the poor may themselves pluck the fruit from my tree: that will cause them
less shame."[14] The Torah and *Tahlmood* teach the concept of *payyah* — leaving over the corner of one's field so the poor can come anonymously and take
what they need without feeling demeaned.

No one who glorifies power and is negative or even indifferent toward
values would have written as you did about the Germans in *The Dawn*:
"Germans: To practice loyalty and, for the sake of loyalty, to risk honor and
blood even for evil and dangerous things."[15] And who is powerful? Just before
you wrote of the Germans, you wrote this of the Jews: "To honor father and
mother and to follow their will to the root of one's soul — that was the tablet
of [self-]overcoming that another people hung up over themselves and
became powerful and eternal thereby."[16] In a draft of *The Birth of Tragedy*, you
wrote of "power that is always evil," and you asked, "Who of you will
renounce power, knowing and experiencing that power is evil?"[17] And the
*Tahlmood* asks, "Who is strong?" and then answers, "He who subdues his
impulses."[18]

With Christianity, you make it clear over and over again that you have no
quarrel with the values of its beginnings; the problem is what it became: "One
has only to recall what Christianity has gradually become through the greed
of the State. Christianity is certainly one of the purest revelations of the
impulse to culture and especially of the impulse to the ever-renewed production of the saint; but since it has been employed in a hundred ways to propel
the mills of the state power, it has gradually become sick to the very marrow,
hypocritical and untruthful, and degenerated into a contradiction of its original goal."[19]

And the casual reader plucks out of context your words on Cesare Borgia, again missing the subtleties. Kaufmann explains: "It is...a common misconception that Nietzsche admired Cesare Borgia and glorified him. Nietzsche found it ridiculous to consider a Cesare Borgia unhealthy in contrast to an emasculated man who is alleged to be healthy. When he was criticized on that point, Nietzsche clarified his point in another book three years later. He now explained that he did not favor "the abolition of all decent feelings" but that he was not sure "whether we have really become more moral. Perhaps we have just become emasculated and our failure to do evil is to be ascribed merely to our inability to do evil."[20]

The words "blond beast" were much in vogue with the Nazis, and so you have been maligned for using those words, Nietzsche. But in what context did you use them? Again we turn to Kaufmann:

> Nietzsche's few references to the "blond beast" are to be understood in the same sense as his reference to Borgia. The Borgias and the beast are both ideograms for the conception of unsublimated animal passion. Nietzsche did not glorify either of them. He derides emasculation and scorns the Church for having "hunted down" the Teutonic barbarians — "blond beasts" — only to put them behind bars in monasteries. This alleged historical process is viewed supra-historically as an allegory or symbol of the extirpation of the impulses. The blond beast is not a racial concept and does not refer to the "Nordic race" of which the Nazis later made so much. Nietzsche specifically refers to Arabs, Japanese, Romans and Greeks, no less than ancient Teutonic tribes when he first introduces the term, and the "blondness" obviously refers to the beast, the lion, rather than the kind of man.[21]

There was nothing ambivalent about your attitude toward Germans and the abuse of power. In *The Gay Science*, you wrote of how the word "German" is "constantly being used nowadays to advocate nationalism and race hatred and to be able to take pleasure in the national scabies of the heart and blood poisoning that now leads the nations of Europe to delimit and barricade themselves against each other."[22] And in *Twilight of the Idols*: "One pays heavily for coming to power: power makes stupid. The Germans — once they were called the people of thinkers: do they think at all today? The Germans are now bored with the spirit; politics swallows up all serious concern for really spiritual matters. *Deutschland, Deutschland über alles* — I fear that was the end of German philosophy."[23]

From the *Tahlmood* comes the advice "Love labor and hate authority and do not become intimate with the authorities."[24] What are other values of the Bayt Meedrahsh? The prophet Hosea says to "observe kindness and justice."[25] From the prophet Micah we read the famous question and answer: "O man, what is good? What does Hahshehm require of you but to do justice, to love kindness and to walk humbly with your God?"[26] Also from the *Tahlmood*: "Shimon *hah-Tzahdeek* [Simon the Just] was one of the last men of the Great Assembly. He used to say, the world stands on three things: on Torah, on divine service, and on kindness."[27]

Did you write of such values, Nietzsche? Clive, as we have seen, complains about your "vindictive contempt for the weak." He doubtless overlooked this: "Hatred for mediocrity is unworthy of a philosopher: it is almost a question mark against his 'right to philosophy.'"[28] A little later in the same work, you wrote, "Well-meaning, helpful, good-natured attitudes of mind have not come to be honored on account of their usefulness, but because they are states of richer souls that are capable of bestowing and have their value in the feeling of the plenitude of life."[29]

Perhaps your casual readers also missed this, in *The Antichrist*: "It would be completely unworthy of a more profound spirit to consider mediocrity, as such, an objection. In fact, it is the very first necessity if there are to be exceptions: a high culture depends on it. When the exceptional human being treats the mediocre more tenderly than himself and his peers, this is not mere politeness of the heart — it is simply his duty."[30]

Had you known of the culture of the Bayt Meedrahsh, you might have had the Jews of this culture in mind when you wrote, "Cheerfulness, the good conscience, the joyful deed, confidence in the future — all of them depend, in the case of the individual as of a nation, on the existence of a line dividing the bright and discernible from the unilluminable and dark."[31] Also, you might have been thinking of the Jews when you penned this: "The most spiritual beings, if we assume they are the most courageous, also experience by far the most painful tragedies: but just for that reason they honor life because it pits its greatest opposition against them."[32]

What about benevolence and friendliness? Surely these are values of the culture of the Bayt Meedrahsh. "Say little and do much and receive all men with a cheerful countenance," advises the *Tahlmood*.[33] And one might assume that the following passage also comes from the *Tahlmood*: "Among the little but immeasurably frequent and thus very influential things to which science ought to pay more attention than to the great, rare things, benevolence too is to be reckoned; I mean those social expressions of a friendly disposition, those smiles of the eyes, those handclasps, that comfortable manner with which almost all human action is as a rule encompassed.... Good-natured-ness, friendliness, politeness of the heart are never-failing emanations of the unegoistic drive and have played a far greater role in the construction of culture." No, not the *Tahlmood*, Nietzsche, but from your *Human, All Too Human*.[34]

You had little nice to say about prayer, but you suggested, in place of prayer, the following: "The first thought of the day. — The best way of begin-ning each day well is to think on awakening whether one cannot this day give pleasure to at any rate one person."[35] Here are two quotes that casual readers of your works and of the *Tahlmood* would have difficulty distinguishing: (1) "The good four. Honest with ourselves and with whatever is friend to us; courageous toward the enemy; generous toward the vanquished; polite — always: that is how the four cardinal virtues want us;"[36] and (2) "Rejoice not when your enemy falls, and let not your heart be glad when he falls."[37] The first quote is from *The Dawn*; the second is from the *Tahlmood*.

It cannot have been a radical, everything-goes thinker who wrote, "Measure and moderation. — Of two very exalted things — measure and moderation — it is best never to speak. Some few know their significance and power through inner sacred paths of experience and conversion: they revere in them something divine and refuse to speak of them aloud."[38] Not long after this aphorism in *Human, All Too Human*, you returned to reinforce these positive values: "Cleanliness. — The sense for cleanliness should be kindled in a child to the point of passion: later it will flame up in ever new transforma-tions almost to the height of every virtue and at least appear, as an attendant to all talents, like an aureole of purity, moderation, gentleness, character — bearing happiness within it, spreading happiness around it."[39] And you extolled similar values: "It will be noted that by 'spirit' I mean care, patience, cunning, simulation, great self-control..."[40]

These values are repeated throughout the Torah and *Tahlmood*; in the section of the *Tahlmood* called the Sayings of the Fathers, many of these values are taught in concise, pithy aphorisms — a form of which you, Nietzsche, were also a master. Here is an example: "Rabban Shimon Gamliel said: The world exists because of three things: justice, truth and peace, as it is written, 'Render truth and the judgment of peace in your gates.'"[41] The last part of the quote is from *Zechariah* 8:16.

In *D'vahreem* — Deuteronomy — the last book of the Torah, as Moses is reviewing for the people of Israel all they have been instructed to do, he is talking about setting up judges and officers of the court when he thunders the mighty call to justice: "*Tzehdehk, Tzehdehk Teerdohf*! — Justice, justice, shall you pursue!"[42] The *Tahlmood* has many interpretations and commentaries on this phrase. Another source of commentary on justice, rich in its prose, comes from your own pen: "In truth, no one has a greater claim to our veneration than he who possesses the drive to, and strength for, justice. For the highest and rarest virtues are united and concealed in justice as in an unfathomable ocean that receives streams and rivers from all sides and takes them into itself. The hand of the just man who is empowered to judge no longer trembles when it holds the scales."[43]

I use all these many quotations to get beyond any possible charge of having merely taken a few examples out of context to prove a specious point. Your praise of virtues is spread throughout your writing, as is your condemnation of unworthy actions that show a failure to overcome the negative will to power:

- *Quiet fruitfulness.* — The born aristocrats of the spirit are not too zealous; their creations appear and fall from the tree on a quiet autumn evening unprecipitately, in due time, not quickly pushed aside by something new. The desire to create continually is vulgar and betrays jealousy, envy, ambition. If one is something one does not need to make anything — and one nonetheless does very much. There exists above the "productive" man a yet higher species.[44]

- *Lack of friends.* — A lack of friends may be put down to envy or presumption. Many owe their friends only to the fortunate circumstance that they have no occasion for envy.[45]

- *Retarded and anticipatory men.* — The unpleasant character who is full of mistrust, consumed with envy whenever competitors or neighbors achieve a success, and violently opposes all opinions not his own, demonstrates that he belongs to an earlier stage of culture and is thus a relic.[46]

- *Acknowledging heirs.* — He who has founded something great in a self-less attitude of mind takes pains to rear heirs for himself. To see an opponent in every possible heir of one's work and to live in a state of self-defense against them is a sign of a tyrannical and ignoble nature.[47]

- *What is needed first.* — A man who refuses to become master over his wrath, his choler and revengefulness, and his lusts, and attempts to become a master in anything else, is as stupid as the farmer who stakes out his field beside a torrential stream without protecting himself against it.[48]

And here are some parallel aphorisms from the Sayings of the Fathers:

- They [the Men of the Great Assembly] said three things: Be deliberate in judgment; raise up many students...[49]

- Provide yourself with a teacher; win for yourself a companion; and judge every man in a favorable, meritorious light.[50]

- Let your fellow man's honor be as dear to you as your own; do not be easily moved to anger.[51]

Praise for the tender concepts of love and friendship flowed from your pen: "Anyone who believes in culture is thereby saying: 'I see above me something higher and more human than I am; let everyone help me to attain it, as I will help everyone who knows and suffers as I do...for it is love alone that can bestow on the soul, not only a clear, discriminating and self-contemptuous view of itself, but also a desire to look beyond itself and to seek with all its might for a higher self as yet still concealed from it.'"[52] And you wrote of love and honor: "Love desires, fear shuns. That is why one cannot be loved and honored by one and the same person, at least not at the same time. For he who honors recognizes power, that is to say he fears it. Love, however, recognizes no power, nothing that separates, contrasts, ranks above and below. Because love does not honor, ambitious men are, secretly or openly, recalcitrant towards being loved."[53]

In the Sayings of the Fathers, the *Tahlmood* differentiates between selfish and unselfish love: "If love depends on some selfish end, when the end fails, love fails; but if it does not depend on some selfish end, it will never fail."[54] In *The Gay Science*, you wrote this about love:

> Our love of our neighbor — is it not just a lust for new possessions? And likewise our love of knowledge, of truth, and altogether any lust for what is new? Gradually we become tired of the old, of what we safely possess, and we stretch out our hands again.... Sexual love betrays itself most clearly as a lust for possession: the lover desires unconditional power and sole possession of the person for whom he longs.... Here and there on earth we may encounter a kind of continuation of love in which this possessive craving of two people for each other gives way to a new desire and lust for possession — a shared higher thirst for an ideal above them. But who knows such love? Who has experienced it? Its right name is *friendship*.[55]

In exploring the concept of love in the culture of the Bayt Meedrahsh, let us look first to your Zarathustra, who approached, yet pulled back from, defining that which is "higher" as "God": "And when I wandered alone, for whom did my soul hunger at night, on false paths? And when I climbed mountains, whom did I always seek on the mountains, if not you? And all my wandering and mountain climbing were sheer necessity and a help in my helplessness: what I want with all my will is to fly, to fly up into you."[56]

It is clear that you celebrated life yet longed for something "higher." Even if you did find such a friend on this earth, there is also some limitation that would yet leave a yearning for a deeper, higher, more inspiring relationship. In the culture of the Bayt Meedrahsh, you would have found the higher human being, for they find one another; yet there remains the quest for a spiritual experience not available in this life.

You would have loved the Kahbahlists, Nietzsche! These were giants of Torah and *Tahlmood* study who sought, in addition to the insights and guidance to be gleaned from these God-given texts, a meditative, spiritual kinship with Hahshehm, *d'vaykoot* — clinging to Hahshehm. One seeks the closest possible relationship with Hahshehm, who represents the ultimate in intellectual, emotional, and spiritual excellence. We must mention again that Hahshehm has no such characteristics and no physical representation; anthropomorphisms and anthropopathisms are the best that mere mortals can do to reach an understanding of Hahshehm. Jews of the culture of the Bayt Meedrahsh live with these subtleties, these antinomies.

Love of one's fellow man is inseparable from love of Hahshehm. One superior being has created us all, and thus, the commandment to "love your fellow man as yourself,"[57] coupled with the knowledge that Hahshehm created man in His own image,[58] is the basis for the legendary closeness of the Jewish people — the responsibility that one Jew feels for another. We have mentioned the first Rabbi Menahkhem Mendel Schneerson, known as the *Tzehmakh Tzehdehk*. The third rebbe of the Lubavitch movement, he lived in your time and died in 1866. He wrote a treatise, steeped in the concealed wisdom of the Kahbahlah, on the commandment to love one's fellow Jew as oneself: "We are therefore commanded to love every individual Jew, since each one includes all the souls of Israel, as in the above analogy of the bodily organs. Thus, a person incorporates also his fellow, so he should love his fellow as he does himself.... Then [his soul] can ascend in favor before *Hashem* in His blessed Wisdom, which contains all the souls actually as one. Inasmuch as his soul is also unified with all others, it can ascend into the general, all encompassing Light that is its source and root."[59] The *Tzehmakh Tzehdehk* was referring to *all Jews*, not just those Jews of the culture of the Bayt Meedrahsh.

Love and friendship are bound up with the desire of the closest possible *d'vaykoot* — longing for, clinging to, Hahshehm. Yet this is a longing of the soul that must be controlled by man's intellect. The highest level of *d'vaykoot* may be achieved by a select few, but it is temporary, and one returns to the task of *teekoon ohlahm* — the task of partnership with Hahshehm in perfecting this world.

With this desire for a "higher" world, for communion with a higher being, how can one live with, let alone embrace, this world with all its imperfections? How does one "justify" earthly life? Kaufmann relates his understanding of your evolution, Nietzsche: "It was not until August 1881, near Sils Marie, '6,000 feet beyond man and time,' that the thought came to Nietzsche that the man who perfects himself and transfigures his physis achieves ultimate happiness and experiences such an overwhelming joy that he no longer feels concerned about the "justification" of the world: he affirms it...forward, backward and 'in all eternity.'"[60] This is "inextricably connected with the possession of power, and where the one is found, the other must be too.

Nietzsche can say: 'My formula for the greatness of a human being is *amor fati*: that one wants nothing to be different — not forward, not backward, not in all eternity. Not merely to bear what is necessary, still less conceal it…but love it.'"[61]

We have mentioned Rabbi Ahkeevah, perhaps the most quoted, most honored rabbi of the *Tahlmood*, who lived an exemplary life of *amor fati*. He had a teacher named Nahkhoom Eesh Gahm Zoo. Whatever fate befell him, he would say, "*gahm zoo l'tovah* — also this is for the good." Whatever Hahshehm creates in this world is for the good; it is up to man to seek the message and learn from it.

One story tells of Rabbi Ahkeevah walking with his colleagues after the destruction of the second Holy Temple. They heard the roar of Roman crowds in the distance, and all wept except Rabbi Ahkeevah, who laughed and asked why his companions were crying. They asked why they should *not* cry, since the idol-worshipping heathens were rejoicing and living in security and comfort while the Jews, despite their obedience to Hahshehm, saw their Holy Temple in ruins. Rabbi Ahkeevah said, "For the same reason I laugh. If it is so for those who transgress His will, how much more so will it be for those who do His will."[62]

On another occasion, Rabbi Ahkeevah and his colleagues walked past the ruins of the Holy Temple and saw a fox coming from the ruins. Again the colleagues wept, and again Rabbi Ahkeevah laughed. They wept from the pain over the recent loss of the Temple. Rabbi Ahkeevah explained that he laughed because he now knew that the prophecy of Zechariah would be fulfilled. What was Zechariah's prophecy? "Thus said *Hashem*, Master of Legions: Old men and old women will once again sit in the streets of Jerusalem, each with his staff in his hand because of advanced age; and the streets of the city will be filled with boys and girls playing in its streets."[63]

And how did Rabbi Ahkeevah know that Zechariah's prophecy would be fulfilled? Because he was witnessing the fulfillment of the prophecy of Uriah the Kohen at the time of the destruction of the First Temple. This prophecy, recorded in Micah, foresees the day when "Zion will be plowed over like a field; Jerusalem will become heaps of rubble and the Temple Mount will become like stone heaps in the forest."[64] Rabbi Ahkeevah knew that since the first prophecy had come true, so, too, would the second prophecy, foretelling the return to Jerusalem.[65]

The *Tahlmood* also instructs, "Just as one should pronounce a blessing for the good, one should also do so for the bad."[66] Hahshehm created the world with good and bad aspects, as we have discussed; this provides man with free will. He can choose either direction: one leading to the negative, corrupted will to power, and the other to "overcoming" and leading a moral, ethical life.

Another sage, fabled in Khahseedic literature, exemplified these overlapping concepts of "also this is for the good" and "just as one should bless for the good, one should also bless for the bad." His name was Rahv (Rabbi) Zoosyah. When a certain student asked his teacher why one should bless the bad as well as the good, his teacher told him to seek out Rahv Zoosyah. The student arrived at the door of a run-down shack and knocked on the door. Rahv Zoosyah opened the door, and the student saw an old, stooped-over man whose house was but sparsely furnished, and most of what was inside was broken. The student explained how he happened to be there, and Rahv Zoosyah replied, "But why would he send you to me? I have never had a bad day in my life."

You yourself, Nietzsche, overcame long periods of illness during which you were bedridden for days, with long periods of vomiting and insomnia. I won't go on, for the details are not what matters — what matters is your response to illness: "I took myself in hand, I myself made myself healthy again.... A being who is typically morbid cannot become healthy.... I discovered life as it were anew, myself included, I tasted all good and even pretty things in a way that others could not easily taste them — I made out of my will to health, to life, my philosophy."[67]

In *The Gay Science*, you wrote, "For the new year. — I still live, I still think: I still have to live, for I still have to think.... I want to learn more and more to see as beautiful what is necessary in things; then I shall be one of those who make things beautiful. *Amor fati*: let that be my love henceforth! I do not want to wage war against what is ugly. I do not want to accuse; I do not even want to accuse those who accuse. Looking away shall be my only negation. And all in all on the whole: some day I will to be only a Yes-sayer."[68]

In describing your work that led to *The Birth of Tragedy*, you derided the morality of pity and the "shallow-pated chatter about *optimism contra pessimism*" and explained how you discovered the antithesis — "an affirmation without reservation even of suffering, even of guilt, even of all that is strange and questionable in existence.... This ultimate, joyfulest, boundlessly exuberant Yes to life is not only the highest insight, it is also the profoundest, the insight most strictly confirmed and maintained by truth and knowledge."[69]

Your "yes to life" is an echo from the Torah; I do not know if you were aware of this when you wrote these words. All the Jews you knew well were far into the assimilating process. You may never have seen one of them raise a cup and say "*L'khahyeem* — to life!" This is the perpetual toast of the Jews. It comes from the Torah, setting out the choice that Hahshehm gives to the Jewish people: "I have placed before you life and death, blessing and curse; therefore choose life, so that you will live, you and your offspring — to love Hahshehm your Lord, to listen to His voice and to cleave to Him, for He is your life and the length of your days, to dwell upon the land that Hahshehm swore to your forefathers, to Abraham, Isaac, and Jacob, to give to them."[70]

When next I write, we will talk more about the land that Hahshehm swore to give to the Jewish people.

Yours,

Ben Moshe

# Letter Thirteen

March 23, 2006                                    כ"ג באדר א' תשס"ו

Dear Nietzsche,

In a previous letter about psychology and Sigmund Freud, we mentioned Joseph Paneth, a Viennese-born Jewish scientist, for he was a link between you and Freud. Paneth much enjoyed his conversations with you during the months from December 1883 to March 1884. You were most interested in his expertise in the natural sciences, as well as in his thoughts about Jews. Paneth, though not wanting to convert to Christianity, was a consciously assimilating Jew. We have interesting insights into his conversations with you from corre-spondence between Paneth and his bride-to-be. When you asked, "What kind of expectations and hopes exist among Jews?" he reports, "I replied that I and others who shared my views did not wish to be regarded as a race or as Jews but as distinct individuals; that the belief in being a chosen people depended strictly upon one's acceptance of the [divine] origin of the five books of Moses [the Torah]; that nowhere do we find a Jewish entity or centrality; but that it is impossible nowadays not to acknowledge being a Jew unless one wished to court accusations of cowardice."[1] Here is the painful ambivalence that accompanies so many assimilating Jews. He does not want to be accused of cowardice; thus, he does not deny being a Jew. However, after another generation or two, his descendants feel no cowardice in shedding their Jewish identity.

Through your conversations, Paneth gleaned that you felt that "the Jews possessed special ideals as a nation. When I displayed indifference to such an idea, he was disappointed, and disappointed as well by my rejection of any claim to exclusivity. The restoration of Palestine [as a Jewish realm] through peaceful or violent means, I decidedly brushed aside."[2]

Although you were interested in the subject of Palestine as a reconstituted home for the Jews, your clearest view of what was good for Europe was that Jews should intermix and thereby raise the level of European culture — add to those who were "good Europeans." Paneth picked up on this aspect of your thought when he wrote of your wish that "Jews connect with the best and noblest families of all countries and transmit their best characteristics, something that all nations ought to be concerned with at any rate."[3]

We have seen that all the Jews you knew and admired were Jews who themselves, or whose parents or grandparents, had left the culture of the Bayt Meedrahsh. They carried with them many of the values of that culture. However, as they assimilated fully into the European culture, many converted to Christianity, and many distinguished themselves in the pursuit of wealth and power. In this way they no longer carried with them the values of the culture of the Bayt Meedrahsh; in your terms they were no longer "good Europeans," for they failed to overcome their negative will to power.

You wrote, "The goal of humanity cannot lie in the end but only in its highest specimens." And Kaufmann asserts, "Perhaps there is no more basic statement of Nietzsche's philosophy than this sentence."[4] Nietzsche, we have discussed a number of these "highest specimens," over thousands of years, who were leaders of the culture of the Bayt Meedrahsh. It is commonplace for their descendants, also, to be exceptional scholars, practitioners, and exponents of the values of the culture of the Bayt Meedrahsh. These family trees extend into the twenty-first century.

It is also true that many Jews who have crossed from this culture into the stream of assimilating Jewry establish themselves as what you might consider "highest specimens," for example, Heinrich Heine or Moses Mendelssohn. Heine was not born into the culture of the Bayt Meedrahsh and ultimately converted to Christianity. Mendelssohn, while raised in the culture of the Bayt Meedrahsh, decided to raise his children in a more "modern" culture. In a few short generations, the Jewish family tree ends, and another few generations later, the descendants are no longer even aware of stemming from a Jewish family tree. We will see many more examples of this when we get to the contribution of many Jewish geniuses whose families had passed out of the culture of the Bayt Meedrahsh and who made some of the truly monumental breakthroughs in science.

We must assume that you knew of the existence of some contemporary "old-fashioned" Jews who worshipped Hahshehm; yet you did not know this culture. Indeed, you wrote them off. Once one writes off the culture of the Bayt Meedrahsh and acknowledges that the exceptional men among assimilating Jews, such as Heine and Mendelssohn, do not for very long have descendants who identify as Jews, then one inevitably must believe there is no ongoing impact of Jews on the world's culture.

However, this is not the case. Jews of the culture of the Bayt Meedrahsh continue to make a major impact, as do those of their offspring who, over time, assimilate before completely disappearing as Jews. There is a striking dynamic between these two groups of Jews; together they have an enormous impact on every generation. What is patently clear is that if the Jews of the culture of the Bayt Meedrahsh should disappear, there would soon be *no* source for Jews of any kind on the face of the earth.

Nowhere is this dynamic between assimilating Jews and the Jews of the culture of the Bayt Meedrahsh more dramatically illustrated than in the subject of the reestablishment of a Jewish homeland in the land of Israel — a subject you tried unsuccessfully to discuss with Paneth. In your time, Nietzsche, there were important assimilating Jews who carried the torch for a return to Zion. Yet, without the centuries-old longing for this return, the holiness that the Jews of the culture of the Bayt Meedrahsh attached to the land, and the physical migration of these Jews to the land of Israel, where they gained a small but significant presence, there would have ceased to be any thought of reestablishing the nation.

In your lifetime, the Jews became a majority of the population in Jerusalem. By the time of your death in 1900, the Jews constituted approximately 60 percent of the estimated population of fifty-five thousand. You may have been aware of Rabbi Tz'vee Hirsch Kalisher's book *The Demand for Zion,* published in 1862, and Moses Hess's *Rome and Jerusalem,* published in the same year. In the wake of anti-Jewish pogroms in Russia, which, in 1881, ravaged the several million Jews from Odessa to Warsaw, who lived mostly in poverty in areas that were permitted to them, Leon Pinsker published *Auto-Emancipation: An Appeal to His People by a Russian Jew.*[5]

So we enter into the "push-pull" ideas of sociologists in determining factors of emigration and immigration. The pogroms in Russia and the persecutions against Jews throughout history were clearly "push" factors, causing Jews to want to leave these areas of discrimination and threat to life. In many cases, there were no "pull" factors; Jews fled a country of danger to countries where there was some degree of welcome. When the welcome was worn out in the new countries, the Jews fled elsewhere. It was unique to the Jews of the culture of the Bayt Meedrahsh that the land of Israel in general, and Jerusalem in particular, has for millennia exerted an enormous *pull*.

The relationship of the Jewish people to the land of Israel is thousands of years old, and it is unique; there is no other such spiritual attachment of a people to a land in the annals of human history. Jerusalem and other areas of the land of Israel are mentioned hundreds of times in the *Tahnahkh* — the Jewish Bible. Here are a few examples from Psalms:

> Great is Hashem and much praised in the city of our Lord, mount of His Holiness, fairest of sites, joy of all the earth, Mount Zion.... May Mount Zion be glad, may the daughters of Judah rejoice.[6]

> For the Lord will save Zion and build the cities of Judah, and they shall settle there and possess it.[7]

> I rejoiced when they said to me, "Let us go to the House of Hashem." Our feet stood firm within your gates, O Jerusalem. The built-up Jerusalem is like a city that is united together. For there the tribes ascended, the tribes of God, a testimony for Israel, to give thanks to the name of Hashem. For there sat thrones of judgment, thrones for the house of David. Pray for the peace of Jerusalem; those who love you will be serene. May there be peace within your walls, serenity within your palaces. For the sake of my brethren and my comrades, I shall speak of peace in your midst. [8]

Isaiah's prophecy spanned more than eighty years in the seventh and sixth centuries before the Common Era. The following three quotes are well known, the last ringing prophecy being one of the most famous passages in all of scripture:

> For Zion's sake I will not be silent, and for Jerusalem's sake I will not be still, until her righteousness emanates like bright light, and her

salvation blazes like a torch. Nations will perceive your righteousness and all the kings your honor.[9]

Be glad with Jerusalem and rejoice in her, all you who love her; exult with her in exultation, all you who mourned for her; so that you may nurse and be sated from the breast of her consolations; so that you may suck and delight from the glow of her glory. For thus said Hashem: Behold I will extend peace to her like a river and the wealth of nations like a surging stream, and you will suckle; you will be carried on the side and dandled on the knees. Like a man whose mother consoled him, so will I console you, and in Jerusalem you will be consoled.[10]

And it shall come to pass in the end of days
that the mountain of God's house
shall be set over all other mountains
and lifted high above the hills
and all the nations shall come streaming to it.
And many people shall come and say:
Come, let us go up to the Mountain of God
to the house of the God of Jacob
and He will teach us of His ways
and we will walk in His paths.
For out of Zion shall go forth the Torah
and God's word from Jerusalem.
And He will judge between nations
and decide between peoples.
And they will beat their swords into plowshares
and their spears into pruning hooks,
Nation shall not lift up sword against nation
neither will they learn war anymore.[11]

While there is no explicit mention in the Torah, Nietzsche, of *Mahshee'ahkh* — "the anointed" — this last passage and many other passages in the Torah with references to "the end of days" are believed to refer clearly to the coming of the Messianic era. The "end of days" is a common translation of the Hebrew "*ahkhareet hahyahmeem.*" This is crucial to understanding the immigration of Jews of the culture of the Bayt Meedrahsh to the land of Israel over many centuries.

Let us reiterate the importance of using the term "Hahshehm" instead of "God," since the latter word invites comparison to the godheads of other cultures. We avoid the term "religion" for the same reason: the culture of the Bayt Meedrahsh is not "one of the three great Western religions." By the same token, we do not refer to "Judaism," since that is the name of the "religion" to which many refer. Also to be avoided is the term "Orthodox" as an adjective defining the word "Judaism."

When speaking of the "end of days," we must carefully avoid using the term "messiah," as the Christian concept of messiah as "savior," in the person of Jesus, is indelibly ingrained in the English language. The *Mahshee'ahkh* longed for by Jews of the culture of the *Bayt Meedrahsh* is an ordinary human being with no superhuman qualities. The coming of *Mahshee'ahkh* will signify the coming of the ultimate time of peace in the world. If a man appears whom some believe to be *Mahshee'ahkh*, but he dies in the absence of the signs of the "end of days," it will be clear that he was not *Mahshee'ahkh*. The only man thought to be *Mahshee'ahkh* by leaders of the culture of the Bayt Meedrahsh of his time was Bahr Kokhbah, who led the rebellion against the Romans in the second century of the Common Era. When he died without the ultimate era of peace being ushered in, it was accepted by all that he was not *Mahshee'ahkh*.

The Christian view of Jesus as messiah obviously does not meet the criteria of the Bayt Meedrahsh for the coming of *Mahshee'ahkh*; the Romans ruled the land of Israel and oppressed the Jews before and after the time of Jesus; they were still doing so at the time Bahr Kokhbah, who failed in his rebellion against the Romans.

While we will know that *Mahshee'ahkh* has arrived when the proper conditions are met, we cannot know in advance when that era will be. This has not prevented the anticipation of this deeply longed-for time throughout the centuries. Much speculation about the time of *Mahshee'ahkh* has come from interpretations of the esoteric wisdom — the Kahbahlistic literature. One tradition draws on an important line in Psalms: "For a thousand years in your sight are but as yesterday when it is past."[12] The world was created in six days; therefore, human history will encompass six thousand years.

These six thousand years were interpreted as containing three distinct periods. During the first two thousand years, represented by the first part of Genesis, corruption ruled the land, and there was no knowledge of Hahshehm. In the second two thousand years the Torah was given, and the Jewish people accepted the precepts of the Torah and abided by them. The third period resulted from the abandonment of these precepts and began with the destruction of the Temple and exile from the land of Israel.[13] In the fifth millennium of the six thousand years, with the continuation of exile, stirrings of expectation intensified.

Among those who believed that the coming of the age of *Mahshee'ahkh* would be hastened by proper actions was Rabbi *Yeh'hoodah* Hahlayvee, who lived at the end the eleventh century and the first forty years of the twelfth century. In his masterwork, the *Koozahree*, which is still intensively studied a thousand years later, he drew on this passage from Psalms: "You will surely arise and take pity on Zion, for it is time to be gracious to her; the appointed time has come. Your servants take delight in its stones and cherish its dust."[14]

For Hahlayvee, "This means that Jerusalem can only be rebuilt when Israel yearns for it to such an extent that they embrace her stones and dust."[15] We have mentioned Rabbi Moses ben Maimon, the Rahmbahm, one of the greatest Jewish figures of the culture of the Bayt Meedrahsh. The Rahmbahm is known as a rationalist, yet he wrote in 1169, "I have a wondrous tradition that prophecy will return to Israel in the year 4972 [1212]. And there is no doubt that the restoration of prophecy in Israel is one of the signs of the *Mahshee'ahkh*...and this is the truest of 'ends' that have been told to us."[16]

One of the dates targeted by Kahbahlistic tradition for the ultimate redemption was 1240 C.E.; this corresponded to the year 5000 (after the creation) in the Hebrew calendar. Thus, when the Muslim leader Saladin took control of Jerusalem on October 2, 1187, after defeating the Crusader forces in most of the surrounding area, messianic fervor was heightened. Jews were again welcomed back to Jerusalem. During your lifetime, Nietzsche, the Cairo Geniza was found hidden in a synagogue in Egypt. It was a treasure trove of Jewish books and documents.

Among the documents in the Cairo Geniza was a letter sent to the Jews of Cairo, describing a new prophecy of the coming of *Mahshee'ahkh* before the end of the fifth millennium: "Letters have come from France...[saying] that there has arisen among them a prophet...who has said that in the year 4986 [1226] the great ingathering will begin, and our master Elijah, of blessed memory, will come.... And in the year 4993 [1233], the *Mahshee'ahkh*, son of David, will come...and kingship will return to the house of Jerusalem."[17]

The Hebrew word "*ahleeyah*" means "going up," and this has always been the word to describe the immigration of Jews to the land of Israel. Early in the thirteenth century, groups of Jews were arriving from all over the world. What has been called "the *ahleeyah* of the three hundred rabbis" included major Tahlmoodic scholars. An unsigned pamphlet written at the time proclaimed that the time of *Mahshee'ahkh* had already arrived, and called for *ahleeyah* to pave the way for greeting him: "Let no one say that the King Messiah will be revealed in an impure land...and let no one make the mistake of saying that he will be revealed in the Land of Israel among the gentiles. Rather, the matter is clear: In the Land of Israel there will be Torah scholars and pious men of good deeds from the four corners of the earth, a handful from every city and every family, and then the King Messiah will be revealed among them."[18]

The *ahleeyah* of the three hundred rabbis was not successful, and the country was racked by warfare between Christians and Muslims. Few of the descendants of the rabbis remained in the land of Israel. The fifteenth century saw a major renewal of messianic hopes. Rabbi Yom-Tov Lipmann Mulhausen, a rabbi and an authority on the Written and Oral Law as well as on the hidden wisdom of the Kahbahlah, produced calculations setting 1410 and 1430 as important years involving the coming of *Mahshee'ahkh*. Those years passed by without incident, but when the Ottoman Turks felled the Christian Byzantine Empire in 1453, this rekindled expectations. Rumors of the discovery of the ten lost tribes of Israel spread. Spanish Jewry, which was already suffering widespread persecution well before the proclamation of the Holy Inquisition later in the fifteenth century, formed an important part of *ahleeyah*. Revered leaders from France and Italy were also part of this movement, prompting a papal order in 1428 forbidding ship captains from taking Jews to Palestine.[19]

Near the end of the fifteenth century, many years of cruel treatment of Jews in Spain ended, in 1492, in their outright expulsion from Spain. This was another crushing blow for the Jews, but in the spirit of *gahm zoo l'tovah* ("this, too, is for the good") — or, in your words, Nietzsche, *amor fati*, the Jews looked for the good in the evil, the positive in the negative, and focused on the Promised Land. One of the great personalities of his generation — and,

indeed, among all generations, for his commentaries on Jewish texts live on
— was Rabbi Don Isaac Ahbrahvahnel, who had worked for Spain's King
Ferdinand and Queen Isabella. He wrote, "And in the year 5252 [1492], the
Eternal roused the spirit of the kings of Spain to expel from their land all of
the Jews, some three hundred thousand souls, in such a manner that all of
them would leave...and all of them would pass before the Land of Israel, not
only the Jews but also the Conversos [i.e., Jews who had converted to Christianity under the Spanish persecutions]...and in this way they would gather
upon the holy soil."[20]

We have this detailed description of life in Jerusalem from an Italian Jew
visiting early in the sixteenth century:

> There is but a single synagogue in Jerusalem; it is beautiful, with four
> supporting columns. It is sixty-three feet long and twenty-eight wide,
> and behind the Torah ark there is a room where more than sixty
> Torah scrolls are housed. They pray facing east, that is, facing the
> Temple.... The congregation has all types of Jews: there are fifteen
> Ashkenazi householders, and many Sephardim, and Mustarabs, they
> are Moriscos, the ancient inhabitants of the land, and Maarabim
> [Maghrebis] who come from Barbary, all together some three
> hundred households.... Those who receive charity number more
> than two hundred persons, and much charity is sent from Egypt and
> Turkey and elsewhere, but the Ashkenazi poor are not included —
> their support comes from Venice.[21]

In your own country, Nietzsche, Martin Luther was a frightening voice
against Jews. Very much driven by the need for power and control, Luther
was seemingly benevolent to the Jews as long as he believed they would leave
their convictions behind and follow him. But when they did not do so, he
turned on them in fury. His anti-Jewish *ressentiment* surfaced as early as 1517
but came over him in full force in 1543:

> What then shall we Christians do with this damned, rejected race of
> Jews?... First, their synagogues or churches should be set on fire, and
> whatever does not burn should be covered or spread over with
> dirt.... And this ought to be done for the honor of God and of Chris-
> tianity in order that God may see that we are Christians, and that we

> have not wittingly tolerated or approved of such public lying, cursing,
> and blaspheming of His Son and His Christians.... Secondly, their
> homes should likewise be broken down and destroyed... They ought
> to be put under one roof or in a stable, like gypsies, in order that they
> may realize that they are not masters in our land.[22]

You recognized easily that Luther failed to overcome his negative will to power. In *The Antichrist*, you wrote, "'Faith' was at all times...in Luther, only a cloak, a pretext, a screen behind which the instincts played their game — a shrewd blindness about the dominance of certain instincts. 'Faith' — I have already called it the characteristic Christian shrewdness — one always spoke of faith, but one always acted from instinct alone."[23]

News of Luther reached Palestine. We have the words of Rabbi Abraham Hahlayvee, the head of the Sephardee *Y'sheevah* in Jerusalem in the first part of the sixteenth century: "There have recently arrived in Jerusalem faithful Jews from the lands of Ashkenaz [Germany] and Bohemia...who tell of the man...named Martin Luther...who began in the year 5284 [1524] to reject the creed of the uncircumcised and to show them that their fathers had inherited a lie."[24]

We do not have evidence that Luther's anti-Jewish *ressentiment* led directly to an *ahleeyah* of German Jews. That persecution in Germany had, before Luther's time, prompted Jews to move to the Promised Land, we do know from a German Jew who moved to Jerusalem. In 1454, he wrote to friends in Germany, imploring his brethren to join him: "I have heard of the afflictions, more bitter than death, that have befallen our brethren in Germany.... Is it not better for you to live under Muslims than under Christians? Here every man may dwell at peace under his own vine and fig tree. Here you are allowed to wear the most precious garments. In Christendom, on the contrary, you dare not even venture to clothe your children in red or blue, according to our taste.... Arise! And leave this accursed land forever!"[25]

Solomon Molkho was a Portuguese Jew born into a family of Conversos, those who, under persistent persecution in Spain and Portugal, converted from Judaism to Christianity. When he returned to the culture of the Bayt Meedrahsh, he became deeply involved in the esoteric wisdom of the Kahbahlah. Among others, he calculated from hints in Jewish sources that 1540 — 5300 on the Hebrew calendar — would be the year of redemption.

"The year 5300 will complete the appointed number of days, and over it will rule the house of David."[26] A significant number of Jews came to Palestine in the years leading up to 1540. This was the beginning of Jewish settlement in the city of Tz'faht in the Galilee.

All the emigration, or *ahleeyah*, to the land of Israel that we have reviewed so far, Nietzsche, repeatedly established the textual and deeply spiritual attachment of the Jews to the Promised Land. It was in Tz'faht that a group of exceptional men, whom you would easily have recognized as *Übermenschen*, put the most indelible and lasting stamp on this attachment to the land. The city Tz'faht (Safed) was known in Tahlmoodic times as Tz'feeyah, and it is said the *Mahshee'ahkh* will pass through this holy city on his way to Jerusalem. The man most responsible for the establishment of Tz'faht in the sixteenth century was Rabbi Jacob Berahb, who was driven out of Spain during the persecution of the Jews. He lived in Algeria, Damascus, and Egypt before coming to the Galilee. Rabbi Berahb had studied with the great Spanish rabbinic teacher and scholar Isaac Aboo'ahb, known as "the last *Gah'ohn* of Castile."[27]

Rabbi Berahb headed the most important synagogue and *y'sheevah* in Tz'faht. He had the inspired idea of reviving the old Tahlmoodic practice of *s'meekhah* — certification of a high level of learning for students in the culture of the Bayt Meedrahsh. To be granted *s'meekhah* was a prerequisite for becoming a member of the Sanhedrin, the ruling body of scholars, and Berahb apparently had in mind reestablishing the Sanhedrin for the first time in over a thousand years. He ran afoul of a requirement that, in order for a scholar to receive *s'meekhah*, there had to be unanimous agreement of all sages in the Land. Berahb had acted without the agreement of the chief rabbi of Jerusalem. However, he brought justification for his actions, and a few of the scholars to whom he granted *s'meekhah* then did likewise to two others — the Tahlmoodic maximum for any one person.

Solomon Alkabetz, Moses Cordovero, Joseph Karo, and Isaac Luria are luminaries of sixteenth-century Tz'faht whose light has only grown stronger with the passing centuries. When one walks the streets of Tz'faht in the twenty-first century, they are there. They and the community around them demonstrate again, Nietzsche, how the esoteric wisdom of the Kahbahlah is integrated with the wisdom of the Torah and the *Tahlmood*. One does not become an authority on Kahbahlah without first being steeped in the knowledge of Torah and *Tahlmood*.

Alkabetz was an important student among a group of Kahbahlists in Salonika. He traveled as a teacher in a number of places before arriving in Tz'faht. There he established himself as a master teacher of Kahbahlah, as well as a prolific writer of biblical commentary. He is enshrined forever in the history of Jewish liturgy as the author of *Lekhah Dohdee*, the singing of which is part of the welcoming of Shahbaht in every Jewish synagogue, every Friday night, all over the world. The refrain between the verses rings out in Jewish time and space that knows no dimensions: "Come, my beloved, to greet the bride, the Sabbath presence, let us welcome!"

Alkabetz was the teacher and brother-in-law of Moses Cordovero, who went on to become the head of the community in Tz'faht. Cordovero is also known as the *Rahmahk*, an acronym for his name in Hebrew. The Rahmahk was an extremely prolific writer. His earliest work, *Pahrdayss Reemoneem — Orchard of Pomegranates* — brought him acclaim as a writer and thinker. His magnum opus was *Ohr Yahkahr — Precious Light* — a sixteen-volume commentary on the literature of the *Zohahr*, the primary Kahbahlistic text of interpretations of the Torah.

Tz'faht owes the leadership of Rabbi Joseph Karo directly to the expulsion of the Jews from Spain in 1492. Karo is the epitome of the inspired Jewish mystic combined with the disciplined codifier of Hahlahkhah — Jewish law. He was an outstanding leader in Turkey for many years before making *ahleeyah* — immigrating to the land of Israel. He worked for twenty years on his compilation of Jewish law known as *Bayt Yosehf — House of Joseph*. This work is itself a commentary on a previous compilation of Jewish law, the *Ahrbah'ah Tooreem — the Four Orders*. This is a famous fourteenth-century work by Rabbi Jacob ben Asher, also known as "the Toor." To make the multivolume *Bayt Yosehf* more accessible, Karo condensed it into the *Shoolkhahn Ahrookh — Prepared Table*.[28]

In an earlier letter, Nietzsche, we presented a long list of Jewish scholars of the culture of the Bayt Meedrahsh. As I said, it was a very limited list of Jewish luminaries, and it is important to reiterate that those names, like the names of the scholars mentioned in this letter, along with their famous works, are known to *every* high school-age student in the culture of the Bayt Meedrahsh.

How is it that a man who lived in Tz'faht for less than three years and was virtually unknown before that time emerges as one of the most noted and revered figures of the culture of the Bayt Meedrahsh? He is remembered as *HahAhree* — the Lion, the holy *Ahree*, and the *Ahree zahl* — the Lion of blessed memory. "*Ahree*," meaning "lion," is also an acronym for the Hebrew words meaning the "Godly Rabbi Yeetzkhahk." His name was Isaac Looreeah. Born in Jerusalem, he left with his mother for Egypt when he was a young child. His father had died, and his mother moved to be near her brother, a wealthy Egyptian merchant. Looreeah's uncle supported the studies of his brilliant nephew. The Ahree spent an extended time in total solitude, studying the esoteric wisdom on an island of the Nile River.[29]

Arriving in Tz'faht in 1570, he overlapped less than a year with Cordovero and studied under him before the older rabbi's death. HahAhree, or Looreeah, was not a writer, but we have his teachings from Khahyeem Veetahl, a faithful student. Looreeah taught detailed expositions of the primary Kahbahlistic work, the *Zohahr*. His teaching was not merely commentary but contained a great deal of original thought. This led many to consider his teachings a separate "text" of Kahbahlah, known as *Looree'ahnic* Kahbahlah. However, theory and commentary were not what preoccupied HahAhree — a point emphasized by one of his biographers: "The virtually exclusive preoccupation with Isaac Luria's mythic conceptions has prevented us from seeing that what mattered to Luria and his disciples themselves were not predominantly speculative systems and scholastic debates. What mattered to them was the religious life to be lived and practiced in relationship to his teachings about the origins and nature of the cosmos."[30]

Rabbi Khahyeem Veetahl was Looreeah's student who compiled his teachings into texts for future generations. He also left behind important testimony about his beloved teacher: "As regards the attribute of charitableness and generosity, I observed that my teacher, of blessed memory, was not concerned with his own vanity, as expressed in the wearing of especially fine clothes. In his eating, as well, he would consume very little. However, when it came to his wife's apparel, he was exceedingly careful to honor her and to clothe her well.... The most important of all worthy traits consists in an individual behaving with humility, modesty, and with the fear of sin to the greatest possible degree. He should also, to the utmost degree, keep his distance from pride, anger, fussiness, and evil gossip; and even should he have a significant reason for behaving harshly, he ought to refrain from acting in this way."[31]

While the observance of Jewish law, to many Jews, is rejected as a great burden, a central tenet of the culture of the Bayt Meedrahsh is to carry out Hahshem's will *b'seemkhah* — with great joy. Another of HahAhree's students learned from his master that "One ought to be happier in the service of the Holy One, blessed be He, His precepts and His Torah, than in possessing all the money in the world.... No joy in the world equals the joy associated with performing the commandments."[32]

We look again at your own unfulfilled desire, Nietzsche: "I have been on the lookout for learned, bold and industrious comrades in arms — I am still looking. The object is to explore the huge, distant and thoroughly hidden country of morality, morality as it has actually existed and actually been lived."[33] If only you had not been so negatively influenced by Christianity, the "thoroughly hidden country of morality," for what you longed to find was there all the time. *Khahvahl, khahvahl* (what a pity) that you did not find it!

The next period of fervor for the coming of redemption was 1648 — 5408 on the Hebrew calendar. The *Zohahr* arrived at that date as the time of the resurrection of the dead, an event firmly tied to the coming of *Mahshee'ahkh*: "In the sixth millennium, in the 408th year, all those who dwell in the dust will rise.... And the verse calls them 'the children of Heth,' because they shall arise in the year 408, as it is written, 'in this jubilee year each of you shall return to his property.' And when 'this' is completed, which is 5408, each man will return to his property, to his soul, which is his property and his inheritance."[34]

As the fateful year approached, there was another movement of *ahleeyah*. A significant number of the migrants were Kahbahlists, followers of Rabbi Cordovero and HahAhree. Tz'faht was a final destination for many of them, but not for all. One important figure stayed in Tz'faht only a short time before moving to Jerusalem, the historical capital of the Jewish people. This was Rabbi Isaiah Horowitz, also known as the *Shehlah*, an acronym for the Hebrew letters of his famous work *Sh'nay Lookhot Hahbreet* — the *Two Tablets of the Covenant*. He wrote, "For thank God [*Bahrookh Hahshehm*] it has become crowded in Jerusalem. For the Ahshkenahzi community in Jerusalem is already twice that of Tz'faht; may it be speedily rebuilt in our days....

Also the Sephardim in Jerusalem increase greatly, to literally hundreds [of families]."[35]

In another letter, Rabbi Horowitz wrote, "Every day we see the ingathering of the exiles. Day by day they come. Wander about the courtyards of Jerusalem: All of them, praise God, are filled with Jews, may their Rock and Redeemer protect them, and with houses of study and schools filled with small children."[36] Ultimately, these hopes, too, were crushed by new persecutions by Mohammed Ibn Fahrookh, a Turkish governor who gained control of Jerusalem.

After two years, Ibn Fahrookh was no longer ruling Jerusalem, and the Jewish fervor clearly persisted, as we see from an anonymous work of 1631, *The Ruins of Jerusalem*:

> For from the day the Temple was destroyed, did God not take an oath — and He will not go back on it — that He will not enter the heavenly Jerusalem until He enters the earthly Jerusalem? And before the coming of Ibn Fahrookh, children from the four corners of the earth fluttered like birds in their eagerness to settle in Jerusalem. And to us, this was an evident sign of the beginning of the ingathering of the exiles.... All the more so, now that God has remembered His people and His land and expelled before our eyes the enemy Ibn Fahrookh; they hover like an eagle, and the children will return to their borders.[37]

However, 1648, instead of bringing the longed-for redemption, saw instead the slaughter of tens of thousands of Jews by the Cossacks, under Bogdan Chmielnicki, during an uprising against the Polish government. This was followed by the disillusioning experience of the most noted false *Mahshee'ahkh* in Jewish history, Shahb'tai Tz'vee, who ultimately gave in to threats by the Turks and converted to Islam.

Yet, as we see over and over again, Nietzsche, for the Jews of the culture of the Bayt Meedrahsh it is not a question of *whether* Hahshehm will fulfill his promises, but only of *when*. This long-term perspective is unique to Jews of the culture of the Bayt Meedrahsh — yet another example of the different dimension of time and space in which they exist. Jews from all over the world physically live in many far-flung countries, but spiritually they all live in the land of Israel, praying and studying in the past and future language of the Jewish nation.

As we move into the 1700s, we find a new reason for messianic expectations. One of the foremost authorities on Looree'ahnic Kahbahlah, Rabbi Immanuel Hai Ricchi, estimated the coming of redemption between 1740 and 1780. From the descent into darkness would come the rise into the period of ultimate light. Jews suffered persecution in Russia in the latter part of the century as the Russians fought on a number of fronts to extend their empire, and Jews continued to move to the Promised Land to spur the coming of *Mahshee'ahkh.*

Arie Morgenstern, a modern-day scholar, discovered this document from the late eighteenth century:

> May it be remembered by the later generations what happened in the year 5537 [1777], how a rumor came about that the Messiah son of David had come. Then the rabbis living abroad began to go up to the city of Jerusalem, may it speedily be rebuilt.... And the reason they believed that the Messiah son of David had come was that at that time the evil nation of Moscow [Russia], that bitter people, a people whose language has not been heard, stretched its hand over the entire world, so that there was no place left that was not caught in war. And they thought that this was the time of the end of days, as promised by the prophets.[38]

The spiritual impetus for hope in your century, Nietzsche, derived from two sources pointing very close to the time you were born: "Rabbi Dosa predicted that the messianic age would begin in the last four hundred years of the sixth millennium — that is, starting around 1840. A statement in the *Zohahr* lent support to this belief: "When the sixth millennium comes, in the six hundredth year of the sixth millennium, the gates of wisdom shall be opened above, and founts of wisdom below.... And the Holy One shall raise up the congregation of Israel from the dust of exile, and remember it."[39]

Despite the failure of *Mahshee'ahkh* to appear, hope was not lost. Morgenstern describes the continued *ahleeyah* — the immigration to the Promised Land: "Most were pious, traditional Jews who sought refuge from the influences of the Haskala, the Emancipation, and the Reform movement, which at that time was spreading throughout Europe. As a result of this continuing wave of immigration, the number of Jews in Palestine increased dramatically: By the 1870s, the Jewish population in Jerusalem was already greater than that of the Muslims and Christians combined. For the first time since the destruction of the Temple, Jews formed a majority in the city."[40]

The modern Zionist movement that began during the latter part of your life, Nietzsche, came from assimilationist Jews. That they looked to the Promised Land, as opposed to some other area of the world, as a refuge from constant persecution is obviously due to the influence of the culture of the Bayt Meedrahsh, and the messianic hopes that led pious Jews to move to that land, ruled for centuries by hostile powers.

In the next letter we shall discuss a Jew whose name became synonymous with genius, a man much interested in the Zionist movement. He was born in Ulm, Germany, in 1879. Although his parents were firmly in the assimilating stream of Jews, and he lived almost all his life in that milieu, according to his sister, he "went through a period of significant religiosity as a child which ended when he was twelve. During this period, for example, he refused to eat pork, a non-kosher animal." His sister testified that "a liberal spirit, undogmatic in matters of religion, brought by both parents from their respective homes prevailed within the family.... Nevertheless he was so fervent in his religious feelings that, on his own, he observed religious prescriptions in every detail."[41]

Did this man's familiarity with the different time frame inhabited by Jews of the culture of the Bayt Meedrahsh influence his breakthrough discovery of the relativity of time and space? We will look more deeply into the amazing world of twentieth-century science — a period of discovery greatly influenced by assimilating Jews. It is fascinating how the scientific discoveries of this century wrenched science and religion from their assumed parallel, never-to-meet trajectories and demonstrated a convergence that convinces some assimilating Jews to draw closer to the culture of the Bayt Meedrahsh.

Yours always,

Ben Moshe

# Letter Fourteen

April 3, 2006                                    ה׳ בניסן תשס״ו

Dear Nietzsche,

His name was Albert Einstein. He came to be called "Doctor" and "Professor," yet these titles were attached to his name as honoraria only after he became the most famous scientist in the world. One can only wonder if Einstein's grounding in the ageless time frame of the Jews of the culture of the Bayt Meedrahsh influenced his intuitive grasp of time and space and his lifelong fascination with how they correlate. This question is especially interesting in that not only Einstein but a disproportionate number of the mathematicians, physicists, and cosmologists who excelled in early work on the theory of relativity and used it to describe what has come to be known as the "big bang" were assimilating Jews. Another central figure we will meet in these intriguing discoveries was a physicist and a Catholic priest. Did his dual competencies figure into his ability to name what the others could not?

One thing is clear: these scientists were fully aware that the wonders unfolding before their eyes and instruments carried them beyond pure science, beyond established fact that could be verified without reservation by mathematical or scientific data. Einstein wrote that among the variables in physical theories were "free inventions of the human intellect."[1] He was present at the dawn of a new physics known as quantum mechanics, a discipline that explicated the makeup of the atom, once thought to be the smallest unit of matter. Now it is a given that the subatomic particles called protons and neutrons are in turn composed of smaller particles known as quarks, which "have never been seen and never will be seen."[2]

Niels Bohr, a Danish physicist, whose mother came from a prominent Jewish family, has often been quoted as saying that if one is not confused by quantum physics, one does not understand it. We will not try to unravel the intricacies of quantum mechanics. The point is that science and faith begin to merge to a degree that would have been unbelievable to you, Nietzsche, and the scientists of your day. Both science and faith make use of plausibility arguments. Indeed, quantum mechanics, by definition, is a method for dealing with the limitations of measuring the properties of subatomic particles.

As is often the case when confronted with students of prodigious intelligence, young Albert's teachers did not recognize that they were dealing with genius. Unable to get an academic appointment, he worked for seven years as a patent clerk in Bern, Switzerland. What did Einstein do there for seven years? You will love this, Nietzsche: what he did there was *think*. This was pure thinking at a level very few people ever reach — or, perhaps better said, that many of us may experience, though only in brief spurts. Finding it arduous to operate at that level of abstract thinking, we soon divert our thoughts to the realm of concrete images, so that we can verbalize them, understand them, give expression to an idea. I mentioned in an earlier letter the Kahbahlistic notion of the highest level of functioning, that of *khokhmah*. *Khokhmah* is pure nonverbal thought, before it gives way to understanding.

To the discomfort he experienced at this rarefied level of *khokhmah*, Einstein gave poignant testimony: "I must confess that at the very beginning when the special theory of relativity began to germinate in me, I was visited by all sorts of nervous conflicts. When young, I used to go away for weeks in a state of confusion, as one who at the time had yet to overcome the state of stupefaction in his first encounter with such questions."[3]

The special theory of relativity recognized that time is not static but flexible; it exists relative to the position of the observer. Someone standing by a railroad track and watching a train whiz by at a very fast speed appreciates time in a very different way from someone inside that train looking out at the bystander. Einstein was able to intuit how time and space fuse together, and this notion led him ultimately to posit that there were not three dimensions to the universe but four, the fourth being time.

Einstein developed his theory in the first decade of the 1900s, but a French philosopher of your era, Nietzsche — another Jew whose family had passed from the culture of the Bayt Meedrahsh — had already come to this conclusion. While you were working on *Thus Spoke Zarathustra, Beyond Good and Evil*, and *On the Genealogy of Morals*, Henri Bergson was working on his *Essai*, published as *Time and Free Will*. Bergson differentiated between duration as a linear progression in time and what he called "pure duration":

> Pure duration is the form which the succession of our conscious states assumes when our ego lets itself live, when it refrains from separating its present state from its former states. For this purpose it need not be entirely absorbed in the passing sensation or idea; for then, on the contrary it would no longer endure. Nor need it forget its former states: it is enough that, in recalling these states, it does not set them alongside its actual state as one point alongside another, but forms both the past and the present states into an organic whole, as happens when we recall the notes of a tune, melting so to speak into one another. Might it not be said that, even if these notes succeed one another, yet we perceive them in one another, and that their totality may be compared to a living being, whose parts, although distinct, permeate one another just because they are so closely connected?[4]

We have no indication, Nietzsche, that you were aware of Bergson's work or that he was aware of yours, but one of your biographers sees an important connection: "Bergson, like Nietzsche, developed a philosophy of the creative will, although he, of course, stopped short of naming it 'will to power.' Nonetheless, the manner in which the two philosophers linked the individual to the universal was similar. Everything that acts in the world and in nature as a whole simultaneously acts as a creative energy for the individual."[5]

Thus, Bergson anticipated Einstein's thought by several years. They were both peerless thinkers. To follow Einstein's ideas from their beginnings through to science's realization that the Torah was right all along about the creation of the universe, we need to go back two centuries before your time. In 1657, Otto von Guericke, inventor of the first vacuum pump, performed a dramatic experiment before an audience. He put a ringing bell in a glass jar and sucked the air out. Observers could no longer hear the bell ringing, thus proving that sound waves could be conducted only through a medium of matter (be it air, liquid, or solid). This outcome was expected, but the observers could still *see* the clapper hitting the bell! How could this be? Could light travel through *nothing*?[6]

Being reasonable people, scientists developed a theory that for two centuries became "fact": the "luminiferous ether." Albert Michelson, who later became America's first Nobel Prize winner in physics, devised an experiment to prove the ether's existence. That he was an American came about thanks to Prussian persecution of Jews, which prompted his parents to emigrate to America when Albert was only two years old. An expert in optics, Michelson set out in 1880 to be the first to demonstrate the luminiferous ether experimentally. The experiment was very elaborate and involved sophisticated instrumentation, but it failed to find evidence of the ether in the atmosphere. Certain that the apparatus used in the experiment must be at fault, Michelson brought in another scientist to perfect the equipment and his methodology, and over seven years they tried to prove the existence of the elusive ether. In the end, they had to conclude that it did not exist.[7]

In 1896, then sixteen-year-old Albert Einstein, unaware of Michelson's research, conducted an experiment in pure thought that brought him to the same conclusion. Already intrigued by the principle of relativity, he was aware of Galileo's concept of simple relativity, developed more than two hundred years before. Galileo described his ideas very simply and convincingly:

> Shut yourself up with a friend in the main cabin below deck on some large ship, and have with you there some flies, butterflies and other small flying animals. Have a large bowl of water with some fish in it; hang up a bottle that empties drop by drop into an empty vessel beneath it. With the ship standing still, observe carefully how all the little animals fly with equal speed to all sides of the cabin; how the fish swim indifferently in all directions; how the drops fall into the vessel beneath. And, in throwing something to your friend, you need to throw it no more strongly in one direction than another, the distances being equal; and jumping with your feet together, you pass equal spaces in all directions.
>
> When you have observed all these things carefully... have the ship proceed with any speed you like, so long as the motion is uniform and not fluctuating this way and that. You will discover not the least change in all the effects named, nor could you tell from any of them whether the ship moves or stands still.[8]

Drawing on this understanding, the sixteen-year-old Einstein wondered what would happen if he were traveling at the speed of light with a mirror in his hand — would he be able to see his own reflection? All conditions being equal, light, carried by the ether, would never leave his face, since he was also traveling at the speed of light and surrounded by the ether. Thus, his image could not reach the mirror and be reflected back to him. Intuitively, Einstein was certain that he would see his reflection — either he was mistaken or there was a conceptual flaw elsewhere.

If a boy shoots a pea from a peashooter while standing still, it will strike a distant object at a given speed. If the boy climbs onto a bicycle and rides rapidly toward the distant object and then fires the pea, the pea, projected from the shooter at a greater speed than when the boy was standing still, will strike the target at a greater speed. This was a given for Einstein, but he reconstructed the thought experiment using light instead of a pea. Einstein intuited that the beam from the bicycle's headlight, unlike the pea, would arrive at the distant target at the same speed, whether the bicycle was standing still or advancing rapidly toward the target; the speed of light, he was sure, was not relative to external conditions but was relative only to the observer. Thus, it did not matter if he and his mirror and the light surrounding them were all traveling at the same speed — he would see his image because the light was traveling relative only to himself as the observer.

Though Einstein had broken through with his theory of special relativity, he was yet unsatisfied. His theory so far dealt only with objects moving at a constant speed — neither accelerating nor decelerating. He wanted to go further. The world-renowned physicist Max Planck warned Einstein against undertaking this challenge: "As an older friend, I must advise you against it for, in the first place, you will not succeed, and even if you succeed, no one will believe you."[9] Einstein withdrew over a number of years into *khokhmah* space — that realm of unformed thought that represents the highest level of the will. Perhaps you would agree, Nietzsche, that this is the loneliest and most noble expression of the will to power. He expressed his anguish during this period in letters to friends. To one he pleaded, "You must help me or else I'll go crazy!" To another friend he described his work as "a rain of fire and brimstone," and to a colleague he wrote that he had "again perpetrated something about gravitation theory which somewhat exposes me to the danger of being confined to a madhouse."[10]

In 1917, Einstein wrote the first treatise applying the physics of time and space to the universe as a single unit. Accepted principles of physics suggested that the universe should be simple, homogeneous in its makeup, and symmetrical, which is to say, at whatever point one is located in the universe, the universe spreads out symmetrically from that point in the same manner as it would from any other point. Einstein's final conjecture is where opinions diverged: he assumed that the universe was static, a closed space. He postulated an antigravity force that compensated for gravity, with the result that it fit his hypothesis that all bodies in the universe were at rest.

Enter Alexander Friedmann, a Russian mathematician, who examined Einstein's calculations, presented his own equations, and considered Einstein's conclusions along with an alternative possibility. Friedmann was not intimidated by Einstein's now worldwide renown as the greatest scientific genius of all time. He submitted an article to the most respected physics journal of the time, the *Zeitschrift für Physik*. In the article, Friedmann stated baldly that Einstein's general theory of relativity was applicable only in a specific location and time: "Einstein's cosmological equations alone [which showed a static universe], without additional assumptions, are insufficient for reaching a conclusion about the finiteness of the world."[11] Einstein initially rejected Friedmann's findings but ultimately had to recant and admit that they were correct.

And now, Nietzsche, in the midst of this struggle between these two Jewish physicists we must introduce a Catholic priest. Georges Lemaître was born in Charleroi, Belgium, in 1894, received a degree in theoretical physics before he became an ordained priest in 1923, and kept busy in both worlds for the rest of his life. "There are two ways of arriving at the truth," he explains. "I decided to follow them both."[12]

Lemaître took a keen interest in cosmology and went beyond Friedmann's tentative thought about the creation of a world from "nothing." He took Einstein's theory of relativity and Friedmann's model of a nonstatic universe and, according to the author Simon Singh, "concluded that the universe began in a small compact form, from which it exploded outwards and evolved over time to become the universe in which we find ourselves today. Indeed, he believed that the universe would continue to evolve into the future."[13] Lemaître called his theory "the primeval atom hypothesis" and characterized it as "a cosmogenic hypothesis which pictures the present universe as the result of the radioactive disintegration of an atom.... The evolution of the universe can be likened to a display of fireworks that has just ended: some few wisps, ashes and smoke. Standing on a well-cooled cinder, we see the fading of the suns, and try to recall the vanished brilliance of the origins of the worlds."[14] At a conference in 1927, Lemaître explained his ideas to Einstein, who dismissed them as he had initially rebuffed Friedmann: "Your calculations are correct, but your physics is abominable."[15]

In the wake of experiments by the Austrian scientist Christian Doppler, who demonstrated what can be called the theory of relativity of sound waves, and other scientists who showed that some heavenly bodies were *moving away* from earth, Einstein had to admit that his theory of a static universe was wrong and that Friedmann and Lemaître had been correct. This was six years after he had dismissed Lemaître's physics as "abominable."[16]

When Alexander Friedmann was jousting with Einstein over the status of the universe, he had a student who took up the baton of the big bang theory after Friedmann's premature death. In 1934, George Gamow, then in the United States at George Washington University, published articles from a perspective of nucleosynthesis. How were so many different substances formed, and why were some so much more abundant than others? Why was the universe so rich in hydrogen and helium?

Lemaître, the Catholic priest whose work Gamow admired, viewed the big bang as beginning with a single massive atom, which then exploded. All else being equal, the elements would indeed break up further, because larger nuclei are inherently unstable, but they would logically have settled out in the middle range of the periodic table, which could not account for the abundance of hydrogen and helium. Gamow reversed Lemaître's thinking. Rather than beginning with a huge superatom, what if the universe began with an abundance of hydrogen atoms that exploded outward? If the starting point were 100 percent hydrogen, would this not account for the universe's present composition of 90 percent hydrogen?[17]

Gamow began with the assumption that the intense heat of the big bang would have broken the universe down into its simplest elements of protons, neutrons, and electrons. As the world expanded, what could have happened to cause these elements to coalesce and form the many and varied elements of our world? Gamow's disadvantage was that he lacked the mathematical knowledge to move his theoretical research forward. He met and brought into his work a teenage prodigy, Ralph Alpher. Alpher's father had come to America from the Ukrainian seaport city of Odessa, as had Gamow. However, the younger Alpher had run afoul of the age-old *ressentiment*, Nietzsche — he was Jewish. In 1937 he was granted a scholarship to the Massachusetts Institute of Technology (MIT). When discussing his family history with an alumnus of this distinguished center of higher learning, he mentioned that he was Jewish, and the scholarship was withdrawn. Alpher related, "My brother had told me not to get my hopes up, and he was damn right. It was a searing experience. He said it was unrealistic to think that a Jew could go anywhere back then."[18]

Starting with the assumption of extreme heat at the instant of the big bang, with a subsequent dissipation of heat, Gamow and Alpher realized that only after some degree of cooling could the protons and neutrons combine to form nuclei. Since free neutrons have a very limited life span, "less than 2% of the original neutrons would be left one hour after the moment of creation, unless the neutrons had already reacted with protons to form stable nuclei.... Because neutrons are a vital ingredient in nucleosynthesis, both the neutron half-life and the rate of neutron creation were critical factors in determining the amount of time during which nucleosynthesis could take place after the Big Bang."[19]

It took Alpher three years to become convinced that his mathematical calculations could logically describe the formation of helium in the early moments after the big bang. Alpher and Gamow's first publication caused quite a stir. On April 14, 1948, the *Washington Post* headline read, "WORLD BEGAN IN 5 MINUTES."[20]

So we see, Nietzsche, that while Albert Einstein may have received some of his insatiable curiosity about the universe from his family roots, which reached back three or four generations into the culture of the Bayt Meedrahsh, he did not receive from those roots the understanding of the wondrous expanse and grandeur of the universe. Until provided with irrefutable mathematical proof, he clung to his theory of a static, limited universe.

Just as the Kahbahlistic wisdom provided the impetus for the movement of Jews of the culture of the Bayt Meedrahsh from all over the world to the land of Israel, the same wisdom inspired a clear understanding of the vastness of Hahshehm's creation — the universe, created from nothing.

This esoteric wisdom is mentioned in the *Tahlmood* and referred to in the

*Tahnahkh* — the Jewish Bible — but only in limited, cryptic terms. There is always a tension between the necessary limits to revealing this wisdom and the necessity that the wisdom be passed from one generation to the next. In the *Tahlmood*, we read of the "Work of the Chariot" and "Work of Creation." These terms are allusions to the esoteric wisdom of the Kahbahlah. It is not something learned apart from *Tahlmood* and Torah, but something taught to some when they are "old enough," which is to say when they are well versed in the Torah and *Tahlmood* and have reached an age and wisdom sufficient to understand the esoteric knowledge.

When it comes to science and Torah, there is controversy in the culture of the Bayt Meedrahsh. Many authorities want to emphasize the separateness of science and Torah, and discourage talk about the age of the universe and other cosmological topics. But there are, in fact, references to such topics in Jewish sources and commentaries, and the culture of the Bayt Meedrahsh is diverse enough to encompass all sides of the controversy.

In your day, Nietzsche, Rabbi Israel Lipschitz, a respected authority in the culture of the Bayt Meedrahsh, wrote about creations of the world *before* the creation that began with Adam. This thought is based on a Kahbahlistic teaching in the *Tahlmood* that there are cycles of creation — the world will exist six thousand years and then is destroyed, to await another such cycle of creation.[21] According to many authorities, we are now in a seventh cycle; therefore, forty-two thousand years preceded Adam.

Rabbi Lipschitz, far from being threatened by scientific discoveries, cited discoveries of dinosaurs and other extinct creatures as evidence that they lived during previous cycles of creation. "See how the teachings of our Torah have been vindicated by modern discoveries," he wrote.[22]

The teaching that the world was forty-two thousand years old at the time of Adam's creation is cited in an important document from Rabbi Isaac of Ahkko, who lived in the thirteenth and fourteenth centuries. He wrote that the Sabbatical cycles of seven thousand years must be measured in divine, not human, years. Many sources consider a divine day as equal to one thousand of our days; this is based on Psalms 90:4, which proclaims, "...a thousand years in your eyes are but a bygone yesterday."

Rabbi Aryeh Kaplan, a physicist as well as an authoritative twentieth-century scholar of the Torah, *Tahlmood*, and Kahbahlah, found the document of Rabbi Isaac of Ahkko and wrote of its possible implications: "

startling consequences, for according to many Midrashic sources, a divine day is 1,000 earthly years long, and a divine year, consisting of 365¼ is equal to 365,250 earthly years. Thus, according to Rabbi Isaac of Akko, the universe would be 42,000 x 365,250 years old. This comes out to be 15,340,500,000 years, a highly significant figure. From calculations based on the expanding universe and other cosmological observations, modern science has concluded that the big bang occurred approximately 15 billion years ago. But here we see the same figure presented in a Torah source written over seven hundred years ago!"[23]

The point, Nietzsche, is not to look for secret codes in Jewish sources; it is, rather, that the Torah, *Tahlmood*, and Kahbahlah, far from being a system of rigid laws, contain revealed wisdom that encourages wide-ranging abstract thinking — thinking that reaches "higher" than what can inspire us in our everyday, mundane lives. This is the "higher" that you were always seeking.

We have seen that Isaac of Ahkko and other sources point to an age of the universe far beyond that most often accepted by the culture of the Bayt Meedrahsh. The traditional idea is that Hahshehm created the world at the time of Adam and that the earth is therefore not yet six thousand years old. This concept views each day of creation described in Genesis as a twenty-four-hour day. However, not all respected commentators see the "days" of creation as twenty-four-hour days.

Rabbi Ohvahdee'ah ben Jacob S'forno, better known as "the S'forno," was a revered Italian rabbi, physician, philosopher, and commentator on sacred Jewish texts in the 1500s. His works are still widely known and studied in the culture of the Bayt Meedrahsh. In his commentary on the first book of the Torah, Genesis, he closely examines the story of Creation and anticipates scientific discoveries that were yet four hundred years in the future:

"And the earth was 'desolate and void' — Genesis 1:2. The S'forno writes that the desolation was 'primeval matter' and void 'primeval form.' The Torah indicates that primeval matter was a totally new creation (there being no matter preceding the world's creation). The matter in this initial amalgam is called desolation, for it only possesses potential but no actuality."[24] This closely follows Herman and Alpher's twentieth-century scientific finding of the "foggy plasma state" that existed for the first three hundred thousand years after the big bang — a time when the heat was so intense that the smallest elements of matter could not be differentiated.

In the fourth and fifth verses of Genesis, we read, "And God separated between the light and the darkness and God called the light day and the darkness night." The S'forno explains: "During those days that the primeval light served the world, there were periods of light and periods of darkness without the revolution of the spheres...."[25] The S'forno clearly states that the "days" of Genesis were not twenty-four-hour days. This raises the question, when did "day" as we know it begin?

In his commentary on the beginning of the second chapter of Genesis, the S'forno writes, "God completed all creative activity at the (exact) beginning of the seventh day, at the indivisible moment which marked the inception of future time, but yet was not part of it."[26] Regarding the creation of man (Genesis 2:7), the S'forno tells us, "He was only a living creature, unable to speak, until he was created in (God's) image and likeness."[27] We can see here, Nietzsche, an allusion to earlier forms of man that preceded Adam. We will soon see the remarkable parallel between Genesis and the development of the world as understood by the world's top scientists.

You were prescient about Darwin's ideas of evolution. In your notes, titled "Anti-Darwin," you wrote: "There are no transitional forms.... Every type has its limits: beyond these there is no evolution."[28] Darwin himself conditioned his theory on the concept that the fossil record was imperfect, saying, "He who rejects this view of the imperfection of the geological record will rightly reject the whole theory."[29] Darwin clearly expected that the gaps in the fossil record would be filled in by new findings. However, your intuition, Nietzsche, more than a century ago, has been confirmed by the enormous weight of the data accumulated since then.

Stephen Gould sums up the data with a simple statement: "The evolutionary trees that adorn our textbooks are not the evidence of fossils and...are never 'seen' in the rocks. "Niles Eldredge, a curator of the American Museum of Natural History, points out, "Large groups — say the orders of mammals (for example, rodents, elephants, carnivores) — appeared too suddenly in the fossil record to admit a rational explanation in terms of gradual adaptive modification."[30]

Life began suddenly and rapidly in the universe and underwent a period of extinction when 90 percent of all living forms were obliterated from the universe; there is no straight-line evolution. Indeed, Darwin, a religious man, developed a theory at odds with the Torah. On the fifth day of creation, God said, "Let the waters swarm with living creatures, and let winged creatures fly above the earth across the firmament of the heaven. And God created the large sea creatures and every living creature that crawls, with which the waters swarmed, after its kind, and every winged creature after its kind."[31]

As Gerald Schroeder, a present-day physicist who lives in the Old City of Jerusalem, explains:

> One-celled life sprang into being as soon as water was present, 3.8 billion years ago. One might have expected that complex multicellular organisms would then have developed in orderly, successive stages. Such was not the case. Instead of a gradual, steady thrust of life evolving complex systems, 3.2 billion years passed during which life remained confined to one-celled organisms.... Then, 530 million years ago in the Cambrian era, with no hint in earlier fossils, the basic anatomies of all life extant today appeared simultaneously in the ocean. The Cambrian explosion of life is one of the [twentieth] century's greatest discoveries.[32]

In other words, science was more and more adapting the terminology of Jewish sources.

The book of Genesis tells us that all the swarming insects and winged creatures were created in one "day." The Torah begins the counting of time with the creation of Adam; thus, the first six days have a different perspective. The time from Adam was Earth-based time since "radioactive dates of archaeological discoveries related to the post-Adam period, such as the early Bronze Age, the beginning of writing, the battle of Jericho, closely match the dates derived from the biblical calendar for those same dates."[33] At the beginning of creation, Nietzsche, all was *tohoo* and *bohoo*; there was no earth, so Schroeder concludes that the only time applicable to the six pre-Adam days was universal time.[34]

Using accepted principles of time dilution dictated by the rapidly expanding universe, we can calculate that the stretching of light waves has slowed the cosmic clock since the big bang. Using Einstein's perspective of relativity, Schroeder explains that "we look back in time. From our perspective using Earth-based clocks running at a rate determined by the condition of today's Earth, we measure a fifteen-billion-year age. And that is correct for our local view. The Bible adopts this Earthly perspective, but only for times after

Adam. The Bible's clock before Adam is not a clock tied to any one location. It is a clock that looks forward in time from the creation.... That cosmic time-piece, as observed today, ticks a million million times more slowly than at its inception."[35]

Using this time-dilution factor and comparing it to the events of the first six days of creation reveals an astounding correlation between biblical events and scientific discoveries. As the universe expands, the time dilution slows, so that from Earth's perspective, each twenty-four-hour day of creation repre-sents fewer and fewer cosmic years. Day one of Genesis began with the big bang over fifteen billion years ago and ends almost eight billion years before Adam. The Torah relates that Hahshehm created the universe and that light was separated from darkness. The corresponding cosmic period began with the big bang and included the cooling of the universe, leading to the develop-ment of atomic nuclei and the beginning of galaxy formation.

Day two of creation saw the formation of the firmament. The correspond-ing cosmic time covers from eight billion to almost four billion years ago, during which the Milky Way took shape, as did the sun.

Day three, as described in the Torah, brings the separation of the oceans and dry land and the appearance of plant life. With the universe expanding, the time dilution slows to cover approximately two billion years, bringing us up to almost two million years before Adam. Science has determined that during this period of time, the cooling of the earth led to the appearance of water and the first forms of life — bacteria and algae.

Biblical day four brings us to 750 million years before Adam, with the parallel appearance of heavenly bodies. Day five finds, in both biblical and paleontological records, the first multicellular animals, then eventually such complex forms as reptiles, followed by birds.

Day six brings us up to the time of Adam, and an exciting parallel between the appearance of *Homo erectus*, an extinct upright creature with a far differ-ent level of development from modern man, and *Homo sapiens*, man as we know him today.[36]

Some hundred thousand years ago, Nietzsche, Neanderthal man suddenly appeared on earth, and just as suddenly, about sixty thousand years later, he was gone. Neanderthal man had a skull roughly the same size as modern man's, but what were the capabilities of the brain inside? Neanderthal man used primitive tools and left behind no evidence of cultural development. The word "ancient" is, of course, relative. The "ancient" cave paintings found in Western Europe were the work of modern humans, not Neanderthals. Was Neanderthal man closer to apes than to modern man? What we have learned is that the question, conditioned by years of acceptance of gradual evolution, is flawed. Neanderthal man was neither ape nor modern man. Physically, "Neanderthals were not less human than modern man.... It is now clear that the Neanderthals had the same postural abilities, manual dexterity, and range and character of movement that modern men do.... [They had] a much stronger grip than that of modern men, but there was nothing gorilla-like in it; their control of movement was evidently the same as ours."[37]

Early modern man showed superior development of tools and weapons for hunting and fishing. He was capable of magnificent cave art. These developments were relatively static for fifty thousand years. According to Schroeder, "Then about 10,000 years ago, another explosion of cultural progress occurred, of even greater dimensions than previously. In fact, this was the most comprehensive series of cultural advances that has ever taken place, covering all aspects of human behavior."[38] What was included in this amazing sprint into a new era of man? "In 3,000 or 4,000 years, the life of man had changed more radically than in all the preceding 250,000 years. Before the Agricultural Revolution, most men must have spent their waking moments seeking their next meal.... As man learned to produce food and store it in the grain bin and on the roof, he was able to settle in larger communities.... Such innovations as the discovery of the basic mechanical principles, weaving, the plow, the wheel and metallurgy soon appeared."[39]

The Hebrew word for man is "*ahdahm*," which comes from the same three-letter root as the word for earth, "*ahdahmah*." Hahshehm breathed his spirit into the nostrils of generic *ahdahm (Adam)*, and pre-modern man became modern man with the proper name Adam. And one of Adam's descendants, Jabal, "was the first of those who dwell in tents and breed cattle. The name of his brother was Jubal; he was the first of all who handle the harp and flute. And Zillah, too — she bore Tubal-cain, who sharpened all cutting implements of copper and iron."[40]

The Torah described the agricultural revolution, animal husbandry, and advanced tool development long before the fossil record revealed it. This is no surprise to the culture of the Bayt Meedrahsh; since Hahshehm created the world and gave the Torah to Moses, it follows that the Torah would know that agriculture, animal husbandry, and advanced metallurgy came into existence after modern man.

With the general acceptance of what we know as the anthropic principle, we find scientists straining to explain certain phenomena in secular terms. The anthropic principle asserts itself in two ways: "(1) Very slight changes in the laws of nature would have made it impossible for life to exist, and (2) human life would not have been possible if not for the occurrence in the past of a large number of highly improbable events."[41]

An important area in which we see the anthropic principle at work is in the central place of the sun in our universe. The sun contains only two kinds of atoms: hydrogen and helium. The hydrogen atom is the simplest of all atoms, with a nucleus containing only one proton. Another Jewish refugee from Hitler, Hans Bethe, won a Nobel Prize for discovering how protons produce solar energy. Because of the sun's extreme heat, a proton can change spontaneously into a neutron; the neutron can combine with another proton to produce a deuteron. It is the deuterons that are involved in the thermonuclear reactions that provide the light and heat of the sun, without which we could not exist.

Amazing scientific advances since your time, Nietzsche, inform us that the three fundamental forces governing our universe are (1) gravity, (2) electromagnetic force, and (3) nuclear force. The strength of the nuclear force determines whether two protons can combine — an event that would destroy the sun in a huge explosion. What if the nuclear force were just a little bit weaker or stronger than it is in the universe?

If the nuclear force were very slightly weaker, it would not be possible for a proton to combine with a neutron to make a deuteron. In this case, the sun would not provide the light and heat to sustain the world. If the nuclear force were very slightly stronger, then protons would combine, producing the destructive explosion just mentioned. How does it happen that these extremes were so narrowly averted? Scientists *do not know.*

Astronomers have provided us with another example of the anthropic principle. They have discovered that Earth's two closest neighbors, Venus and Mars, used to have abundant water, as our planet does. The key words here are "used to." Now they have no water and, therefore, no life. Venus is a little too close to the sun; thus, its water evaporated; Mars is a little too far away from the sun, so its waters froze. Because earth is just the right distance from the sun, it has escaped the fate of its neighbors and is the only planet in our solar system that can sustain life. Noting these and many other examples of the anthropic principle, one prominent scientist commented, "As we look out into the universe and identify the many peculiarities of physics and astronomy that have worked together for our benefit, it almost seems as if the universe must in some sense have known that we were coming."[42] But of course, the Jew of the culture of the Bayt Meedrahsh has known for thousands of years that Hahshehm created the universe for the sake of man.

I mentioned in an earlier letter, Nietzsche, the discovery of DNA, the bewilderingly complex double helix of proteins that governs the life of every cell, from the smallest bacterium to the billions of cells in man. Francis Crick and his colleague, James Watson, shared a Nobel Prize for their description of the structure of DNA. Crick noted, "The origin of life appears to be almost a miracle, so many are the conditions which would have had to be satisfied to get it going."[43] You did not like the word "miracle," but Crick could not find a scientific term to fit the phenomenon.

The second part of the anthropic principle has to do with the improbable events without which life could not be. Dinosaurs are not just bizarre extinct beasts that fascinate children. They dominated the earth for 150 million years. Then, in some cataclysmic event still poorly understood by scientists, some 85 percent of species on earth disappeared. The most convincing theory is that of Luis and Walter Alvarez, who have amassed evidence that a "giant meteor from outer space collided with the earth to cause this worldwide catastrophe."[44]

We know the contempt that scientists and thinkers of your time had for the Torah concept of the creation of the world from nothing. Indeed, we know the contempt with which the Jewish people themselves were regarded in Europe in your time. Those Jews, who rejected the Christian messiah, were destined to wander the face of the earth, eternally homeless. Their long-lamented land of Israel had been in the hands of world powers for over fifteen hundred years. What ruler or scholar would even have entertained the idea that the Jews would be in control of this land before the middle of the twentieth century? Would they have said, "It would take a miracle"?

It is perhaps not so surprising, Nietzsche, that the leaders of the Jews who, in your lifetime, spearheaded the initiative to develop a Jewish cultural home in the land of Israel were deeply influenced by your writings. More than that, I can justifiably say that your writings very much encouraged in them the same sense of personal independence and intellectual striving that ultimately brought such energy to the Zionist movement. It is now more than a century later. Did they succeed? I will write again soon.

Very truly yours,

Ben Moshe

# Letter Fifteen

May 23, 2006

כ"ה באייר תשס"ו

Dear Nietzsche,

What the Jews call the land of Israel, with Jerusalem at its heart, has been a target of conquest for every leader who has aspired to a role on the world stage. Because the Muslim and Christian religions have long sought economic and political hegemony as well as theological supremacy throughout the world, the Middle East has been a battleground. The land of Israel is a bridge joining three continents.

The Jews of the culture of the Bayt Meedrahsh, as we have seen, yearned for the Promised Land with a deep spiritual attachment. Periods of messianic fervor prompted many significant groups of Jews to come to "the Land," but they harbored no notions of Jewish sovereignty apart from the redemption that would accompany the coming of *Mahshee'ahkh* — the Messiah. Near the turn of the twentieth century, a secular leadership arose with visions of a Jewish homeland in Palestine.

A huge statue of Theodor Herzl looks over the city named for him, Herzlyia. He is the "father of modern Zionism." Like other Zionist leaders, Herzl wanted a solution for "the Jewish problem" — the problem of statelessness in a time of rising nationalism. It does not detract from their noble motives to say that they were looking for solutions for themselves as well. Many, like Herzl, were highly educated men of letters who recognized that in Europe their aspirations were limited by their being Jewish. They did not want to reject their heritage outright, but just as you, Nietzsche, wanted a "new European," Herzl and his colleagues wanted a "new Jew." The new Jew could forge his own destiny only in his own homeland.

Herzl's private literary collection is preserved, and in his library are leather-bound editions of your books. Under his editorship, after your death, seven issues of *Neue Freie Presse* were dedicated to you and your work.[1] Among Herzl's peers, with whom he served in a literary social-action society, was Joseph Paneth, the scientist who, in his conversations with you, disavowed any Jewish national aspirations. As a journalist, Herzl had covered the Dreyfus Affair in France, and it is widely believed that this awakened in him his latent Jewish identity.

Dreyfus, from a family of rapidly assimilating Jews, was a captain in the French military. Arrested in 1894 and accused of spying for Germany, he was convicted and sent to the penal colony at Devil's Island. That he was a scapegoat became clear to many after the document that had been the primary incriminating evidence was shown to be the work of another officer. The second man was tried and acquitted. This prompted the author Émil Zola to write his famous *J'Accuse*, in which he bluntly condemned the "odious anti-Semitism of which the great, liberal rights-of-man France will die if she is not cured."[2]

In the middle of the anti-Jewish charge was the Catholic Church — no surprise to you, Nietzsche. In 1898, the Vatican newspaper *L'Osservatore Romano* published this broadside: "Jewry can no longer be excused or rehabilitated. The Jew possesses the largest share of all wealth, movable and immovable.... The credit of States is in the hands of a few Jews. One finds Jews in the ministries, the civil service, the armies and the navies, the universities and in control of the press.... If there is one nation that more than any other has the right to turn to anti-Semitism, it is France, which first gave their political rights to the Jews, and which was thus the first to prepare the way for its own servitude to them."[3]

The Dreyfus Affair certainly had an impact on Herzl, but his thinking was already well shaped by less spectacular but persistent evidence of the chronic European disease of *ressentiment* against the Jews. In 1894 Herzl published a play, *Das Neue Ghetto* (*The New Ghetto*). The principal character is a nominal Jew whose pride pushes him to the realization that by trying to assimilate, he has betrayed himself.[4]

Max Nordau was another well-known early Zionist leader. Like Herzl, he was born in Budapest, and also like Herzl, he was an aspiring writer. He also was well versed in your writings, Nietzsche, though he reacted very negatively to them early in his career. Nordau pinned his hopes on the promise of the Enlightenment. It is also significant that whereas Herzl was from an already assimilated family, Nordau was raised in a family of the culture of the Bayt Meedrahsh. However, he left his religious practices behind and was primed for a fight with anyone who rejected, or even appeared to reject, the Enlightenment. He saw in your criticism of nationalism and Enlightenment romanticism a threat to his ticket out of what he viewed as a Jewish ghetto.

Nordau was the physician of your onetime close friend Lou Andreas-Salomé. We cannot know what influence this relationship may have had on Nordau's views of your work;[5] we know only that as he grew more and more disillusioned with European *ressentiment* toward the Jews, he turned more toward Zionism and seems to have acquired greater appreciation for your writing.

The fear of some early Zionists that you were somehow dangerous to their enterprise arises from an incomplete understanding of your work. And indeed, their misguided notion that you rejected reverence for one's cultural upbringing and roots is refuted in many of your writings. I will cite just a few: (1) *"The unhistorical and the historical are necessary in equal measure for the health of an individual, of a people and of a culture"*;[6] (2) "The profound reverence for age and tradition — all law rests on this double reverence — the faith and prejudice in favor of ancestors…is typical in the morality of the powerful";[7] (3) "History thus belongs…to him who preserves and reveres — to him who looks back to whence he came into being, with love and loyalty; with the piety he, as it were, gives thanks for his existence. By tending with care that which has existed from old, he wants to preserve for those who shall come into existence — and thus he serves life."[8] You have always disappointed those who see in you a rebellious, fire-breathing radical. Nordau, driven by his own dynamics, initially saw you in that way.

Micha Joseph Berdichevski was a promising student of Torah and *Tahlmood* in the culture of the Bayt Meedrahsh when he bolted to the European popular culture of your day. His father-in-law expelled him from his house for this apostasy. As opposed to Nordau, he looked not to the Enlightenment to find his personal expression of who he was, but to you, Nietzsche. He was the first to write in the Hebrew language about your work. He saw the "new Jew" as a thinking individual who would create a new Jewish state and culture in the land of Israel.

In 1899, Berdichevski assertively identified with you when he wrote an essay in Hebrew entitled "The Old and Young Age: A Reevaluation of Values." This brought down on his head the wrath of Nordau and some other early Zionist leaders who felt threatened by what they thought you said.[9]

The pattern we are seeing, Nietzsche, is that these Zionist leaders turned to your writings, and ultimately to Zionism, for personal reasons. It was Nietzsche as psychologist they needed most. We see another example of this need in Martin Buber. Buber was born in Vienna in 1878, where he showed an interest in philosophy at a precocious age. As a teenager, he contemplated suicide.

Buber sang your praises in lyrical prose, making clear what your works meant to him personally, saying that you:

> uncovered the feeble lies of our values and our truths, but the tip of his raised sword glistened purple in the light of the rising sun.... He erected in front of our eyes the statue of the heroic human being who creates his own self and beyond his self. In place of a thin and lame altruism he put the egotism of his own development and the virtue of giving.... He contrasted the ideal of a comfortable and painless life with a stormy and dangerous life, whose powerful beauty is enhanced by the pain. Instead of happiness for the greatest number, he considered the creation of great people and great ideas to be the purpose of humanity.[10]

Buber wrote but never published an essay on Zarathustra at about the time you died, in 1900. He quoted many of your works, then the following lines: "I love you, Friedrich Nietzsche, for your free, fresh, and cheerful, all too human poetry, for your appearing to be like an old master builder.... I love the artist in you and the psychologist...and moralist."[11]

Buber's words recall Otto Rank, a close associate of Freud, whom we discussed in an earlier letter. He wrote about his own personal crisis: "For a long time, I had serious thoughts of suicide which, as Nietzsche says, 'helped me get past many a night and many a day.' Then in reaction came a tremendous love of life and creative joy, which swept me into activity."[12] Buber went on to be a productive writer. He stuck it out in Germany until 1938, when he finally moved to Jerusalem.

Herzl pushed his program of "political Zionism," meeting with many world leaders to discuss the establishment of a Jewish homeland in Palestine. Buber's interests turned from political to cultural Zionism. In the words of Jacob Golomb, a scholar of your works, "Buber is not dealing solely with Jewish resurrection as a nation, but defines as the ultimate and the most essential objective of Zionism a radical transfiguration of the whole personality.... He has in mind, like many other Nietzschean Zionists, an existential revolution more difficult to attain than the cultivation of new and devastated lands: the cultivation of a new type of Jew."[13]

Clearly, all these Zionists were outside the culture of the Bayt Meedrahsh. Those who considered themselves cultural Zionists had no aspirations to form a new Jewish nation. The political Zionists, such as Herzl, would need the cooperation of the major powers to establish a state, and there was little in the history of these powers to encourage Jewish aspirations. Herzl died in 1904 at age forty-four, and the leadership of the drive for Jewish settlement in the land of Israel with the ultimate goal of a Jewish state passed to the hands of an unlikely group of Russian Jews.

I need not give you a complete review of twentieth-century history. What is fascinating, Nietzsche, is that the cultural ideology that drew Russian Zionists in the early 1900s is the same as that behind the dictatorship that triumphed in the Russian Revolution of 1917: Marxist socialism. Not only did you have nothing good to say about socialism, your description of what a socialist state would be like is a surprisingly accurate description of the socialist state that existed in Russia from 1917 until its collapse some seventy years later: "If there should ever be a socialist state, it would enforce an unprecedented iron discipline — they know themselves — and the citizens would put up with their chains because they are self-imposed, and the feeling of...this power is so young and charming to them that they would suffer anything for its sake."[14]

Many countries in Eastern Europe came under communist/socialist regimes, and eventually the citizens whom these regimes controlled brought them down. The leadership of the *yeeshoov* — the collective name for the Jews in Palestine in the first half of the twentieth century — was also made up of socialists and communists.

The movement of Jews to the land of Israel in your lifetime, Nietzsche, is called the First *Ahleeyah* and was limited to approximately thirty-five thousand Jews, mostly from Eastern Europe. It happened during the years 1882–1903. By the end of that period, close to half the pioneers who made the move to Israel had since left. The Ottoman officials in Palestine were alternately hostile, then agreeable, to admitting a limited number of Jews. By 1903, it was clear to most powers that the Ottoman Empire was on its last legs, and carving up that empire would entail war.

The Second *Ahleeyah* began in 1904 and ended with the outbreak of World War I in 1914. While there was some degree of idealism in the First *Ahleeyah* — "pull" factors that drew Jews to "their land" — the Second *Ahleeyah* and subsequent periods of immigration were mostly dictated by "push" factors, that is, anti-Semitism. Your word "*ressentiment*," when applied to feelings toward the Jews at the time, is more apt, because it addresses the underlying dynamics of those afflicted with this "dis-ease."

You were doubtless aware of violent Russian pogroms against Jews in the 1800s. The worst outbreak began in 1903, after your death, and is known as the Kishinev Pogrom. An article in the *New York Times* described the horrors as:

> worse than the censor will permit to publish. There was a well laid-out plan for the general massacre of Jews on the day following Orthodox Easter. The mob was led by priests, and the general cry, 'Kill the Jews,' was taken up all over the city. The Jews were taken wholly unaware and were slaughtered like sheep. The dead numbered 120, and the injured about 500. The scenes of horror attending this massacre are beyond description. Babes were literally torn to pieces by the frenzied and bloodthirsty mob. The local police made no attempt to check the reign of terror. At sunset the streets were piled with corpses and wounded. Those who could make their escape fled in terror, and the city is now practically deserted of Jews.[15]

This description, as you well know, Nietzsche, could come from almost any period of history. Here is a similar report:

> So excessive were the sufferings of our people that anyone who spoke of them [i.e., of the Jews] as undergoing wanton violence and outrage

would be using words not properly applicable. [Such a man would lack] adequate terms to express the magnitude of cruelty so unprecedented that actions of conquerors in war, who are also merciless to the conquered, would seem kindness itself in comparison.... [The pogromists] tied with thongs and nooses, and binding their ankles, dragged them through the middle of the market, leaping on them and not even sparing their dead bodies. For, more brutal and savage than fierce wild beasts, they severed them limb from limb and piece from piece and trampling on them destroyed every lineament, so that not even the least remnant was left which could receive burial.[16]

This description is from Philo of Alexandria in the year 38 of the Common Era. Yet, from long before the time of Philo, through the Hitler era, and to the present day, the culture of the Bayt Meedrahsh continues to thrive.

So far, we have spoken of the land of Israel as a place of strategic importance to world powers in terms of religious dominance and commerce. Into this paradigm we must introduce a new commodity that was in its infancy when you left us, Nietzsche. This commodity looms so large over geopolitical considerations now that most people have no idea that it came to the fore scarcely a hundred years ago. You knew of it as petroleum, or "stone oil."

The First World War raged from 1914 to 1919. In the last two years of the war, the price of a barrel of oil in the United States jumped from two dollars to three, and it was clear that the United States, emerging from the war as a superpower on a global scale, would have to become an importer of oil. The British were more alert to the importance of Middle Eastern oil than were France and Russia, their main competitors for hegemony in the area. In a 1920 agreement, they ceded to the French an enlarged mandate over Syria in exchange for complete control over any oil production in Mesopotamia. It was in Mosul, now part of Iraq, that the first oil was discovered. To the south, Saudia Arabia soon became — and remains to this day — the most important oil exporter in the world.

So, Nietzsche, we have the spheres of influence in the Middle East carved up between France and Britain. The United States, stunned by the 1920 agreement giving Great Britain control over Mesopotamian oil, was determined to compete actively in the area. Amid all these developments, a group of Zionist dreamers gathered in Palestine, now also under British mandate, and dreamed of establishing a Jewish homeland. The majority of Arabs in the area resented any Jewish presence, and though there was some sentimental support for Zionist hopes back in England and, to a lesser extent, in France, those nations' foreign departments were poorly inoculated against the age-old *ressentiment* against Jews — oil and international politics were far more important.

The United States at the beginning of the 1900s was less than a century and a half old. As a country, it did not have a long history of institutionalized *ressentiment* against Jews, as did European countries and Russia. However, Jews were excluded from almost every elite dining and social club, as well as from most corporate boardrooms. There were "Jewish quotas" at privileged universities such as Harvard, Yale, and Princeton. Unfortunately for aspirations for a Jewish homeland in Palestine, the Foreign Service officers of the U.S. State Department were almost exclusively products of these universities and members of the highest social stratum, which excluded Jews from its ranks. There were many opportunities for career service in Arab capitals and, thus, a natural identification with the Arab world's emerging power, based on the importance of oil. A natural part of this identification was a commonly held antipathy toward the idea of a Jewish homeland in Palestine. Thus, the number of "Arabists" in the State Department grew, with no counterweight of Jews or those sympathetic to the dream of a Jewish state. The education and social contacts of these Arabists were largely devoid of experience with Jews, and to them the idea of a Jewish state was chimerical at best.

In the middle of the post-World War I maneuverings among the world powers, the Germans, decisively defeated in that war, were rebuilding. Your anti-*Übermensch*, Adolf Hitler, was busy turning the German nation into a grotesque caricature of nationalism. Germany emerged as a menace to the entire civilized world, right under the noses of an all-too-accommodating Europe.

Under the cover of World War I, Turkey, Germany's ally, carried out a systematic genocide of over one and a half million Armenians. Henry Morgenthau, the United States ambassador to Turkey, was told by one of the Turkish leaders, "We have got to finish with them.... No Armenian can be our friend after what we have done to them."[17] Morgenthau sent suggestions for intervention to the State Department, and after a two-month silence, he received this reply: "However much we may deplore the suffering of the

Armenians, we cannot take any active steps to come to their assistance at the present time."[18]

During the war, France, Great Britain, and Russia formally accused the Turks of "crimes against humanity and civilization." The postwar Treaty of Sevres, without providing any details, gave the Allies the "right to designate the tribunal which shall try the persons so accused [of war crimes]." The British held some accused war criminals on the island of Malta for a time but ultimately replaced the Treaty of Sevres with the Treaty of Lausanne, which omitted any reference to war crimes. Most of the accused Turks took advantage of the asylum offered to them by Germany.[19]

This history lesson was not lost on Hitler, who used the Second World War to systematically murder over six million Jews in Europe. The European and American responses, as Hitler had reason to anticipate, were the same as they had been to the Armenian massacre in World War I. At the end of World War II, world Jewry had lost one-third of its population. Those who survived the Nazi camps were kept in "displaced persons" camps. The overwhelming majority of them wanted to go to Palestine; it was unthinkable that they should return to their European countries of origin, which had stood by while their families were slaughtered. However, the British kept the doors of Palestine closed to Jews and actively fought attempts at underground immigration, imprisoning those they caught in camps on the island of Cyprus.

The Catholic Church's attitude changed little as a result of the mass murders of World War II. Bartley Crum was a member of an official delegation from the United States that toured Europe and the refugee camps where Jewish survivors were being held until a place could be found for them to relocate. Great Britain kept the gates of the Promised Land closed to them. In Vienna, Crum and other delegates met with His Excellency, Monsignor Francis Kamprath, Auxiliary Bishop of Vienna. This is his account:

> I had another experience in Vienna when, with other members, I heard his Excellency. I was present at the beginning, but as the meeting went on, I felt, as a Catholic, such shame at their interpretation of Christianity that I excused myself and left.... Judge Hutcheson asked the two churchmen what they thought was the extent and nature of the Jewish problem in Austria. The two priests made their position

clear. "We have no official opinion, but personally we feel this: we do not hate the Jews, we hate only the Jewish spirit," they said. "We believe that the best solution to the Jewish problem would be to change the Jewish spirit into a Christian spirit. The Jews should become Christians." ...Judge Hutcheson asked, "Has anti-Semitism in Vienna increased, decreased, or remained constant since liberation?" "During the war and in the time of the Nazis there was a great deal of mistaken racial anti-Semitism," came the reply. "Today all anti-Semitism in Austria is religious anti-Semitism. That is justified."[20]

The war ended in 1945, Nietzsche. On May 14, 1948, the independent state of Israel was declared. Arab forces from Egypt, Syria, Transjordan, Lebanon, and Iraq, along with irregular Arab militias, attacked the new Jewish state. Israel won the war. In three subsequent major wars, Arab states tried again and again to overrun the Jewish state. They failed. As this letter is written to you, in 2006, Israel, the Jewish state, is an economic success and *the* major military power in the Middle East. Although you were able to envision a socialist state and accurately describe what it would be like, neither you nor anyone else could imagine a Jewish state, let alone a Jewish state on this strategic and hallowed ground that has been coveted for centuries by world powers.

Historians and political scientists have written volumes about wars and the formation of nations. Little of what they have to say can explain the existence of the state of Israel. The Torah tells us that Hahshehm made a covenant with Abraham, which he renewed with Isaac and Jacob and gave collectively to the people of Israel on Mount Sinai. Conventional analysis of international power politics and warfare cannot explain Israel's existence; only Hahshehm's promise to the Jewish people can explain it.

Since the Jewish state was built on a socialist model and was achieved — despite the many daunting obstacles we just discussed — by secular Jews, what could one predict for Israel? We have already mentioned the fall of the Russian superpower built on a Marxist model, and we have seen what happens over generations to those Jews who move out of the culture of the Bayt Meedrahsh.

Many of the leaders of the *yeeshoov* — the pre-state Jewish community —

were not only nonreligious but vigorously *anti*religious. They were dedicated pioneers and wanted to forge a new Jew — a Jew rooted in the land, proud of traditions in a general way, but determined to reject what they saw as the "ghetto mentality" of the culture of the Bayt Meedrahsh. The Jews of the culture of the Bayt Meedrahsh had indeed kept the focus on the Promised Land by *ahleeyah*, based on messianic expectations, but from 1900 until the establishment of the state, they were largely bystanders.

Most of the rabbinic leaders early in the 1900s rejected the secular leaders of the community, condemning them as transgressors of *hahlahkhah* — Torah law. There was one notable exception, a man who saw the secular pioneers as part of Hahshehm's plan for the reestablishment of a Jewish state in the land of Israel. Over a century later, he is revered by many as one of the most brilliant, pious, and farsighted leaders of the culture of the Bayt Meedrahsh in the twentieth century. Those rabbis who vigorously, even maliciously slandered him are barely a footnote to history. This illustrates, Nietzsche, that it is not Jewish law that is rigid; rather, some of its *interpreters* are rigid.

Avraham Yitzkhak Kook was born in Greiva (Griva), Russia, in 1865. His father, the local rabbi, came from a long line of Khahseedic Jews, while his mother was of Lithuanian lineage — those Jews who, following their great leader, the Ga'ohn of Vilna, initially opposed Khahseedism. The young Avraham Yitzkhak was recognized early as an exceptionally gifted prodigy. He studied with many of the great European rabbis from both Lithuanian and Khahseedic backgrounds, including the Torah giant the Khahfehtz Khahyeem, Rabbi Yisrael Meir of Radin.

Rav Kook imbibed Kahbahlah through intensive study with Rav Solomon Eliashev. There is no understanding this man, Nietzsche, without recognition of the deep spiritual, Kahbalistic soul that dominated his being. Recall that we talked about *t'feeleen*, the phylacteries that men wear as part of the morning service. Rav Kook wore *t'feeleen* all day. So clad, he would travel to the secular *keebootzeem* — collective farms built on a socialist model — and engage the *khalootzeem*, or pioneers, in a wide-ranging discussion of their work, and he would also deliver words of Torah. For Rav Kook, all Jews in the land of Israel were part of the plan for redemption.

Like many of the greats of the culture of the Bayt Meedrahsh who preceded him, Rav Kook was deeply interested in the classical philosophers such as Kant and Schopenhauer, whom he read in German.[21] We also have evidence that he read the philosopher whose books so fascinated the secular leaders of early Zionism — you, Nietzsche. Some scholars have thought they saw your influence in some of Rav Kook's writings, though they had no definite proof. The background for his writing that we will examine is the relentless onslaughts against him by many rabbis of the *yeeshoov* — the Jewish community in Palestine.

In 1985, Rabbi Bezalel Naor, a prominent scholar of Rav Kook's works, came upon a book, *Orot ha-Emunah* (*Lights of Faith*), a compilation of some of Rav Kook's writings. Rabbi Naor writes, "On page 21, I read: 'Sometimes a man may be ruined through books written by those of small faith whose souls have not the holy courage, the flame of holy fire; and books written by absolute atheists, drenched with a spirit of impure courage which comes from disbelief — will mend him and arouse in him his slumbering soul. He will find himself full of life and vigor, flowing with lofty courage and a powerful faith in the Living God.' I think I know which books 'written by an absolute atheist drenched with a spirit of impure courage' the Rav had in mind."[22]

One contemporary Israeli scholar of your work has it right when he says, "There is clearly something special about Nietzsche that enabled his thought to exert such an impact on divergent political streams, educators, political leaders and philosophers — whether religious or atheist, left or right-wing, individualists or collectivists."[23]

Despite Rav Kook's need to append "impure" as a descriptor for your courage, this did not prevent him from acknowledging his debt to you. And despite the fact that Rav Kook was a "believer," that would not have kept you from admiring his depth of knowledge and his character. The two of you would have had much to talk about. Your *Übermensch* had the critical characteristics of being a consummate thinker, true to himself, one who has overcome the negative will to power. There is nothing in your writing to suggest that the *Übermensch* must have a certain intellectual or spiritual orientation to be a confirmed "Nietzschean."

You would have had to know about Hahshehm and the culture of the Bayt Meedrahsh to understand my assertion that you would have found *Übermenschen* there.[24] In the end, it is not relevant what we call your ideal man or what we call the Torah giants who spring up in every generation; what is clear is that you had much in common. Forgive me for the personal reference, Nietzsche, but if you had availed yourself of the opportunity to meet and talk to the Torah giants of your generation, you would not have been so lonely.

Rav Kook's vast knowledge of Jewish sources and his many commentaries on them stand on their own. Yet his phraseology in certain passages certainly suggests that he had your writing in mind — for example, in his writing about Europe: "Europe rightly gives up on God, whom she never knew. Individual humanists adapted to the sublime good, but not an entire nation. No nation or tongue could understand how to aspire to the Good, the All, let alone know how to stamp with this the foundation of its existence. Therefore, when in our day nationalism grew and penetrated the system of philosophy, the latter was forced to place a big question mark over all the content of absolute ethics, which truly came to Europe only on loan from Judaism, and as any foreign implant, could not be absorbed in its spirit."[25]

On Christianity, Rav Kook writes, "Christianity abandoned law, rooted herself in apparent mercy and love that undermines the world and destroys it. By emptying the law of its divine content, it becomes seized by the grossest wickedness. The poison invades the private law of the individual and spreads through the soul of nations, becoming the foundation of national hatred and the depth of evil and bloodshed, without removing the yoke from man's neck."[26]

In a paragraph inviting comparison to your statement that "the goal of humanity cannot lie in the end but only in its highest specimens," Rav Kook wrote this:

> Especially in our nation, for which the sublime spirituality of the ideology that is so much higher than all the present world, is the basis of her soul — it may occur that from every movement of material freedom and compulsion for work in material, practical, social affairs, there resonates in her immediately an inner shudder lest the practical preoccupation lessen her fount.... Therefore, the nation must produce great saints, special in greatness of intellect, who enclose within their midst the spiritual state of the total nation. They, these lofty ones, know that the treasure of the spirit of the nation is within them.[27]

Having called for the nation to produce great men, Rav Kook urges the Jewish people to acknowledge its own greatness. He does not shrink from using the word "chosen": "A great mistake is the turning back from all of our advantage, the cessation of the recognition that, 'You have chosen us.' Not only are we different from all the peoples, distinguished by historical life that has no comparison among other peoples and tongues, but we are exalted and much greater than any other people. If we know our greatness, then we know ourselves, and a people who forgets itself certainly is small and lowly."[28]

In rejecting causal restrictions, it is almost as if Rav Kook had your writing before him. Below, we look first at your words from *Beyond Good and Evil*, then at Rav Kook's writing, echoing your words:

(1) One should not wrongly reify "cause" and "effect," as the natural scientists do.... One should use "cause" and "effect" only as pure concepts, that is to say, as conventional fictions for the purpose of designation and communication — not for explanation. In the "in itself" there is nothing of "causal connections," of "necessity," or of "psychological non-freedom"; there the effect does not follow the cause, there is not rule of "law." It is we alone who have devised cause, sequence, for-each-other, relativity, constraint, number, law, freedom, motive and purpose.... The "unfree will" is mythology; in real life it is only a matter of strong and weak wills.[29]

(2) The causal perspective presents laws that ripple throughout existence. It proceeds from the material world and scales the spiritual heights as it examines their details.... In the chain of causality there is contained a general restriction, a constriction that constrains laws to those pathways.... However, when we ascend to a higher plane of freedom, we are freed of this causal restriction, and the entire structure of laws appears to us as being held together by ethical bonds that are no weaker and are even stronger than those of the causal explanation and whose total value is infinitely more exalted. Then we stand in a world of freedom: when the ethical universe is revealed to us, it uplifts the causal universe, attracts it and enlightens it, flooding it in a sea of living light of ethical laws that far surpass the causal laws.[30]

In 1924, the Mercaz [Center] HaRav Y'sheevah was established in Jerusalem. "HaRav" is Rav Kook. This is a higher learning institute where young men spend long hours every day in the Bayt Meedrahsh studying *Tahlmood*. Rav Kook died in 1935, and Mercaz HaRav remains, in the twenty-first century, a major learning center for Jews of the culture of the Bayt Meedrahsh.

Although Rav Kook was a major figure in the Jewish *yeeshoov*, the overwhelming majority of the leaders of the Jewish community were secular Jews. With great dedication and pertinacity they built the infrastructure for the future state, fought the political battles, and, in 1948, led the nascent Israeli army to victory in the war of liberation. On the eve of the establishment of the state of Israel, Yedaiya HaCohen was a young *y'sheevah* student in K'far HaRo'eh in the north of Israel. His *rohsh y'sheevah* — head of the *y'sheevah* — was a disciple of Rav Kook. One day HaCohen was hitchhiking to Jerusalem and was given a ride by Yitzkhak Ben-Aharon, a socialist/communist leader of the pre-state government. HaCohen recalls, "All the way in the car, he harangued me about being religious. I'll never forget; he said 'this is the last generation of religious Jews.'"[31]

Few people realize how many leaders of the *yeeshoov* were committed socialists and communists. The leader of Russia, for the bulk of its existence as a world superpower, was Josef Stalin. Stalin was a ruthless dictator who ordered the murder of anyone he suspected of opposing his rule. Among those murdered were large numbers of Jews. Despite this reality, when Stalin died, the Israeli leader Yitzhak Ben-Aharon, the leader who gave Yedaiya Cohen a ride, delivered a eulogy expressing his grief over the loss of such a great world leader.

HaCohen estimates that during the years of his studies, there were approximately one thousand students in a few *y'sheevot* (plural of *y'sheevah*) in Israel. Today, in 2006, there are almost that many *y'sheevot*.

HaCohen is typical of the growing segment in Israel's population who are Jews of the culture of the Bayt Meedrahsh. He is an administrator at a prestigious *y'sheevah*. Among his eight children, two sons are heads of *y'sheevot*, two others teach *G'mahrah* in *y'sheevot*, two daughters teach in Jewish educational systems, and one son is a high-ranking officer in the Israeli army. The representation of Jews of the culture of the Bayt Meedrahsh in the Israeli army is close to twice their proportion in the general population. Such studies, as you know, Nietzsche, are often inexact, but the trend is clear:

within two generations, Jews of the culture of the Bayt Meedrahsh will make up a majority of the Jews in Israel. Already Jews in Israel are one half of all Jews in the world, and in two generations, it will only be a question of the *size* of the majority of world Jewry living in Israel.

Among the "religious" Jews in Israel, the Jews of the culture of the Bayt Meedrahsh make up over 98 percent. Jews of the Conservative and Reform movements are only a handful; most of their constituency is in the United States, and as we have seen, their number is shrinking significantly through assimilation. The number of secular Israelis living abroad is approximately seven hundred thousand — more Jews than there were in Israel in 1948 with the founding of the state. Virtually all these *yordeem* (those who have gone "down" from the land) are now assimilating outside the land of Israel.

In an earlier letter, we discussed the attempt in Tz'faht in the 1500s to reconstitute the *Sanhehdreen*, the highest legal body of the Jewish people. The *Sanhehdreen* has not been convened in about sixteen centuries. The attempt in the 1500s failed because the requirement to have the agreement of the leaders of all communities of the culture of the Bayt Meedrahsh could not be met. One of the most significant events of the early twenty-first century is the reestablishment of the *Sanhehdreen*. One of the facts underscoring its importance for the long term is the almost complete absence of knowledge about its reconstitution.

The government of the state of Israel is a secular government and has no intention of conferring any official status on the nascent *Sanhehdreen*. There is a Supreme Court in Israel that constitutes the highest judicial body. Just as the idea of a Jewish state was considered a pipe dream only a hundred years ago, it is now considered a chimerical idea that the *Sanhehdreen* will become the highest recognized judicial authority in Israel. For Jews of the culture of the Bayt Meedrahsh, the reestablishment of the state of Israel was inevitable; it was only a question of time. It is just as inevitable that the *Sanhehdreen* will regain its place as the highest judicial assembly of the Jewish people.

The socialist pioneers were a strong and resilient group of "new Jews" — indeed, in their time, "modern" Jews — but we have seen the fate of socialism worldwide, and the ephemerality of anything "modern." Socialism has failed, and many of the grandchildren of those pioneers seek their fortunes outside the Jewish state. The spiritual significance of the land of Israel eludes them. The grandchildren of Rav Kook, and the grandchildren of the disciples of Rav

Kook and of all the leaders of the culture of the Bayt Meedrahsh, are in Israel because this is *the* land that Hahshehm promised; there is simply no other place to dwell that makes any sense at all.

Yours,

Ben Moshe

# Letter Sixteen

June 1, 2006                                      ה' בסיון תשס"ו

Dear Nietzsche,

In a few hours, at nightfall, it will be the holiday of *Shahvoo'oht*, a day that falls on the sixth day of the Jewish month of *Seevahn*. Now it is the fifth day of *Seevahn;* the sixth day begins with nightfall. It is a Thursday. Stores and restaurants will close; the cars and crowds on gridlocked streets will gradually thin until the city appears all but deserted. It is the time commemorating the giving of the Torah — a joyous time, a time of celebration. It is a time of gratefulness, a time of heightened awareness of the presence of Hahshehm. Many Jews of the culture of the Bayt Meedrahsh will be awake all through the night, studying Torah. For secular Israelis it is June 1 now, and it will be June 1 after nightfall. They know it is *Shahvoo'oht* and are glad because it is a national holiday and they do not have to work tomorrow. For Jews in the Diaspora, outside the land of Israel, only a minority know that it is *Shahvoo'oht*. It will be just another evening, and they will go to work tomorrow.

These differences are the essence of free choice among the Jewish people. It is said, "*Hahkol beey'day Shahmayeem, khootz mee'yeeraht Shahmayeem —* All is in the hands of heaven except for awe of heaven."

Those Jews born into the culture of the Bayt Meedrahsh who opt out of that culture make a conscious choice. They have every right to do so; there is no value judgment to be made. As we have seen, the life of a Jew is not easy, and one may wonder why even more Jews have not chosen to assimilate into the general population.

What do we mean by "general population," Nietzsche? In almost every

realm, whether social, economic, or philosophical, there is a definite sentiment that the "masses," the "herd," the "average," are at best something to be
avoided, a group that makes the wrong decisions. At worst, one sees the
"average" as corrupt, hungry for money and power. Hahshehm judged the
world corrupt in Noah's time and decided to destroy it. He promised never to
do this again. Soon most of Noah's progeny had fallen into the old pattern of
lusting after power and riches.

In the environment of the masses, it is as if Hahshehm decided to try
something new. Into this control group of the general population of individuals lacking a higher moral order, Hahshehm set up an experimental group
and provided clear guidelines for all areas of their lives. There would be no
laws governing how or what they think, but there would be clear laws governing what they shall do and shall not do. In order to make sure it was a group
set apart from the general populace (the control group), Hahshehm
instructed Abram, before changing his name to Abraham, to leave his father's
house, his homeland, and go to a land that Hahshehm would show him. With
Abraham he made a covenant and promised to make of him a great people.
When the foreign prophet Balaam came to curse the people of Israel,
Hahshehm put words into his mouth, and Balaam saw a people destined to
live separate, apart, and "not be reckoned among the nations."[1]

The "nations" noticed. Tacitus complained about the Jews that "they sit
apart at meals and sleep apart."[2] Others complained of their "obstinate attachment to each other," which supported Tacitus's claim that "toward every other
people they feel only hate and enmity."[3] What is fascinating is that it *mattered*
so much what the Jews did! And Christians over the centuries have continued
to condemn the Jews for living apart and not accepting Jesus as their savior.

Arnold Toynbee, a British man of letters of the early 1900s, was more than
a little annoyed at the ongoing presence of the Jews: "Upon the advent of
Christianity or, alternatively, of Islam, the 'mandate' of Judaism and the Jews
'was exhausted' (to use an apt Chinese concept). Now, in God's own good
time, the true 'Chosen people' had arrived on the scene, and the Jews' duty
was clear. They ought to have accepted Jesus or, alternatively, Muhammad."[4]
One can only imagine Toynbee's consternation were he around to see Jews in
control of "the Holy Land."

Thomas Paine, a hero of the American Revolution, asserted that the Jews
were "restless, bloody-minded people" and that "Moses had bound the Jews

to many idle ceremonies, mummeries, and observances of no effect.... Jesus exposed their futility and insignificance."[5]

Frustration over the continued existence of the Jews of the culture of the Bayt Meedrahsh is not limited to Christians. We have mentioned Freud's colleague, Otto Rank, born with the family name Rosenfeld. His deep annoyance with his "outmoded" coreligionists fairly boiled over in this screed: "The observation of the laws in the Old Testament was very simple at the time of its inception.... Today, it is utterly impossible to live in accordance to the viewpoints of that time. The last 'Jew' has been dead for a long time now; yet the descendants, with a mixture of obstinacy, arrogance, malice, [and] self-conceit appropriate to their race, hold fast to their inherited laws and prejudices."[6]

We have also mentioned the pronouncement of a twentieth-century Jewish leader that "rabbinic Judaism has died." That all this *ressentiment* comes from a sense of insecurity, inferiority, and jealousy was clear to you. From outside the culture of the Bayt Meedrahsh, there is a sense of rage that this "outmoded," "dead" culture will not die. The "certainty" of its demise comes from intoxication with the "modern." Since what is "modern" passes, whereas the culture of the Bayt Meedrahsh — though declared "dead" — is always present and vibrant, "modern" becomes a meaningless word. It is meant to be positive; yet, in the context of even three or four generations, "modern" means "deteriorating, outmoded, passing from the scene."

It is only outside the culture of the Bayt Meedrahsh that the state of Israel was ever a "whimsical" notion. Eliezer Berkovits, a scholar of the Bayt Meedrahsh whose wisdom is often quoted in these letters, empathized with those on the outside looking in when he wrote, "One must appreciate the irrationality of it all before one can grasp its significance. In terms of exclusively man-made history, Israel's existence is irregular — a people such as the Jews is not supposed to exist; its survival is anomalous — a people as 'different' as the Jews is not expected to survive; its return to Zion is absurd — the irregular and the anomalous compounded into the impossible realization of a delusion."[7]

So how do we understand these perplexities? Berkovits provides the answer: "Yet, Israel is real. It can be real only because history is enacted on a twofold level: it is man-made, the Kingdom is man's responsibility; it is God-planned, because the Kingdom of God on earth is man's responsibility; it may be delayed by crematoria and death camps, yet come it must, come it will, a-coming it is. The movement of the two levels towards each other is the messianic process of history. Israel is the only nation that lives on both levels."[8]

Scientists have lately discovered the unity of the universe that erupted from the big bang. This unity has been on the lips of Jews for millennia: *Sh'mah Yeesrah'ehl Hahshehm Ehlohaynoo, Hahshehm Ehkhahd* — Hear, O Israel, Hahshehm is our Lord, Hahshehm is One. The secret of the Jews is in this unity of Hahshehm's world, created *ex nihilo*, and the system of values given in His Torah. It is the holiday of *Shahvoo'oht*, Nietzsche, and we are grateful for the unity of Hahshehm's Torah, for the clarity of its message. The message is perfect, but the Jews of the culture of the Bayt Meedrahsh are far from perfect. Rabbi Samson Raphael Hirsch, your contemporary, said it best:

> The Torah…did not spring from the breast of mortal man; it is the message of the God of Heaven and Earth to man; and it was from the very beginning so high above the cultural level of the people to which it was given, that during the three thousand years of its existence there was never a time yet during which Israel was quite abreast of the Torah, when the Torah could be said to have been completely translated into practice. The Torah is rather the highest aim, the ultimate goal toward which the Jewish nation was to be guided through all its fated wanderings among the nations of the world. This imperfection of the Jewish people and its need of education is presupposed and clearly expressed in the Torah from the very beginning. There is, therefore, no stronger evidence for the Divine origin and uniqueness of the Torah than the continuous backsliding, the continuous rebellion against it on the part of the Jewish people…. Thus, the Torah manifests from the very beginning its superhuman origin. It has no development and no history; it is rather the people of the Torah which has a history. And this history is nothing else but its continuous training and striving to rise to the unchangeable, eternal height on which the Torah is set, this Torah that has nothing in common with what is commonly called "religion."[9]

For the same reasons, Rabbi Hirsch explains that the Torah is not a theology or a way of worshipping: "Now it is just because our Houses of God and the Divine Services within them are not the essence of our worship of God, but are rather places and occasions for preparing ourselves for the real worship of God in practical life, that the synagogues are not Israel's holiest places. They take but second place in holiness as compared to the בית מדרש [Bayt Meedrahsh], the houses of learning, which are devoted to the study and teaching of the Torah, i.e., the inquiry into the prescription of the Divine Will as to how a godly life should be led by man."[10]

You never met Rabbi Hirsch, Nietzsche, even though you could have. Perhaps it was important for you not to find "a higher spirit" besides yourself. You put into the mouth of Zarathustra these words: "But let me reveal my heart to you entirely, my friends: *if* there were gods, how could I endure not to be a god! Hence there are no gods. Though I drew this conclusion, now it draws me."[11] If the highest being for you was the *Übermensch*, perhaps you could not endure being one among many. You would have found a friend in Rabbi Hirsch and someone who, by example, would have helped you refine your understanding of an *Übermensch*. So, Nietzsche, let us close this series of letters with more of Rabbi Hirsch's words:

> When we raise aloft this Torah, the revelation of which we celebrate on *Shavuoth*, we jubilantly proclaim "This is the Torah which Moshe gave to Israel," that it is the same Torah which Moses brought to Israel "through the mouth of God, through the hand of Moses" — the same Torah, pure and unadulterated. When we live and die in the conviction that this precious heritage has been preserved pure and genuine amidst all the tempests and vicissitudes of a history of more than three thousand years, or when we rely for the earthly welfare and heavenly salvation of ourselves and our children on the truth of this Torah, what guarantee have we for all this other than the tradition of our fathers? Yes, the selfsame fathers who, together with the Written Torah, handed down to us the Oral Law also? If our fathers have deceived us with the one, how could they be trustworthy with the other? Indeed there is no evidence or guarantee for the truth and reality of a historic fact save our trust in tradition. All sorts of documents and monuments, all kinds of internal and external circumstances, may lead you to the conclusion that it is probable, or almost certain that such and such an event did really happen, but who tells you that what you consider probable or even certain has really

happened? Or that the very documents from which you draw your conclusions are not in fact forged.... The Torah-tradition was entrusted to no special calling or priestly cast, but to the entire Jewish nation. In virtue of the maxim "raise up many disciples," it was the first and most sacred duty taught by tradition to spread the knowledge of the Torah among all classes of the people — every honest Jew, whether he was a "shepherd" or a "weaver at the gate of Jerusalem" was listened to and respected as the bearer of Jewish tradition by the highest legal authorities in Israel.[12]

Your friend,

Ben Moshe

# Partial Bibliography

Aviezer, Nathan, *Fossils and Faith: Understanding Torah and Science* (Hoboken, N.J.: KTAV, 2001).

Bakan, David, *Sigmund Freud and the Jewish Mystical Tradition*, 2nd ed. (**Mineola**: Dover, 2004).

Berghahn, Klaus L., and Jost Hermand, eds., *Goethe in German-Jewish Culture* (Rochester, N.Y.: Camden House, 2001).

Bergson, Henri, *Time and Free Will: An Essay on the Immediate Data of Consciousness*, trans. F. L. Pogson (Mineola, N.Y.: Dover, 2001).

Berkovits, Eliezer, *God, Man and History: A Jewish Interpretation* (New York: Jonathan David, 1959).

Berkovits, Eliezer, *Faith after the Holocaust* (New York: KTAV, 1973).

Berkovits, Eliezer, *Crisis and Faith* (New York: Sanhedrin Press, 1976).

Berkovits, Eliezer, *With God in Hell: Judaism in the Ghettos and Death Camps* (New York: Sanhedrin Press, 1979).

Berkovits, Eliezer, *Not in Heaven: The Nature and Function of Halakha* (New York: KTAV, 1983).

Berlin, Isaiah, *The Power of Ideas*, ed. Henry Hardy (Princeton, N.J., and Oxford, UK: Princeton University Press, 2000).

Buell, Lawrence, *Emerson* (Cambridge, Mass.: Harvard University Press, 2003).

Cahill, Thomas, *Gift of the Jews* (New York: Doubleday, 1998).

Cahill, Thomas, *Desire of the Everlasting Hills: The World Before and After Jesus* (New York: Anchor, 2001).

Cahill, Thomas, *Sailing the Wine-Dark Sea: Why the Greeks Matter* (New York: Doubleday, 2003).

Carroll, James, *Constantine's Sword: The Church and the Jews — A History* (Boston: Houghton Mifflin, 2001).

Clark, Maudemarie, and Brian Leiter, eds., *Daybreak: Thoughts on the Prejudices of Morality* (Cambridge, UK: Cambridge University Press, 1997).

Clive, Geoffrey, ed., *The Philosophy of Nietzsche* (New York: Mentor, 1965).

Cornwell, John, *Hitler's Pope: The Secret History of Pius XII* (New York: Viking Penguin, 1999).

Crum, Bartley, *Behind the Silken Curtain* (Jerusalem: Milah Press, 1996).

Deleuze, Gilles, *Spinoza: Practical Philosophy* (San Francisco: City Lights, 1988).

Dimont, Max I., *Jews, God and History* (New York: Signet, 1962).

Dimont, Max I., *The Indestructible Jews* (New York: Signet, 1973).

Elias, Joseph, *The Nineteen Letters about Judaism: The World of Rabbi S. R. Hirsch* (Jerusalem: Feldheim, 1995).

Ellenson, David, *After Emancipation: Jewish Religious Responses to Modernity* (Cincinnati: Hebrew Union College Press, 2004).

Fine, Lawrence, *Physician of the Soul, Healer of the Cosmos: Isaac Luria and His Kabbalistic Fellowship* (Palo Alto, Calif.: Stanford University Press (2003).

Flannery, Edward H., *The Anguish of the Jews: Twenty-Three Centuries of Antisemitism* (New York: Paulist Press, 1985).

Flusser, David, *Jewish Sources in Early Christianity* (Israel: Naidat Press, 1989).

Gay, Peter, *The Enlightenment: The Rise of Modern Paganism* (New York: Norton, 1966).

Geldard, Richard, *Remembering Heraclitus* (Hudson: Lindisfarne, 2000).

Geller, Victor B., *Orthodoxy Awakens: The Belkin Era and Yeshiva University* (New York: Lambda, 2003).

Goldhagen, Daniel Jonah, A Moral Reckoning: The Role of the Catholic Church in the Holocaust and Its Unfulfilled Duty of Repair (New York: Knopf, 2002).

Golomb, Jacob, *Nietzsche's Enticing Psychology of Power* (Ames: Iowa State University Press, 1988).

Golomb, Jacob, Santaniello Weaver, and Ronald Lehrer, eds., *Nietzsche and Depth Psychology* (New York: SUNY Press, 1999).

Gould, Allan, *What Did They Think of the Jews?* (Northvale, N.J.: Aronson, 1991).

Greely, Andrew M., *The Catholic Myth: The Behavior and Beliefs of American Catholics* (New York: Simon and Schuster, 1997).

Green, Brian, *The Elegant Universe* (New York: Random House, 2003).

Grunfeld, Frederic V., *Prophets Without Honor: A Background to Freud, Kafka, Einstein and Their World* (New York: Holt, Rinehart and Winston, 1979).

HaLevi, Yehuda, *The Kuzari: In Defense of the Despised Faith*, trans. and annotated by N. Daniel Korobkin (Northvale, N.J.: Aronson, 1998).

Helmreich, William B., *The World of the Yeshiva: An Intimate Portrait of Orthodox Jewry* (New York: Free Press, 1982).

Henoch, Chayim J., *Ramban: Philosopher and Kabbalist* (Northvale, N.J.: Aronson, 1998).

Hertzberg, Arthur, *The French Enlightenment and the Jews: The Origins of Modern Anti-Semitism* (New York: Columbia University Press, 1990).

Hirsch, Samson Raphael, *Collected Writing of Rabbi Samson Raphel Hirsch*, Elliott Bondi and David Bechhofer, eds. (New York: Feldheim, 1988).

Hirsch, Samson Raphael, *Chapters of the Fathers*, trans. Gertrude Hirschler (New York: Feldheim, 1989).

Hirsch, Samson Raphael, *The Pentateuch*, Ephraim Oratz, ed., trans. Gertrude Hirschler (New York: Judaica Press, 1990).

Humphreys, Colin J., *The Miracles of Exodus: A Scientist's Discovery of the Extraordinary Natural Causes of the Biblical Stories* (New York: HarperCollins, 2004).

Huskinson, Lucy, *Nietzsche and Jung: The Whole Self in the Union of Opposites* (New York: Brunner-Routledge, 2004).

Jacob, Heinrich Eduard, *Felix Mendelssohn and His Times*, trans. Richard Winston and Clara Winston (Englewood Cliffs, N.J.: Prentice-Hall, 1963).

Johnson, Mark, *The Body in the Mind: The Bodily Basis of Meaning, Imagination, and Reason* (Chicago: University of Chicago Press, 1987).

Kaplan, Aryeh, trans., *The Bahir Illumination* (York Beach, Maine: Weiser, 1979).

Kaplan, Aryeh, *Made in Heaven* (New York: Moznaim, 1983).

Kaplan, Aryeh, *Immortality, Resurrection and the Age of the Universe: A Kabbalistic View* (Hoboken, N.J.: KTAV, 1993).

Kaplan, Aryeh, trans., *Sefer Yetzirah: The Book of Creation* (Northvale, N.J.: Aronson, 1995).

Kaplan, Aryeh, *The Aryeh Kaplan Anthology*, vol. 2: *Illuminating Expositions on Jewish Thought and Practice by a Revered Teacher* (New York: Noble Book Press, 1998).

Kaufmann, Walter, *Nietzsche: Philosopher, Psychologist, Antichrist* (Princeton, N.J.: Princeton University Press, 1974).

Kaufmann, Walter, *Existentialism from Dostoevsky to Sartre* (New York: Meridian, 1975).

Kaufmann, Walter, ed., trans., *The Portable Nietzsche* (New York: Penguin, 1976).

Kaufmann, Walter, *From Shakespeare to Existentialism* (Princeton, N.J.: Princeton University Press, 1980).

Kleiman, Rabbi Yaakov, *DNA and Tradition: The Genetic Link to the Ancient Hebrews* (Jerusalem: Devorah, 2004).

Klein, Dennis B., *Jewish Origins of the Psychoanalytic Movement* (New York: Praeger, 1981).

Klugman, Eliyahu Meir, *Rabbi Samson Raphael Hirsch: Architect of Torah Judaism for the Modern World* (New York: Masorah, 1996).

Kook, Abraham Isaac, *Orot:The Annotated Translation of Rabbi Abraham Isaac Kook's Seminal Work*, ed. Bezalel Naor (Northvale, N.J.: Aronson, 1993).

Koppel, Moshe, *Meta-Halakhah: Logic; Intuition, and the Unfolding of Jewish Law* (Northvale, N.J.: Aronson, 1997).

Kupferberg, Herbert, *The Mendelssohns: Three Generations of Genius* (New York: Scribner and Sons, 1972).

Langmuir, Gavin I., *History, Religion, and Antisemitism* (Berkeley: University of California Press, 1990).

Lehrer, Ronald, *Nietzsche's Presence in Freud's Life and Thought: On the Origins of a Psychology of Dynamic Unconscious Mental Functioning* (New York: SUNY Press, 1995).

Liebes, Yehuda, *Studies in the Zohar*, trans. Arnold Schwartz, Stephanie Nakache, and Penina Peli (Albany: SUNY Press, 1993).

Livingston, Dorothy Michelson, *The Master of Light: A Biography of Albert A. Michelson* (New York: Charles Scribner's Sons, 1973).

Magnus, Bernard, and Kathleen M. Higgens, eds., *The Cambridge Companion to Nietzsche* (Cambridge, UK: Cambridge University Press, 1996).

Mandel, Siegfried, *Nietzsche and the Jews: Exaltation and Denigration* (New York: Prometheus, 1998).

Marius, Richard, *Martin Luther: The Christian between God and Death* (Cambridge, Mass.: Harvard University Press, 1999).

Martin, Malachi, *The Decline and Fall of the Roman Church* (New York: Bantam, 1983).

Nadich, Judah, *The Legends of the Rabbis*: vol. 1, *Jewish Legends of the Second Commonwealth* (Northvale, N.J.: Aronson, 1994).

Nadich, Judah, *The Legends of the Rabbis*: vol. 2, *The First Generation after the Destruction of the Temple and Jerusalem* (Northvale, N.J.: Aronson, 1994).

Nadich, Judah, *Rabbi Akiba and His Contemporaries* (Northvale, N.J.: Aronson, 1998).

Netanyahu, Benzion, *The Origins of the Inquisition in Fifteenth Century Spain* (New York: New York Review of Books, 2001).

Nietzsche, Friedrich, *The Birth of Tragedy* and *The Genealogy of Morals*, trans. Francis Golffing (New York: Anchor, 1956).

Nietzsche, Friedrich, *Beyond Good and Evil*, trans. Walter Kaufman (New York: Vintage, 1966).

Nietzsche, Friedrich, *The Will to Power*, trans. Water Kaufmann and R. J. Hollingdale (New York: Vintage, 1967).

Nietzsche, Friedrich, *The Gay Science*, trans. with commentary, Walter Kaufmann (New York: Vintage, 1974).

Nietzsche, Friedrich, *Thus Spoke Zarathustra*, trans. Walter Kaufman (New York: Penguin, 1978).

Nietzsche, Friedrich, *Ecce Homo: How One Becomes What One Is*, trans. R. J. Hollingdale (London: Penguin, 1992).

Nietzsche, Friedrich, *Untimely Meditations*, trans. R. J. Hollingdale (Cambridge, UK: Cambridge University Press, 1997).

Nietzsche, Friedrich, *Daybreak: Thoughts on the Prejudices of Morality*, ed. Maudemarie Clark and Brian Leiter (Cambridge, UK: Cambridge University Press, 1997).

Nietzsche, Friedrich, *Human, All Too Human: A Book for Free Spirits*, trans. R. J. Hollingdale (Cambridge, UK: Cambridge University Press, 1998).

Padover, Saul K., *Karl Marx: An Intimate Biography* (New York: McGraw Hill, 1978).

Patai, Raphael, and Jennifer Patai Wing, *The Myth of the Jewish Race* (New York: Charles Scribner's Sons, 1975).

Peters, H.F., *Zarathustra's Sister: The Case of Elisabeth and Friedrich Nietzsche* (New York: Crown, 1977).

Pinker, Steven, *The Blank Slate: The Modern Denial of Human Nature* (New York: Penguin, 2002).

Rackman, Emanuel, *One Man's Judaism: Renewing the Old and Sanctifying the New* (Jerusalem: Gefen, 2000).

Rakeffet-Rothkoff, Aaron, *The Rav: The World of Rabbi Joseph B. Soloveitchik*, vol. 1 (Jersey City, N.J.: KTAV, 1999).

Ravven, Heidi M., and Lenn E. Goodman, eds., *Jewish Themes in Spinoza's Philosophy* (Albany: SUNY Press, 2002).

Robert, Marthe, *From Oedipus to Moses: Freud's Jewish Identity*, trans. Ralph Manheim (New York: Anchor Press, 1976).

Roth, Saul, *Halakhah and Politics* (New York: Yeshiva University Press, 1988).

Rummel, Erika, *The Case against Reuchlin: Religious and Social Controversy in Sixteenth-Century Germany* (Toronto: University of Toronto Press, 2002).

Sáenz-Badillos, Angel, *A History of the Hebrew Language*, trans. John Elwolde (Cambridge, UK: Cambridge University Press, 2002).

Safranski Rüdiger, *Nietzsche: A Philosophical Biography*, trans. Shelley Frisch (New York: Norton, 2002).

Santaniello, Weaver, *Nietzsche, God and the Jews: His Critique of Judeo-Christianity in Relation to the Nazi Myth* (Albany: SUNY Press, 1958).

Sarna, Jonathan, *American Judaism: A History* (New Haven, Conn.: Yale University Press, 2004).

Schafer, Peter, *Judeophobia: Attitudes toward Jews in the Ancient World* (Cambridge, Mass.: Harvard University Press, 1997).

Scherman, Nosson, and Meir Zlotowitz, eds., *Kohelet* (New York: Mesorah, 1994).

Schochet, Jacob Immanuel, *The Mystical Tradition*, vol. 1, *The Mystical Dimension* (New York: Kehot, 1995).

Scholem, Gershom, *Kabbalah* (New York: Meridian, 1974).

Schroeder, Gerald L., *The Science of God: The Convergence of Scientific and Biblical Wisdom* (New York: Free Press, 1997).

Schroeder, Gerald L., *The Hidden Face of God: Science Reveals the Ultimate Truth* (New York: Simon and Schuster, 2001).

Schweid, Eliezer, *The Jewish Experience of Time: Philosophical Dimensions of the Jewish Holy Days*, trans. Amnon Hadary (Northvale, N.J.: Aronson, 2000).

Singh, Simon, *Big Bang: The Origins of the Universe* (New York: Harper Collins, 2004).

Snyder, Douglas M., *Freud, Einstein, and Marx: The Influence of Judaism on Their Work* (Beverly Hills, Calif.: Taylor Press, 1998).

Soloveitchik, Joseph B., *Halakhic Man*, trans. Lawrence Kaplan (Philadelphia: Jewish Publication Society, 1983).

Spinoza, Benedict de, *A Theologico-Political Treatise*, trans. R. H. M. Elwes (New York: Dover, 1951).

Spinoza, Benedict de, *Ethics*, trans. R. H. M. Elwes (Buffalo, N.Y.: Prometheus, 1989).

Stein, Murray, *Jung's Map of the Soul: An Introduction* (Chicago: Open Court, 1998).

Steinsaltz, Adin, *The Strife of the Spirit* (Northvale, N.J.: Aronson, 1988).

Steinsaltz, Adin (Even Yisrael), *The Talmud: Reference Guide*, trans., ed. Israel V. Berman (New York: Random House, 1989).

Taguieff, Pierre-André, Rising *From the Muck: The New Anti-Semitism in Europe* (Chicago: Ivan R. Dee, 2004).

Tropp, Eduard A., Viktor Y. Frenkel, and Artur D. Chernin, *Alexander A. Friedmann: The Man Who Made the Universe Expand* (Cambridge, UK: Cambridge University Press, 1993).

Voegelin, Eric, *The Collected Works of Eric Voegelin: Order and History*, vol. 1, *Israel and Revelation* (Columbia, Mo.: University of Missouri Press, 2001).

Von Franz, **Marie-Louise**, *C. G. Jung: His Myth in Our Time*, trans. William H. Kennedy (Toronto: Inner City Books, 1998).

Young, Brad H., *Jesus the Jewish Theologian* (Peabody, Mass.: Hendrickson, 2001).

# Notes

**INTRODUCTION**

1  Robert, Marthe, *From Oedipus to Moses: Freud's Jewish Identity*, translated by Ralph Manheim (New York: Anchor Press, 1976), 18.

2  Cited in Gould, Allan, *What Did They Think of the Jews?* (Northvale, N.J.: Jason Aronson, 1991), 13.

3  Cited in Schafer, Peter, *Judeophobia: Attitudes toward Jews in the Ancient World* (Cambridge, Mass.: Harvard University Press, 1997), 70.

4  Cited in Gould *What Did They Think of the Jews?* 51-52.

5  Ibid., 101.

6  Cited in Gould, *What Did They Thin of the Jews*, 233.

7  Charles Neider, ed., *The Complete Essays of Mark Twain* (New York: Da Capo Press, 2000), 249.

8  Cited in Gould, *What Did They Think of the Jews?* 125.

9  Ibid., 71-72.

10  Ibid, 181.

11  Philo, describing a pogrom in Alexandria, Egypt, in 38 C.E.; quoted in Netanyahu, Benzion, *The Origins of the Inquisition in Fifteenth Century Spain* (New York: New York Review of Books, 2001), 16.

12  Dimont, Max I., *The Indestructible Jews* (New York: Signet, 1973), 19.

13  Hogan, Maurice P., in introduction to Voegelin, Eric, *The Collected Works of Eric Voegelin*, vol.1: *Israel and Revelation* (Columbia, Mo.: University of Missouri Press, 2001), 4.

14  Cited in Gould, *What Did They Think of the Jews?* 453

15  Cahill, Thomas, *Gift of the Jews* (New York: Doubleday, 1998), 3.

16  Ibid., 7.

17  Sarna, Jonathan, *American Judaism: A History* (New Haven, Conn.: Yale University Press, 2004), xvii.

18  Ibid., 374.

19  Sarna, Jonathan, "Intermarriage and Conversion," *Journal of Reform Judaism* (Winter 1990): 7-8.

20 Kaufmann, Walter, *Nietzsche: Philosopher, Psychologist, Antichrist* (Princeton, N.J.: Princeton University Press, 1974), 309.

21 Dimont, Max I., *Jews, God and History* (New York: Signet, 1962), 320.


### LETTER ONE

1 The beginning of this chapter draws heavily on Ben Moshe, David, "Jews and JOTWO: A Letter to Nietzsche," *Jewish Spectator (Spring-Summer 2002)*: 42-45.

2 Nietzsche, Friedrich, *"The Genealogy of Morals" in The Birth of Tragedy and The Genealogy of Morals*, translated by Francis Golffing (New York: Anchor Books, 1956), , # VII, 155-56.

3 Nietzsche, *The Genealogy of Morals*, 281.

4 Nietzsche, Friedrich, *Beyond Good and Evil*, translated with commentary by Walter Kaufmann, "What Is Religious), # 52, pp. 65-66.

5 Nietzsche, Friedrich, *The Dawn*, in Kaufmann, *The Portable Nietzsche*, #205, p. 88.

6 Nietzsche, *Beyond Good and Evil, op. cit.*, "Peoples and Fatherlands", #251, 187.

7 Kaufmann, *Nietzsche: Philosopher, Psychologist, Antichrist*, 45.

8 Martin, Malachi, *The Decline and Fall of the Roman Church (New York: Bantam, 1983)*, 3.

9 Ibid., 40.

10 Ibid., 41.

11 Ibid., 42.

12 Ibid., 77.

13 Chrysostom, John, "Eight Homilies Against the Jews," in *Medieval Sourcebook*, www.fordham.edu/haisall/source/chrysostom-jews6.html. Most recent access date, 11/19/2007.

14 Flannery, Edward H., *The Anguish of the Jews: Twenty-Three Centuries of Antisemitism*, (New York: Paulist Press, 1985), 60-61.

15 Martin, *The Decline and Fall of the Roman Church*, 94.

16 Ibid., 111.

17 Ibid.

18 Netanyahu, Benzion, *The Origins of the Inquisition in Fifteenth Century Spain* (New York: New York Review of Books, 2001), xvi.

19 Ibid., xvii.

20 Ibid.

21 Ibid., 925-26.

22 Ibid., 928.

23 Ibid., 929.

24 Klugman, Eliyahu Meir, *Rabbi Samson Raphael Hirsch: Architect of Torah Judaism for the Modern World* (New York: Masorah, 1996), 7-8.

25 Cited in Kaufmann, *Nietzsche: Philosopher, Psychologist, Antichrist*, 297-98.

26 Ibid., 247-48.

27 Peters, H. F. , *Zarathustra's Sister: The Case of Elisabeth and Friedrich Nietzsche* (New York: Crown, 1977), viii.

28 See Kaufmann, *Nietzsche: Philosopher, Psychologist, Antichrist*, 364.

## LETTER TWO

1 Kaufmann, *Nietzsche: Philosopher, Psychologist, Antichrist*, 53.

2 Mandel, Siegfried, *Nietzsche and the Jews: Exaltation and Denigration* (New York: Prometheus, 1998), 102.

3 Ibid., 241.

4 Ibid., 242.

5 See, for example, Patai, Raphael, and Jennifer Patai Wing, *The Myth of the Jewish Race* (New York: Charles Scribner's Sons, 1975).

6 Mandel, *Nietzsche and the Jews*, 183.

7 Cited in Gould, *What Did They Think of the Jews?* 101.

8 Quoted in Kupferberg, Herbert, *The Mendelssohns: Three Generations of Genius* (New York: Charles Scribner and Sons, 1972), 5.

9 Ibid., 27.

10 Ibid., 28.

11 Ibid., 96–100.

12 Berghahn, Klaus L., and Jost Hermand, eds., *Goethe in German-Jewish Culture* (Rochester, N.Y.: Camden House, 2001), 4.

13 Kupferberg, *The Mendelssohns*, 82–83.

14 Ibid., 108.

15 Ibid., 116.

16 Cited in Kaufmann, *Nietzsche: Philosopher, Psychologist, Antichrist*, 376.

17 Padover, Saul K., *Karl Marx: An Intimate Biography* (New York: McGraw Hill, 1978), 57.

18 Snyder, Douglas M., *Freud, Einstein, and Marx: The Influence of Judaism on Their Work* (Beverly Hills, Calif.: Taylor, 1998), 95–96.

19 Padover *Karl Marx: An Intimate Biography*, 31, cited in Snyder, 108.

20 Ibid., 44.

21 Berkovits, Eliezer, *Faith after the Holocaust* (New York: Ktav, 1973), 118.

22 Snyder, *Freud, Einstein, and Marx*, 188.

23 Carroll, James, *Constantine's Sword: The Church and the Jews — A History* (Boston: Houghton Mifflin Co., 2001), 436.

24 Klugman, *Rabbi Samson Raphael Hirsch*, 20–21.

25 Ibid., 56–57.

26 *Berghahn Goethe in German-Jewish Culture*, 87–89.

27 See Hirsch, *Samson Rafael, Collected Writing of*, vol. 5, ed. Elliott Bondi and David Bechhofer, (New York: Feldheim, 1988), 209.

## *LETTER THREE*

1  A. A. Brill, as cited in *Kaufmann, Nietzsche: Philosopher, Psychologist, Antichrist,* 218.

2  Ibid., 222.

3  Ibid.

4  Ibid., 224.

5  Nietzsche, Friedrich, *Beyond Good and Evil,* trans. Kaufmann, "Epigrams and Inter-ludes," #68, 80.

6  Ibid #39, 49.

7  Mandel, *Nietzsche and the Jews,* 231.

8  Ibid., 194.

9  Parkes, Graham, in Jacob Golomb, Santaniello Weaver, and Ronald Lehrer, eds., *Nietzsche and Depth Psychology* (New York: State University Press, 1999), 208.

10  Ibid., 230.

11  Barbre, Claude, in Golomb et al., *Nietzsche and Depth Psychology,* 249.

12  Ibid., 251.

13  Ibid., 255.

14  Mandel, *Nietzsche and the Jews,* 184.

15  Ibid., 189.

16  Ibid., 194.

17  Snyder, *Freud, Einstein, and Marx,* 15–16.

18  Ibid., 17.

19  Momigliano, Arnaldo, cited in Lehrer, in Golomb et al., *Nietzsche and Depth Psychology,* 186.

20  Lehrer in Golomb, *Nietzsche and Depth Psychology,* 193.

21  Klein, Dennis B., *Jewish Origins of the Psychoanalytic Movement* (New York: Praeger, 1981), 58.

22  Ibid., 59.

23  Ibid., 57.

24  Grunfeld, Frederic V., *Prophets Without Honor: A Background to Freud, Kafka, Einstein and Their World* (New York: Holt, Rinehart and Winston, 1979), 53.

25  Klein, *Jewish Origins of the Psychoanalytic Movement,* 60.

26  Ibid., 110.

27  Cited in Gould, *What Did They Think of the Jews?* 167–69.

28  Grunfeld, *Prophets Without Honor,* 58–59.

29  Ibid., 58.

30  Nietzsche, Friedrich, *The Gay Science,* translated with commentary by Walter Kaufman (New York: Vintage Books, 1974), #377, 339.

31  Nietzsche, *The Twilight of the Idols,* cited in Kaufmann, *Nietzsche: Philosopher, Psychologist, Antichrist,* 297–98.

32  Huskinson, Lucy, *Nietzsche and Jung: The Whole Self in the Union of Opposites* (New York: Brunner-Routledge, 2004), 2-3.

33  Parkes, in Golomb, *Nietzsche and Depth Psychology*, 212.

34  Ibid., 225.

35  Samson Rafael Hirsch, quoted in Snyder, *Freud, Einstein, and Marx*, 21.

36  Nietzsche, *Twilight of the Idols*, in Kaufmann, *The Portable Nietzsche*, #6, 511.

37  Nietzsche, *Human, All Too Human*, trans. R. J. Hollingdale, *(Cambridge, UK: Cambridge University Press, 2000)*, "The Wanderer and His Shadow", # 53, 323.

38  See *Babylonian Talmud, Yoma*, 69b.

39  Hirsch, Samson Rafael, *The Pentateuch, T'rumath Tz'vee*, trans. Gertrude Hirschler (New York: Judaica Press, 1990), 19.

40  Berkovits, Eliezer, *God, Man and History: a Jewish Interpretation* (New York: Jonathan David, 1959), 107.

41  Ibid., 107-108.

42  Ibid, 108.

43  Ibid., 109.

44  Golomb, Jacob, *Nietzsche's Enticing Psychology of Power* (Ames: Iowa State University Press, 1988) 74-75.

45  Cited in Kaufmann, *Nietzsche: Philosopher, Psychologist, Antichrist*, 180.

46  Nietzsche, *Thus Spoke Zarathustra*, trans. Walter Kaufmann (New York: Penguin, 1978), "On the Thousand and One Goals", 58.

47  Kaufmann, *Nietzsche: Philosopher, Psychologist, Antichrist*, 201.

## LETTER FOUR

1   Peters, *Zarathustra's Sister*, viii.

2   Cited in Kaufmann, *Nietzsche: Philosopher, Psychologist, Antichrist*, 63.

3   Peters, *Zarathustra's Sister*, 41.

4   Ibid., 51.

5   Ibid., 122.

6   Ibid., 129.

7   Ibid., 133-34.

8   Ibid., 149.

9   Cited in Kaufmann, *Nietzsche: Philosopher, Psychologist, Antichrist*, 247-48.

10  Letter dated 3/22/1933, Central Zionist Archives, Wise papers, Reel 82, quoted in Morrison, David, *Heroes AntiHeroes and the Holocaust: American Jewry and Historical Choice*, second printing (Jerusalem: Gefen Publishing, 1999), 25.

11  Ibid., letter dated 3/29/1933, Reel 115, 26.

12  Letter dated 4/1/1933, quoted in Voss, Carl Herman, ed., *Stephen Wise: Servant of the People: Selected letters* (Philadelphia: Jewish Publication Society of America, 1969), 177.

13 Telegram dated 4/22/1933, quoted in Morrison, *Heroes Antiheroes and the Holocaust*, 28.
14 Letter dated 5/22/1933, Ibid., 30.
15 Ibid., 220.
16 Ibid., 221.
17 Ibid., 224.
18 Cornwell, John, *Hitler's Pope: The Secret History of Pius XII* (New York: Viking Penguin, 1999), viii.
19 Ibid.
20 Ibid., 3.
21 Ibid., 10.
22 Ibid., 11.
23 Ibid., 13.
24 Ibid., 28.
25 Ibid.
26 Ibid., 41.
27 Ibid., 114.
28 Ibid.
29 Ibid., 70.
30 Ibid., 110.
31 Ibid.
32 Ibid., 149.
33 Quoted in Morrison, *Heroes, Antiheroes, and the Holocaust*, 127.
34 Ibid.
35 Cornwell, *Hitler's Pope*, 208.
36 "The Vanishing American Jews," *Look Magazine*, May 5, 1964.
37 della Pergola, Sergio, "New Data on Demography and Identification Among Jews," in Paul Ritterband, ed., *Jewish Intermarriage in Social Context*, cited in Elliott Abrams, *Faith or Fear: How Jews Can Survive in a Christian America* (New York: Free Press, 1997, 5.
38 Cited in Abrams, *Faith or Fear*, 8.
39 "Reform Jewish Leaders, Intermarriage and Conversion," *Journal of Reform Judaism* (Winter 1990): 7–8.
40 See Goldstein, Sidney, "Profile of American Jewry: Insights from the 1990 National Jewish Population Survey," *American Jewish Year Book*, 1993, 77–173.
41 della Pergola, Sergio, "The Jewish People Today: A Demographic View," *Congress Monthly* 59, no. 4 (May/June 1992), cited in Abrams, *Faith or Fear*, 7.
42 Quoted from the speech of Irwin Kula. For a more complete critique of this address, see Morrison, David, "Irwin Kula's Hospice Judaism," in the *Jewish Spectator*, Vol. 63, no. 2, fall 1998.

*LETTER FIVE*

1    Nietzsche, *The Antichrist*, in Kaufmann, *The Portable Nietzsche*, #25-#26, 594-97.
2    Nietzsche, Friedrich, *Ecce Homo*, trans. R. J. Hollingdale (New York: Penguin, 1992), *Why I Am a Destiny*, #7, 102.
3    Yovel, Yirmiyahu, *Dark Riddle: Hegel, Nietzsche, and the Jew*, (University Park: Pennsylvania State University Press, 1998), 160-61.
4    Hirsch, The Pentateuch, T'rumath Tz'vee, 2.
5    Nietzsche, *Ecce Homo*, trans. Hollingdale, "Thus Spoke Zarathustra", #3, 72-73.
6    Ibid., #7, 78.
7    *Proverbs* 1:10-29.
8    Nietzsche, *Thus Spoke Zarathustra*, #3, 171.
9    Nietzsche, *The Gay Science*, #125, 181.
10   Ibid., #343, 279.
11   Nietzsche, *The Antichrist*, in Kaufmann, *The Portable Nietzsche*, # 47, 627.
12   *Ecclesiastes* 3:1-12.
13   *Meedrahsh Tahnkhooma, Tetzaveh* 5, and *Song of Songs* 1:1.
14   *Song of Songs* 4:1-6.
15   Cited in Gould, *What Did They Think of the Jews?* 146.
16   Martin, *The Decline and Fall of the Roman Church*, 30.
17   Ibid., 31.
18   Flusser, David, *Jewish Sources in Early Christianity* (Tel Aviv: Naidat Press, 1989), 27.
19   *Babylonian Talmud, Pirkei Avot (Sayings of the Fathers)*, ch. 1.
20   *Ezra*, 7:10. This entire paragraph is from the *Babylonian Talmud*, Tractate *Sanhedreen*, 21b.
21   Koppel, Moshe, *Meta-Halakhah: Logic, Intuition and the Unfolding of Jewish Law* (Northdale, N.J.: Jason Aronson), 62.
22   Ibid., fn., 62.
23   Ibid., 37.
24   Koppel, *Meta-Halakhah*, 69.
25   *Babylonian Talmud, Sookah*, 20a.
26   Nietzsche, *Human, All Too Human, Man Alone With Himself*, #588, 189.
27   Ibid., *From the Souls of Artists and Writers*, #210, 97.
28   Ibid., *Man Alone With Himself*, #577, 188.
29   Rackman, Emanuel, *One Man's Judaism: Renewing the Old and Sanctifying the New* (Jerusalem: Gefen, 2000), 185.
30   *Babylonian Talmud, Bava Metzia*, 59a-59b. The final quote in the paragraph is from *Exodus* 23:2.
31   *Pesikta Rabbati*, cited in Koppel, *Meta-Halakhah*, 71.

## LETTER SIX

1  *Babylonian Talmud, Khahgeegah*, 14b.

2  Steinsaltz (Even-Yisrael), Adin, *Talmud Reference Guide* (New York: Random House, 1989).

3  *Babylonian Talmud, Pehsahkheem*, 49b.

4  *Babylonian Talmud, Ketooboht*, 62b-63a.

5  See Kaplan, trans., *Sefer Yetzirah*, xvii.

6  Ibid., 38.

7  Ibid., 39.

8  Ibid., 40.

9  Steinsaltz, Adin, *The Strife of the Spirit* (Northdale, N.J.: Jason Aronson, 1988), 59.

10  Transliterated with a double "s" on the end, so that it is not read as the plural of "Shah," as in "Shahs of Iran," but rather as the "ss" in "hiss."

11  Steinsaltz, *Talmud Reference Guide*, 9.

12  Koppel, *Meta-Halakhah*, 47.

13  Rackman, *One Man's Judaism*, 17.

14  Berkovits, Eliezer, *Not in Heaven: The Nature and Function of Halakha* (New York: Ktav, 1983), 118.

15  Hirsch, Samson Raphael, *Collected Writings of*, vol. I., 199.

16  Nietzsche, *Human, All Too Human*, trans. Hollingdale, #266, 126.

17  Ibid., "Assorted Opinions and Maxims", #91, 232.

18  Ibid., *"From the Soul of Artists and Writers"*, #164, 88.

19  Nietzsche, *The Antichrist*, in Kaufmann, *The Portable Nietzsche*, #4, 571.

20  Nietzsche, *The Gay Science*, trans. Kaufmann, #102, 157.

21  Berkovits, Eliezer, *God, Man and History*, 10.

22  Ibid.

23  Henoch, Chayim J., *Ramban: Philosopher and Kabbalist* (Northvale, N.J.: Jason Aronson, 1998), 14.

24  *Ibid.*

25  Ibid., 53.

26  *Babylonian Talmud, Avodah Zahrah*, 56b.

27  Nietzsche, *Human All Too Human*, #528, 183.


## LETTER SEVEN

1  The best single source for a concise presentation of the history of Lithuanian Jewry is Greenbaum, Marsha, *The Jews of Lithuania* (Jerusalem: Gefen, 1995).

2  Rakeffet-Rothkoff, Aaron, *The Rav: The World of Rabbi Joseph B. Soloveitchik*, vol. 1 (New York: KTAV, 1999), 147.

3  Ibid., 148.

4  An excellent reference for this period is Geller, Victor B., *Orthodoxy Awakens: The Belkin Era and Yeshiva University* (New York: Lambda, 2003).

5  Helmreich, William B., *The World of the Yeshiva: An Intimate Portrait of Orthodox Jewry* (New York: Free Press, 1982).

6  Ibid., 277.

7  Ibid., 278.

8  Ibid.

9  Ibid., 9–10.

10  Kleiman, Rabbi Yaakov, *DNA and Tradition: The Genetic Link to the Ancient Hebrews* (Jerusalem: Devorah, 2004), 47.

11  Ibid.

12  Ibid., 17–18.

13  Ibid., 53.

14  Ibid., 19.

15  Ibid. The complete articles are found in the appendix, 179–185.

16  Ibid., quoting an article in *The New York Times*, Jan. 7, 1997.

17  Ibid., 22.

18  Ibid., 23.

19  Ibid., 106.

20  *Ecclesiastes*, 1:4–10.

21  See Kaufmann, *Nietzsche: Philosopher, Psychologist, Antichrist*, 317.

22  Nietzsche, *The Gay Science*, trans. Kaufmann, #341, 273–274.

23  Ibid., #276, 223.

## LETTER EIGHT

1  1 Maimonides, *Mishneh Torah*, vol. 1, translation and commentary by Rabbi Eliyahu Touger (Jerusalem: Moznaim, 1919), 146–47.

2  Ibid., 148.

3  Nietzsche, *Human, All Too Human*, trans. Hollingdale, "The Wanderer and His Shadow", #3, 302.

4  Elias, Joseph, *The Nineteen Letters about Judaism: The World of Rabbi S. R. Hirsch* (Jerusalem: Feldheim, 1995), 41–42.

5  Ibid., 50, fn.

6  Rackman, *One Man's Judaism*, 15.

7  Ibid., 15–16.

8  Ibid., 85.

9  From the preliminary prayers of the morning *Shahkhareet* service.

10  Ibid.

11  Ibid.

12  Ibid.

13  Steinsaltz, Adin, *Strife of the Spirit*, 110–111.

14  Ibid., 32.

15  Nietzsche, *Thus Spoke Zarathustra*, trans. Walter Kaufmann, "*Before Sunrise*", #3, 164.

16  *Psalms* 27:4.

17  Nietzsche, *Thus Spoke Zarathustra*, "Upon the Blessed Isles", #2, 86.

18  Berkovits, Eliezer, *God, Man and History*, 100.

19  Ibid., 102.

20  Tatz, Akiva, and David Gottlieb, *Letters to a Buddhist Jew* (Southfield, Mich.: Targum Press, 2004), 47.

21  *Babylonian Talmud, Khahgeegah*, 14b.

22  Nietzsche, *Human, All Too Human*, trans. Hollingdale, "Tokens of Higher and Lower Culture", #224, 107.

23  The first paragraph of the *Shehmah* is from *D'vahreem* (Deuteronony) 6:4–9; the second paragraph is from *D'vahreem* 11:13–21; the third paragraph is from *Bahmeedbahr* (Numbers) 15:37–41.

24  Humphreys, Colin J., *The Miracles of Exodus: A Scientist's Discovery of the Extraordinary Natural Causes of the Biblical Stories* (New York: HarperCollins, 2003).

25  *Joshua* 3:15–16, as translated in Humphreys, *The Miracles of Exodus*, 15.

26  Humphreys, *The Miracles of Exodus*, 19.

27  Ibid., 20–21.

28  *Numbers* 33:1–38.

29  Humphreys, *The Miracles of Exodus*, 157.

30  Ibid., 207.

31  Ibid.

32  Ibid., 212.

33  Ibid., 184–85.

34  Ibid., 199.

35  *The Exodus Decoded*, documentary film written and directed by Simcha Jacobovici and produced by James Cameron, 2006. (CD available for purchase at: http://theexodusdecoded.com/index1.jsp. Last accessed 11/19/2007.

## *LETTER NINE*

1  Cited in Gould, *What Did They think of the Jews?* 101.

2  *Ibid.*, 181.

3  Schweid, Eliezer, *The Jewish Experience of Time: Philosophical Dimensions of the Jewish Holy Days*, trans. Amnon Hadary (Northdale, N.J.: Aronson, 2000), 3.

4  *Babylonian Talmud, Rosh Hashanah*, 2a.

5  Nietzsche, *Beyond Good and Evil*, trans. Kaufmann, #251, 187–188.

6  *Ibid.*

7   *Sh'moht* (*Exodus*), 12:2.

8   Hirsch, Samson Raphael, *The Pentateuch, T'rumath Tz'vee*, 250.

9   As cited in Morrison, David, *The Gush: Center of Modern Religious Zionism* (Jerusalem: Gefen, 2004), 146–47.

10  *Babylonian Talmud, Tractate Shahbaht*, 119a.

11  Schweid, *The Jewish Experience of Time*, 37–38.

12  Rackman, *One Man's Judaism*, 54–58.

13  Nietzsche, *Human, All Too Human*, trans. Hollingdale, #624, 197.

14  Rackman, *One Man's Judaism*, 58–59.

15  Kaplan, Aryeh, *The Aryeh Kaplan Anthology, vol. 2: Illuminating Expositions on Jewish Thought and Practice by a Revered Teacher* (New York: Mesorah, 1998), 110–11.

16  *B'raysheet* (Genesis) 48:20.

17  Rackman, *One Man's Judaism*, 16.

18  *Ibid.*, 27–28.

19  Kook, Abraham Isaac, *Orot :The Annotated Translation of Rabbi Abraham Isaac Kook's Seminal Work*, Bezalel Naor, ed. (Northvale, N.J.: Aronson, 1993), 155.

20  *Babylonian Talmud, Pirkei Avot (Sayings of the Fathers)*, ch. 3, *meeshnah* 4.


*LETTER TEN*

1   Nietzsche, *Human, All Too Human*, #91, 232.

2   *Babylonian Talmud, Nahzeer*, 23b.

3   *Berkovits, God, Man and History*, 109.

4   Nietzsche, *Human, All Too Human*, #53, 323.

5   *Ibid.*, vol. 1, 9:521, 182.

6   Nietzsche, *Untimely Meditations*, 73–74.

7   Nietzsche, *The Genealogy of Morals*, in Golffing, *The Birth of Tragedy and The Genealogy of Morals*, #VII, 155–56.

8   Nietzsche, *Untimely Meditations*, 72–73.

9   See discussion of HaRav Aharon Lichtenstein in *By His Light: Character and Values in the Service of God*, based on some of his lectures and adapted by Rabbi Reuven Ziegler (Newark, N.J.: KTAV, 2003), 109–11.

10  Nietzsche, *Untimely Meditations*, 162–63.

11  Cited in Gould, *What Did They Think of the Jews?* 101.

12  *Babylonian Talmud, Shahbaht*, 127a.

13  Nietzsche, *Human, All Too Human*, 323.

14  Rahmbahm, *Heelkhot Tzeetzeet*, ch. 3.

15  Italicized words in the original. See Nietzsche, *The Gay Science*, #14, 88–89.

## LETTER ELEVEN

1 Nietzsche, *Human, All Too Human*, #378, 150.
2 Nietzsche, *Thus Spoke Zarathustra*, #24, "On the Old and New Tablets, 211.
3 *Babylonian Talmud, Keedoosheen*, 29b.
4 *B'raysheet* (Genesis) 24:65; See Kaplan, Aryeh, *Made in Heaven* (New York: Moznaim, 1983), 125.
5 *Ibid.*, 1:28; see Kaplan, *Made in Heaven*, 144.
6 See Kaplan, *Made in Heaven*, 158.
7 Cited in Kaplan, *ibid.*, 168.
8 *Ibid.*, 181.
9 *Ibid.*, 179.
10 *Sh'moht* (Exodus) 20:15; see Kaplan, *ibid.*, 195.
11 *Babylonian Talmud, K'tooboht*, 6b.
12 *B'raysheet* (Genesis), 1:22.
13 Adapted from *Otzarot HaRe'eeyah*, vol. 2, 518–19.

## LETTER TWELVE

1 Clive, Geoffrey, editor and author of introduction, *The Philosophy of Nietzsche* (New York: Mentor, 1965), ix.
2 *Ibid.*, x.
3 *Ibid.*, xi.
4 *Ibid.*, xvi.
5 Dimont, *Jews, God and History*, 320. Also see introduction to this book.
6 Nietzsche, *The Gay Science*, trans. Kaufmann, #4, 79.
7 *Ibid.*, fn.
8 Samson Raphael Hirsch, quoted in Snyder, *Freud, Einstein, and Marx*, 21.
9 Kaplan, Aryeh, translator, *Sefer Yetzirah: The Book of Creation*, 60.
10 Nietzsche, *The Antichrist*, in Kaufmann, *The Portable Nietzsche*, #16, 582–83.
11 *Ibid.*, #17, 584.
12 Nietzsche, *Beyond Good and Evil*, trans. Kaufmann, #23, 31.
13 *Ibid.*, 31–32.
14 Nietzsche, *Thus Spoke Zarathustra*, trans. Kaufmann, 88–89.
15 See discussion in *Kaufmann, Nietzsche: Philosopher, Psychologist, Antichrist*, 201–2.
16 *Ibid.*
17 Quoted in Kaufmann, *ibid.*, 180.
18 *Babylonian Tahlmood, Pirkei Avot* (Sayings of the Fathers), part 4, meeshnah 1.
19 Nietzsche, *Untimely Meditations*, trans. Hollingdale, 166.
20 Kaufmann, *Nietzsche: Philosopher, Psychologist, Antichrist*, 224.
21 *Ibid.*, 225.

22 Nietzsche, *The Gay Science*, trans. Kaufmann, #377, 339.

23 Nietzsche, *Twilight of the Idols, in Kaufmann, The Portable Nietzsche*, #2, 506.

24 *Babylonian Talmud, Pirkei Avot (Sayings of the Fathers)*, ch. 1, meeshnah 9.

25 Hosea 12:7.

26 Micah 6:8.

27 *Babylonian Talmud, Pirkei Avot* (Sayings of the Fathers), ch. 1, meeshnah 2.

28 Nietzsche, Friedrich, *The Will to Power*, trans. Walter Kaufmann and R. J. Hollingdale, (New York: Vintage Books, 1968), #893, 476.

29 Ibid., #932, 492.

30 Nietzsche, *The Antichrist, in Kaufmann, The Portable Nietzsche*, #57, 647.

31 Nietzsche, *Untimely Meditations*, trans. Hollingdale, 63.

32 Nietzsche, *Twilight of the Idols*, in Kaufmann, *The Portable Nietzsche*, #17, 524.

33 *Babylonian Talmud, Pirkei Avot* (Sayings of the Fathers), ch. 1, *meeshnah* 12.

34 Nietzsche, *Human, All Too Human, trans.* Hollingdale, #49, 38.

35 Ibid., #589, 189.

36 Nietzsche, *The Dawn*, in Kaufmann, *The Portable Nietzsche*, #556, 91.

37 *Babylonian Talmud, Pirkei Avot (Sayings of the Fathers)*, ch. 4, meeshnah 24.

38 Nietzsche, *Human, All Too Human*, trans. Hollingdale, #230, 272.

39 Ibid., #288, 280.

40 Nietzsche, *Twilight of the Idols*, in Kaufmann, *The Portable Nietzsche*, #14, 523.

41 *Babylonian Talmud, Pirkei Avot (Sayings of the Fathers)*, ch. 1, meeshnah 15.

42 *D'vahreem* (Deuteronomy) 18:20.

43 Nietzsche, *Untimely Meditations*, trans. Hollingdale, 88.

44 Nietzsche, *Human, All Too Human*, trans. Hollingdale, #210, 97.

45 Ibid., #559, 186.

46 Ibid., #614, 194-95.

47 Ibid., #577, 188.

48 *Ibid.*, #65, 326.

49 *Babylonian Talmud, Pirkei Avot* (Sayings of the Fathers), ch. 1, *meeshnah* 1.

50 Ibid., ch. 1, *meeshnah* 6.

51 Ibid., ch. 2, *meeshnah* 15.

52 Nietzsche, *The Untimely Meditations*, trans. Hollingdale, 162-63.

53 Nietzsche, *Human, All Too Human*, #603, 192.

54 *Babylonian Talmud, Pirkei Avot (Sayings of the Fathers)*, ch. 5, *meeshnah* 19.

55 Nietzsche, *The Gay Science*, trans. Kaufmann, #14, 88-89.

56 Nietzsche, *Thus Spoke Zarathustra*, trans. Kaufmann, 164.

57 *Yayeekrah* (Leviticus) 19:18.

58 *B'raysheet* (Genesis) 1:27.

59 Schneerson, Menahkhem Mendel (the Tzemakh Tzedek), *The Mitzvah to Love Your*

*Fellow as Yourself*, trans. Zalman I. Posner and Nissen Mandel, ed. Eliezer Danzinger and Avraham Vaisfiche (New York: Kehot, 2002), 26.

60  See Kaufmann, *Nietzsche: Philosopher, Psychologist, Antichrist*, 323–24.

61  Ibid., 283.

62  *Babylonian Tahmood, Mahkot*, 24a-b.

63  Zechariah 8:4–5.

64  Micah 3:12.

65  *Babylonian Talmud, Mahkoht*, 24a-b.

66  *Babylonian Talmud, B'rahkhot*, 60b.

67  Nietzsche, *Ecce Homo, trans.* Hollingdale, #2, 10.

68  Nietzsche, *The Gay Science*, trans. Kaufmann, #276, 223.

69  Ibid., 49–50.

70  *D'vahreem* (Deuteronomy) 30:19–20.

## LETTER THIRTEEN

1  Mandel, *Nietzsche and the Jews*, 185–86.

2  Ibid., 188.

3  *Ibid.*, 187.

4  See Kaufmann, *Nietzsche: Philosopher, Psychologist, Antichrist*, 149.

5  See Hazoni, Yoram, *The Jewish State: The Struggle for Israel's Soul* (New York: Basic Books, 2000), 98ff.

6  From Psalms 48.

7  From Psalms 60.

8  From Psalms 122.

9  Isaiah 62:1–5.

10  Ibid., 66:10–13.

11  Micah 4:1–3 .

12  Psalms 90:4.

13  See Morgenstern, Arie, "Dispersion and the Longing for Zion, 1240–1840," *Azure* 12 (Winter 2002): 77.

14  Psalms 102:14–15.

15  Cited in Morgenstern, "Dispersion and the Longing for Zion," 78–79.

16  Ibid., 79.

17  Ibid., 81.

18  Quoted in Morgenstern, ibid., 82.

19  Ibid., 86–88.

20  Quoted in Morgenstern, ibid., 91.

21  Fine, Lawrence, *Physician of the Soul, Healer of the Cosmos: Isaac Luria and His Kabbalistic Fellowship* (Palo Alto, Calif.: Stanford University Press, 2003), 26.

22  Cited in Gould, *What Did They Think of the Jews?* 51–52.

23  Nietzsche, *The Antichrist*, in Kaufmann, *The Portable Nietzsche*, #39, 613.

24  Cited in Morgenstern, "Dispersion and the Longing for Zion," 91.

25  Fine, *Physician of the Soul*, 20–21.

26  Morgenstern, "Dispersion and the Longing for Zion," 92.

27  Fine, *Physician of the Soul*, 53.

28  Ibid., 54.

29  Ibid., 35

30  Ibid., 9.

31  Ibid., 89–90.

32  Ibid., 91

33  Nietzsche, *The Genealogy of Morals*, in Golffing, *The Birth of Tragedy and The Genealogy of Morals*, #VII, 155–56.

34  Cited in Morgenstern, "Dispersion and the Longing for Zion," 98.

35  Ibid., 98–99.

36  Ibid., 100.

37  Ibid., 103.

38  Ibid., 108.

39  Ibid., 111.

40  Ibid., 116.

41  Snyder, *Freud, Einstein, and Marx*, 81.

## LETTER FOURTEEN

1  Cited in Snyder, ibid., 56.

2  Aviezer, Nathan, *Fossils and Faith: Understanding Torah and Science* (Hoboken, N.J.: KTAV, 2001), 2.

3  Cited in Singh, Simon, *Big Bang: The Origins of the Universe* (New York: Harper Collins, 2004), 108.

4  Bergson, Henri, *Time and Free Will: An Essay on the Immediate Data of Consciousness*, trans. F. L. Pogson (Mineola, N.Y.: Dover, 2001), 101.

5  Safranski, Rüdiger, *Nietzsche: A Philosophical Biography*, trans. Shelley Frisch (New York: Norton, 2002), 326.

6  Singh, *Big Bang*, 93.

7  Ibid., 94–97.

8  Ibid., 99–100.

9  Ibid., 123.

10  Ibid.

11  Tropp, Eduard A., Viktor Y. Frenkel and Artur D. Chernin, *Alexander A. Friedmann: The Man Who Made the Universe Expand* (Cambridge: Cambridge U. Press, 1993), 168.

12  Singh, *Big Bang*, 156–57.

13 Ibid., 158.

14 Ibid., 159–60.

15 Cited in Singh, ibid, 60.

16 Ibid., 276.

17 Ibid., 307–9.

18 Ibid., 315.

19 Ibid., 316.

20 Ibid., 322.

21 Kaplan, Aryeh, *Immortality, Resurrection and the Age of the Universe: A Kabbalistic View* (Hoboken, N.J.: KTAV, 1993). 5–8.

22 Ibid.

23 Ibid., 9. Kaplan cites many other sources supporting this concept in the traditional literature.

24 Scherman, Nosson, and Meir Zlotowitz, eds., translation and notes by Rabbbi Raphael Pelcovitz, *Sforno Commentary on the Torah: Genesis/Exodus* (New York: Mesorah, 1987), 11.

25 Ibid., 13

26 Ibid., 21.

27 Ibid., 23.

28 Kaufmann, *Nietzsche: Philosopher, Psychologist, Antichrist*, 328.

29 Quoted in Aviezer, Nathan, *In the Beginning: Biblical Creation and Science* (Hoboken, N.J.: KTAV, 1990), 54–55.

30 Ibid., 55.

31 *B'raysheet* (Genesis) I:20–22.

32 Schroeder, Gerald L., *The Science of God: The Convergence of Scientific and Biblical Wisdom* (New York: Free Press, 1997), 29–30.

33 Ibid., 51.

34 Ibid.

35 Ibid., 58.

36 The data for the first six days is culled from a table in Schroeder, ibid., 67.

37 Ibid., 95.

38 Ibid., 97.

39 Ibid., 98.

40 *B'raysheet* (Genesis) 4:20–22.

41 Aviezer, Nathan, *Fossils and Faith*, 21.

42 Ibid., 26.

43 Ibid., 27.

44 Ibid., 28.

## LETTER FIFTEEN

1   Golomb, Jacob, *Nietzsche and Zion* (Ithaca, N.Y.: Cornell University Press, 2004), 25.

2   Carroll, *Constantine's Sword*, 453.

3   Ibid., 457.

4   See Golomb's discussion in *Nietzsche and Zion*, 30–31.

5   Ibid., 47–48.

6   Nietzsche, *Untimely Meditations*, trans. Hollingdale, 63.

7   Nietzsche, *Beyond Good and Evil*, trans. Kaufmann, #260, 205–6.

8   Nietzsche, *Untimely Meditations*, trans. Hollingdale, 72–73.

9   See Golomb on Berdichevski, *Nietzsche and Zion*, 73–86.

10  Schmidt, Gilya Gerda, *Martin Buber's Formative Years: From German Culture to Jewish Renewal, 1897-1909* (Tuscaloosa: University of Alabama Press, 1995), 24–25.

11  Golomb, Jacob, *Nietzsche and Zion*, 164.

12  Barbre, Claude, in *Nietzsche and Depth Psychology*, ed. Golomb, Jacob, Santaniello Weaver, and Ronald Lehrer, 249.

13  Ibid., 167.

14  Nietzsche, *The Dawn*, cited in Kaufmann, *Nietzsche: Philosopher, Psychologist, Antichrist*, 191.

15  Cited at http://en.wikipedia.org/wiki/Pogrom., last accessed 11/19/2007.

16  Philo, describing a pogrom in Alexandria, Egypt, in 38 C.E.; quoted in Netanyahu, Benzion, *The Origins of the Inquisition in Fifteenth Century Spain*, 16.

17  Morrison, David, *Heroes, Antiheroes and the Holocaust*, 49.

18  Ibid.

19  Ibid., 49–51.

20  Crum, Bartley, *Behind the Silken Curtain* (Jerusalem: Milah Press, 1996), 134.

21  Jacob Golomb's assertion (*Nietzsche and Zion*, 194) in his discussion of Hillel Zeitlin's exposure to western philosophy, that "such an exposure happens only to one who has already begun to lose his faith" is refuted by the experience of many great leaders of the culture of the Bayt Meedrahsh, past and present.

22  Introduction to Kook, *Orot*, 46.

23  Ohana, David, "Zarathustra in Jerusalem: Nietzsche and the 'New Hebrews,'" *Israel Affairs* 1, no. 3.

24  Golomb's assertion that "The tzaddik cannot by any means be regarded as belonging to the category of Nietzschean *Übermensch* because he is not living, acting, thinking beyond the prevalent ethos of good and evil" is based on a misperception of the culture of the Bayt Meedrahsh as demonstrated throughout this book (see Golomb, *Nietzsche and Zion*, 194). His repeated use of terms such as "Nietzsche's atheistic ideal of the *Übermensch*," (ibid., 210) and reference to Nietzsche's "radical atheistic stance" (ibid., 111) make more of the issue of atheism than did Nietzsche. Contrast this with Kaufmann: "Nietzsche's atheism is…a corollary of his basic

commitment to question all premises and to reject them unless they are for some reason inescapable. The issue has been confused by Nietzsche's scorn for the Christian conception of God. "What differentiates *us* is not that we find no God...but that we do not feel that what has been revered as God is 'godlike'" (Kaufmann, *Nietzsche: Philosopher, Psychologist, Antichrist*, 101). And Nietzsche says explicitly, "The greatest recent event — that 'God is dead,' that the belief in the *Christian* god has become unbelievable — is already beginning to cast its first shadows over Europe" [emphasis added]. See *The Gay Science*, trans. Kaufmann, #343, 279.

25  Kook, *Orot*, 150–51.

26  Ibid., 105–6.

27  *Ibid.*, 152–53.

28  Ibid., 155.

29  Nietzsche, *Beyond Good and Evil*, #21, 29.

30  *Orot*, 103.

31  Morrison, David, *The Gush*, 100.


## LETTER SIXTEEN

1  *Bahmeedbahr* (Numbers) 23:9.

2  Cited in Gould, *What Did They Think of the Jews?* 13.

3  Ibid.

4  Ibid., 453.

5  Ibid., 74.

6  Klein, *Jewish Origins of the Psychoanalytic Movement*, 110.

7  Berkovits, *Faith after the Holocaust*, 147.

8  Ibid.

9  Hirsch, *Collected Writing of Rabbi Samson Raphael Hirsch*, vol. 1, 185.

10  Ibid., 192.

11  Nietzsche, *Thus Spoke Zarathustra*, trans. Kaufmann, 86.

12  Hirsch, *Collected Writing of Rabbi Samson Raphael Hirsch*, vol. 1, 196–97.

# Index